THE CITY
IN THE GREEK AND
ROMAN WORLD

THE CITY
IN THE GREEK AND
ROMAN WORLD

E. J. Owens

London and New York

First published in 1991

Paperback edition first published in 1992
by Routledge
11 New Fetter Lane, London EC4P 4EE

Set in Bembo by Columns of Reading
Printed in England by Biddles Ltd, Guildford

British Library Cataloguing in Publication Data
Owens, E.J.
The city in the Greek and Roman world.
1. Classical world. Cities
I. Title
307.7640938

Library of Congress Cataloging in Publication Data
Owens, E.J.
The city in the Greek and Roman world / E.J. Owens.
p. cm.
Includes bibliographical references.
1. Cities and towns, Ancient-Rome. 2. Cities and towns,
Ancient-Greece. I. Title
HT114.093 1991
307.76'0938—dc20 90–8305

ISBN 0–415–08224–2

CONTENTS

LIST OF ILLUSTRATIONS

PREFACE

Haverfield laid the foundations for the modern study of ancient town planning in his book *Ancient Town Planning*, published in 1913. In 1924 the German scholar, A. von Gerkan, produced his fundamental study of planning in the Graeco-Roman world, entitled *Griechische Städteanlagen*. Since then aerial and ground survey and continuing excavation have added greatly to the knowledge and understanding of ancient Greek and Roman towns and town planning. Continuing research has produced a wealth of stimulating articles, books and monographs on towns, planning and urban architecture. R. Martin's *L'Urbanisme dans la Grèce antique*, second edition, 1974, remains an outstanding study of the Greek city. F. Castagnoli's fundamental review of regular town planning, *Orthogonal Town Planning in Antiquity*, was translated from the Italian in 1971. There followed J. B. Ward-Perkins' short but excellent synopsis of Classical planning, *Cities of Ancient Greece and Italy: Planning in Antiquity*, published in 1974. Articles and books on town planning, urban architecture and related subjects continue to appear.

The present study is a synthesis. Its overall aim is to give a synoptic account of the development of urban planning in the Graeco-Roman world. As such it relies on the achievements of the past, but it also takes into account new evidence and the latest interpretations. The first two chapters set the scene for the rest of the study, which assesses the contribution of the Greeks, Etruscans and Romans to the field of urban planning.

In studying the history of urbanisation it always has to be remembered that urban life was not exclusive to the Greeks and the Romans in the Mediterranean. The Phoenicians and the Carthaginians were both prolific builders of cities with novel and stimulating ideas. Nevertheless, the contribution of the latter to the development of cities in the Mediterranean has not been studied in detail. The reason for their omission is that, whilst Graeco-Roman planning traditions came into contact with and in some cases eventually fused with the established traditions of the Carthaginians and Phoenicians in parts of Sicily and Africa, in reality their urban traditions are more firmly rooted in the achievements of the Near East in general, and as such form a separate study.

The bibliography on the ancient city is extensive, and every year brings more evidence as excavation and survey continue. Thus the chapter notes tend to refer to the more accessible evidence, wherever possible in English. This is for convenience. Fuller bibliographic details can be found in the books and works to which reference is made in the text and the bibliography. In addition, C. Stillwell (ed.), *The Princeton Encyclopedia of Classical Sites* (Princeton, 1976), is an invaluable source of reference, which describes the majority of Classical sites with full bibliographical references. Current archaeological journals and archaeological reports must be consulted for the most up-to-date work on a particular site.

The plans, all of which have been redrawn, illustrate a selection of the cities which are discussed. Further detailed illustrations are usually available in the original excavation reports.

Finally, there is the ever-present difficulty of trying to achieve uniformity in the spelling of ancient names and places. The present study has found no solution to the problem. It errs on the side of transliteration of ancient names, except when a spelling has become so entrenched in modern usage that the straight transliteration of the word is both pedantic and indeed unsightly. The end result, as ever, is inconsistency.

ACKNOWLEDGEMENTS

First and foremost, I would like to thank Richard Stoneman for his patience and perseverance throughout the writing of this book. Thanks are also due to the British Academy for the grant which I received to enable me to visit many of the sites in Italy which are discussed below. I would also like to thank my wife for her help in reading the manuscript. Thanks are also due to Dr David Hannell for his useful criticism of the early drafts of several chapters, and in particular to Linda Keyes, a postgraduate student in the Department of Classics and Ancient History at Swansea, for her willing assistance both in typing parts of the text and in reading the final draft of the manuscript, and suggesting improvements. They cannot be held in any way responsible for the mistakes and inconsistencies which remain. Finally, my parents must also be mentioned for their support over the years. To them and to my wife, Linda, I dedicate this book.

1

INTRODUCTION

The city was one of the fundamental institutions of the ancient world and as such was not confined to the civilisations of Greece and Rome. Cities had long been the basis of civilisation in the Near East, and indeed in this region urban life antedates by several centuries the emergence of cities in the Greek and the Roman world.[1] Nevertheless, the importance of the city in the political, religious and social life of both the Greeks and the Romans cannot be emphasised too strongly. The city was synonymous with civilisation and in opposition to barbarity and chaos. Two of the accusations which Homer levels at the uncivilised Cyclopes were that they had no assemblies for making laws and they had no sense of community beyond their immediate family.[2] Both of these qualities were considered crucial for orderly urban life. Thucydides equated urban life with stability, security and prosperity. In the introduction to his history of the Peloponnesian War, where he described the unsettled, dangerous and poverty-stricken times of early Greece, he maintained that the threat of invasion resulted in a transitory population, who did not build large cities and lacked substantial resources.[3] Furthermore, the city was the agency through which the Graeco-Roman way of life was disseminated throughout the Mediterranean, Europe and the Near East. An urban building programme was one of the ways in which Tacitus' father-in-law, Agricola, helped to pacify and civilise the province of Britain.[4]

The criteria which defined a city in the eyes of the Greeks and Romans differed. To the Greeks the *polis* needed no definition. The city was essentially a community of citizens, sharing common political, religious and social traditions. Alcaeus stated that it was not well-roofed houses, well-built walls, docks and

1

harbours, which constituted a city, but men able to use their own opportunity.[5] Both Herodotus and Thucydides express similar sentiments. When, after the sack of Athens, the Greek commanders met to decide where to oppose the Persian fleet, Themistocles argued vehemently that they should fight at Salamis and not at the Isthmus of Corinth. During the debate the Corinthian general, Adeimantos, tauntingly replied that a man without a city had no right to vote, and even suggested that Themistocles should not participate in the discussions until he had regained his city. In reply Themistocles said that the Athenians had a far greater city than the Corinthians in two hundred fully manned warships.[6] Over sixty years later, in a speech delivered to the defeated remnants of the Syracusan expedition, the Athenian general Nicias maintained that men made a city, not walls or ships without men inside them.[7]

To the Greeks of the Archaic and Classical periods the city was a community, and its physical attributes – well-built houses, walls, docks, other buildings and to a certain extent even its locality – were secondary in importance. It was the concept of the city as a community which made the abandonment of Athens at the time of the Persian Wars, however reluctantly, acceptable, especially when the Athenians realised that their protecting deity, in the guise of a snake, had already left the Acropolis.[8] Presumably it also convinced Eurybiades, the overall commander of the Greek forces, of the reality of Themistocles' threat that the Athenians would abandon the Greek cause and settle at Siris in Italy, if he refused to engage the Persians at Salamis.[9]

Although to the Greeks the *polis* was essentially the people, the words of Alcaeus, Adeimantos and Nicias also acknowledge that the city had a physical aspect. As cities grew, especially under the patronage of the Hellenistic kings and their Roman successors, fine public buildings, sumptuous houses and impressive civic amenities became the hallmark of urban life. Pausanias' comments on the small city of Panopeus in Phocis, whilst recalling Classical sentiments, reflect second-century Roman attitudes. How, he asks, can Panopeus be considered a city when it has no state buildings, no theatre and no market square, when it has no running water at a water head, and the people live on the edge of a torrent in hovels like mountain huts.[10] Pausanias' words reveal the contrast between the old Greek concept of the *polis* as a community and the importance attached by the Romans to providing for the material well-being of the citizens. Indeed Pausanias' comments on Panopeus offer a veritable check-list of what constituted a successful city in the eyes of the second-century inhabitants of the empire. The fact that Pausanias felt that it was appropriate to comment upon the failings of a relatively small, insignificant city in Phocis indicates the significance to the Romans of the physical amenities of urban life. It was such impressive public buildings and other urban amenities, which, in *The Golden Ass*, the noble woman, Byrrhaena, praised in her own town of Hypata in Thessaly.[11] Aelius Aristides expressed similar sentiments when he praised the achievements of the Romans in fostering urban life throughout the empire.[12]

Within the Graeco-Roman world the city fulfilled various functions, and these functions affected its physical and architectural development. Until the reality of the *pax Romana*, the need for defence remained paramount. Cities were located with a view to the natural defensive qualities of the site. The acropolis with its Roman equivalent, the arx, remained both the symbol of a city's independence and the last place of refuge for its inhabitants even after the advent of city walls.

The political, economic, social and religious functions of the city[13] are reflected in its public buildings and their location within the urban environment. The political and administrative role of the city is witnessed most of all in the agora and forum. They were the heart of the Greek and Roman city respectively, linked to the rest of the town by the network of streets. Like the acropolis, the agora and forum were an indication of a city's political and administrative independence, and remained so even at the height of the Roman Empire. The agora/forum also doubled as the town's social centre. Entertainment, competitions and other leisure activities were put on within their precincts until more specialised buildings were developed.

The importance of economic activity in the ancient city is often understated. Cities had an important economic role both locally and in some cases on a much wider scale. Ultimately the physical development of the city was conditioned by its resources. Within the city itself economic foci were positioned in relation to harbours, gates, the agora or forum, and other areas where crowds were to be found. As time went on large, purpose-built commercial buildings were developed.

A city was also a religious community. Temples, shrines and

3

other sacred places were an integral part of the urban framework. Some places within the city were naturally sacred and attracted cult practice. The agora/forum was one place which attracted temples; the acropolis/arx was another. The siting of temples on the acropolis and other high points emphasises the protective nature of a city's gods.

The orderly arrangement of the elements which made up the ancient city was the task of the town planner. But despite the extensive evidence of cities and urban buildings, knowledge of ancient town planning theory remains limited. It is not until the fifth century BC that history first records the name of a town planner. He was Hippodamos of Miletos, erroneously credited with the invention of town planning. The names of a few other planners and the cities on which they worked are subsequently recorded.

Written evidence regarding planning is not totally deficient. Concerned with the nature of the ideal city, philosophers speculated about the form that such a city should take. Thus the treatises of Plato and Aristotle are helpful. Often sociological factors were combined with planning concepts. Plato advised that temples should be located around the agora and in a circle around the city to act as a protective ring in order to maintain the purity of the city and its centre.[14] The houses of public officials and the law courts, because they too were sacred, were also to be located in close association with the temples.

On the question of defence Plato argues against the construction of city walls both for reasons of health and on moral grounds, in that the citizens might place too much trust in them. One is reminded of Sparta's boast that her men were her walls. If, however, the citizens want urban defences, he recommends that the city should be so arranged that it presents a unified appearance. He advises that the houses themselves should be so built that they act as the city wall. They should be regularly constructed and they should all face the street. His reason for such an arrangement is that it would not only offer protection but also the overall effect would be aesthetically pleasing.[15] Plato concludes his discussion of his ideal city by defining some of the duties of the *astynomoi* with regard to the encroachment by individuals on public property and the general cleanliness of the city.[16]

Aristotle's account of his ideal city is more comprehensive than Plato's.[17] His discussion includes advice on the choice of site and the best orientation for the city both for reasons of health and for the political and military well-being of the inhabitants. Availability of water was one of the essential factors which he felt should influence choice of site.

Regarding the town plan Aristotle admired what he called the new 'Hippodamian' method, but felt that the old haphazard arrangement was better for defence. He himself preferred a combination of the two systems; an arrangement which offered both security and was aesthetically pleasing. On the question of defence he disagreed with Plato over the construction of city walls, considering them to be advantageous both in war and peace. He ends by discussing the locations of individual types of building within the town and the types of agora which a town should possess.

Plato and Aristotle were concerned with the theoretical, sociological and moral concepts of establishing an ideal state. Nevertheless, their comments illustrate some of the considerations which governed the work of the town planner. They include the overall layout, the siting and orientation of buildings, defence, the health of the citizens, and the aesthetic qualities of the arrangement of the town and its buildings.

From the Hellenistic and Roman periods there is available a large body of technical literature relating to various aspects of towns and town planning. The manuals of the Roman land surveyors are helpful. Vitruvius wrote a treatise on architecture and related subjects. Frontinus wrote a comprehensive account of the water supply of Rome in the reign of Domitian. Practising doctors also commented on aspects of town planning which they felt would be advantageous to the well-being of their patients. Thus, for example, Hippocrates advised on the best alignment of the streets to ensure the health of the inhabitants.[18]

In addition to the professional and technical literature which is available, there are descriptions of cities and their monuments from travellers and geographers. Sometimes the accounts are first hand; sometimes they are collated from other sources and consequently their accuracy is questionable. The selectivity of the author in the choice of the monuments which he describes is another difficulty. The laws and statutes passed by individual cities also reveal some of the practical problems of urban life with which city authorities had to contend.

The relevance and importance of this information for the study of urbanisation and town planning is variable, dependent upon the interests of the writer and the chance survival of the material. Indeed, at times accounts can even be confusing, as the logical outcome of Vitruvius' advice on the siting and orientation of cities reveals.[19] Yet throughout, the documentary evidence again emphasises the importance of practical considerations in the planning and building of a city. They include the exploitation of the natural advantages of the site for protection and for an assured supply of water.[20] Practical considerations governed orientation[21] and the location of individual buildings within the townscape.[22] Vitruvius' account of the religious practices connected with the foundation of a new city, and in particular the inspection of the entrails of the sacrificial victims from the site, has the practical importance of deciding the healthiness of the chosen location.[23] Aristophanes' portrayal of Meton as a town planner is an indication of the importance and application of geometry in the laying out of a town.[24] The evidence indicates that Graeco-Roman planning was rooted in practical experience.

Despite its variable quality, documentary evidence remains an important source of information regarding cities and aspects of urban life. The other major source of evidence is the physical remains of the cities themselves. Whereas the written evidence offers descriptions and comment, excavation and aerial photography reveal the actual towns and individual buildings. Although there are dangers and deficiencies in studying the material remains, they offer evidence concerning the cities and the urban environment which is often lacking in the written accounts. Archaeology and aerial photography illustrate the plans of the cities and the relationships between buildings and different areas. They allow the study of the architecture of the cities and the amenities which were provided, and permit the reconstruction of the buildings.

When considering town planning it is usual to think in terms of the 'Hippodamian' gridded cities which were a widespread feature of the Graeco-Roman world. However, town planning involves more. The overall aim of the town planner should be to improve and ameliorate the conditions of urban life by providing for the material well-being of the inhabitants and by creating an aesthetic and visually pleasing urban environment.

Indeed, although widely used, regular town planning was not without its critics. For various reasons the 'old' towns without formal arrangement were preferred. Certainly regular planning had disadvantages. Grid planning remained essentially functional and consequently there was the ever-present danger of monotony and repetition. It was a simple and straightforward means of laying out a new town; but sometimes its application was totally unsuitable to the conditions of the site. Its use on steep ground was neither always appropriate nor always successful. The planners who laid out such cities as Priene and Norba can be admired for the skill which they displayed in overcoming the difficulties of the sites. Yet in reality the towns are an uneasy, not to say impractical, union of the gridded plan with the terrain. One is left to wonder what they might have achieved if they had fully exploited the natural and visual advantages of the locations in the same way as the planners of such cities as Halicarnassus, Pergamon and Cuicul.

The development of town planning came about as the direct result of the creation of new cities, or the refurbishment of existing ones if conditions allowed. Colonisation was one means of creating a new town. Greek and Roman colonisation needs little explanation. From the middle of the eighth century BC onwards, the Greek city-states sent out groups of permanent settlers who founded new cities, at first throughout the Mediterranean and then later along the coast of the Black Sea. The same principles of direct occupation, albeit for different reasons, were followed by the Romans when they began to expand initially throughout Italy and later throughout the Mediterranean.

Synoecism was another method of establishing a new town. Synoecism was the process whereby a new town was artificially created or an existing city was increased in size by the influx of the local population. It was essentially a political act, sometimes, as in the case of Attica, involving only the political union of the people but not their physical concentration in one place. Alternatively, it involved the creation of a new urban centre or the refurbishment of an existing one. The synoecism of Messene and Megalopolis and the reconstitution of Mantinea were undertaken by Thebes to act as a check on and a bulwark against Sparta. Not all new creations were successful. One only has to compare Rhodes and Megalopolis. Rhodes, on the one hand, created in 408 BC by the synoecism of three neighbouring communities, became one of the greatest cities in the Aegean until its defeat at the hands of the Romans. Megalopolis, on the other hand, despite its name was never really a success. From its initial foundation in 368 BC it suffered from Spartan aggression, the hostility and jealousy of fellow Arcadian cities, and the reluctance of the population which had been drafted in from surrounding towns, to remain in the city. By Strabo's time it was a joke that the 'great city was a great desert'.[25]

Although different, the processes of colonisation and synoecism were not necessarily mutually exclusive. Certainly the Greeks tended to drive out the existing native population when founding a new colony.[26] The Romans sometimes expelled the natives but often they incorporated them into the new settlement.[27] A number of colonists formed the nucleus of the city and at the same time elements of the local population were drafted in, or the new colonists were added to the population of the existing town.

The reasons for establishing a new city were numerous and often complex, involving political, economic and strategic factors. Greek and Roman colonies were planted for reasons of trade, to exploit the agricultural potential or the natural resources of a region, sometimes to remove surplus population, and for military purposes. Existing cities were moved to new locations due to changing geographical or economic factors. This happened in the case of Priene, Knidos and Astypalaia on Cos in the fourth century BC.[28] Sometimes the population was reluctant to move and force had to be used. Lysimachos compelled the Ephesians to abandon their original site by blocking up the drains and flooding the city when it rained.[29] The *pax Romana* allowed cities to move from their defensive sites to more accessible locations.[30] After the battle of Issus, Alexander the Great commemorated the victory by establishing a new town which he called Nicopolis. This act established a precedent and the concept of the 'victory' city was followed not only by Alexander and his successors but also by Roman generals and emperors. The city became a symbol of power and prestige, reflecting and enhancing both the regime and the individuals who built it.

For the Greeks and the Romans the creation of a city was a political and a secular act, conceived and executed by man.[31] It had a fixed foundation date and the name of the founder was often venerated. It must never be forgotten, however, that religion and sacred ritual were an integral part not only of the foundation of a city but also of its subsequent development. Before a new city was established the favourable concurrence of the gods was sought. The Delphic oracle was a great store of practical knowledge and the oracle played an important role in the process of Greek colonisation. Once the decision had been made to send out a colony, the settlers took fire from their mother city and sacred oaths bound the new colony to its mother city. Often the founder was deified and hero-cult worship grew up around him.

The Romans, according to legend, followed Etruscan ritual in founding cities and in extending the sacred boundary of existing towns. First, auspices were taken, and then the perimeter of the town was marked out with a bronze plough. The furrow afforded sacred protection to the inhabitants from the gods of the underworld. At the point where the gates were to be located, the plough was lifted in order to permit access without having to cross the magic line of protection. The centre of the town was also marked by a circular pit in which were placed offerings, and a sanctuary was established to the Roman Triad of Jupiter, Juno and Minerva. The founding of a new city was a complex process in which ritual and the practical went hand-in-hand.

Because of the overall uniformity within the Graeco-Roman world there is always the danger of overgeneralisation. The physical development of cities was not equal. Thucydides' comparison of Athens and Sparta, the two most prominent cities of Classical Greece, offers a warning of the disparity which might exist between two cities.[32] Even the apparent uniformity which the Romans brought throughout the empire is less substantial when the cities are examined in detail. The rate at which cities developed differed not only in different provinces but even within the same province. Cities and urbanised existence varied throughout the empire.

Economic factors are important in explaining the variations. Many of the urban building programmes were expensive, and so obtaining the necessary funding was crucial. The Periclean building programme at Athens in the fifth century BC relied heavily on the financial resources of the Delian League. The Greek cities of the west were generally more prosperous than their counterparts in the Aegean and the difference is reflected in larger temples and other public buildings, and generally a better standard of urbanised life.[33]

From the Hellenistic period onwards cities depended upon the contributions and the generosity of kings, emperors, wealthy patrons and their own leading citizens. Public projects were undertaken as a necessary part of an individual's civic responsibility. In return, the individual wanted reward and so often tended to support the sort of projects that brought enhanced prestige and a better position. Thus, the willingness of individuals to contribute and the ability of the city to attract benefactions were crucial in the physical and architectural development of the city. The result is anything but uniformity.

2

URBAN DEVELOPMENT AND THE 'OLD' CITIES OF GREECE

Athens and Rome were in many respects unworthy of their reputations as leading cities of Greece and Italy, and as capitals of their respective empires. Both cities were characterised by cramped, overcrowded conditions. The streets were narrow, insinuating themselves between irregular blocks of houses and public buildings. An ancient traveller to Athens was amazed that such a badly arranged city with its haphazard and irregular streets, its lack of water and its mean houses could be the most famous town in Greece.[1] Conditions were much the same at Rome. Tacitus states that Rome's winding narrow streets and irregular house blocks assisted the spread of the great fire of Rome in AD 64;[2] and if Juvenal is to be believed, even Nero's efforts to improve conditions after the great fire were not successful.[3]

Athens and Rome were not unique but merely reflected conditions in many of the old towns of Greece and Italy which had grown up over a long period of time. Cicero contrasted the well-laid-out cities of Campania with the ill-arranged, crowded hill towns of Latium.[4] The irregularity of these towns did have advantages. Some Romans were scornful of Nero's attempts to improve and modernise Rome because the high buildings and the narrow streets of the old city provided some protection from the heat of the sun.[5] There were also military advantages. The irregularity often hindered and confused any enemy troops who managed to gain entry.[6] Pyrrhus' attack on Argos, in which the king himself was killed, was thus thwarted. The narrow, sinuous streets, rutted with water channels, disturbed the cavalry and generally confused and disorientated the attackers. Forced from the agora into the narrow streets, Pyrrhus' troops found it difficult to manoeuvre. Hard-pressed, the king summoned support, but in the confusion his orders were misinterpreted and the entry of these additional troops into the city only added to the confusion and congestion. The whole situation was made worse when one of Pyrrhus' elephants fell and blocked the city gate through which the soldiers were to retreat. In the narrow streets Pyrrhus was killed when he was struck by a roof tile thrown by a woman from a roof top.[7] One hundred and fifty years earlier the Theban troops who entered Plataea at the beginning of the Peloponnesian War had faced similar difficulties. They became lost and disorientated in the dark and muddy streets. The defenders, on the other hand, knew the city and avoided the streets by digging through the walls of adjacent houses.[8]

The origins and evolution of the unplanned towns of Greece are becoming increasingly understood. The collapse of Mycenaean civilisation in the course of the twelfth century BC profoundly affected conditions in Greece. The strong, centralised political control of the palace system disappeared. There was widespread depopulation and abandonment as many of the bronze-age centres were destroyed, and many technical and artistic skills were lost.

The focal point of a Mycenaean town was usually a fortified citadel, which contained the ruler's palace or the local governor's residence. The town itself, densely packed with houses and served by narrow alleys, crowded around the palace for protection.[9] The poverty-stricken and uncertain times of post-bronze-age Greece brought a significant change in settlement pattern. The densely packed towns of the Mycenaean age were replaced by settlements with a looser, less concentrated arrangement.[10] The need for protection remained crucially important. For this purpose an easily defensible hill acted as a fortified retreat and the place of residence of the chieftain. Occupation then developed sporadically at convenient points around the lower slopes of the hill, creating in effect loosely-knit villages.

In his discussion of the early history of Greece, Thucydides comments on the sporadic nature of occupation in the early cities of Greece, which, he states, were unprotected by walls and for the most part consisted of nothing more than scattered villages.[11] Even in the fifth century BC the village origins of Sparta were still clearly recognisable,[12] and the institution of the joint monarchy presumably reflects a period when the villages were in fact politically distinct.[13] Archaeology at such major centres as Athens, Corinth, Argos and Eretria is beginning to confirm the same

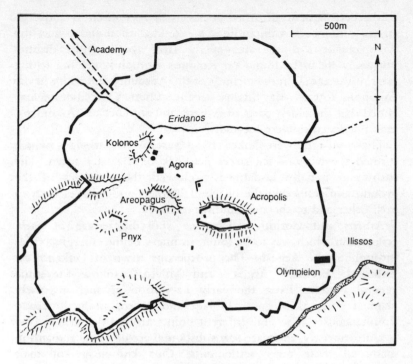

Figure 1 Athens

general picture of scattered, sporadic occupation.

The site of Corinth offered many benefits. Situated 2 kilometres from the sea and therefore relatively safe from pirate raids, the acropolis of Acrocorinth, towering above the city, was a safe, easily defensible refuge against any invader. Early occupation spread over the lower northern and north-eastern slopes of the acropolis which were abundantly supplied with water, whilst the surrounding territory was highly fertile and productive. The benefits and advantages of the site were clearly recognised by its first inhabitants. In the course of the ninth century BC occupation began on the so-called temple hill terrace and shortly afterwards other small communities had established themselves throughout the area of the later city, especially where supplies of water were abundant and easily available.[14]

Early Athens presents a similar picture of sporadic habitation (Figure 1).[15] Occupation began initially in the course of the ninth century BC on the lower slopes of the Acropolis, undoubtedly one

13

of the best naturally fortified positions in ancient Greece. By the eighth century BC habitation had extended to the slopes of the Areopagus and to the area of the later agora. Other distinct villages were to be found on Kolonos Agoraios, the hill to the west of the agora, in the vicinity of the Academy and south of the Acropolis towards the Illissos stream, where Thucydides maintained that the oldest parts of Athens and some of the Athenians' oldest sanctuaries were located.[16]

These villages were linked by a system of pathways which formed the basis of the street network of the later town. The pathways, initially ill-defined, followed the contours of the ground and connected the different hamlets and villages both to each other and to the surrounding territory.

Athens and Corinth reflect the sporadic nature of early occupation which was to be found in many of the emerging cities throughout the Aegean. The prosperous town of Lefkandi on Euboea,[17] Eretria,[18] Argos[19] and Miletos[20] follow the same general pattern. Even the early habitation at such regularly planned cities as Megara Hyblaea and Naxos in Sicily began simultaneously at several different points around the sites.[21]

Unfortunately, there are few substantial architectural remains in many of these early settlements. Our knowledge of their habitation pattern derives mainly from graves, wells and scattered occupation debris. The loose-knit nature of the settlements suggests only loose-knit political control. Indeed it is not even certain whether such villages, albeit sharing a common defensive point, considered themselves a unified settlement.[22] Even political unification did not necessarily bring physical unity. Consequently the level of urbanisation in these early communities was often extremely low.

The post-Mycenaean period, however, was not one of total demoralisation. Slowly, contacts with the higher civilisations of the Near East were renewed and these contacts brought new impetus and fresh initiatives which laid the foundation for the eventual recovery of Greece. The effects are clearly seen in the eighth century BC. This century is marked by rapid expansion and dramatic changes in both the quality and tempo of life. New contacts were made as the Greeks themselves began to explore and colonise the Mediterranean and seek new markets. At home, as the population increased, so existing settlements expanded and new places were occupied. The use of more substantial building materials and better design brought improvements in architecture. At the same time other characteristic features of the *polis* were emerging.

The effects of these developments are apparent at Old Smyrna on the west coast of Asia Minor. The site was first inhabited by Greeks around 1000 BC and had slowly developed over the next two centuries. By the end of the eighth century BC the increased population and uncontrolled expansion had brought serious difficulties.

The site, close to the modern village of Bayrakli, now lies *c.* 450 m from the sea. In antiquity it stood on a low, oval-shaped peninsula at the mouth of the River Hermus. A freshwater spring on the eastern side of the city assured adequate supplies of drinking water.[23] Initially occupation, like that in other cities, was sporadic and scattered without order throughout the peninsula. However, unlike other Greek settlements along the coast of Asia Minor, the peninsula had no natural defences. Instead towards the middle of the ninth century BC the inhabitants of Old Smyrna constructed a city wall, the first of three defensive circuits to be built by the Smyrnaeans and the oldest urban fortifications in the Aegean.[24] The defences themselves were not only an imposing architectural structure but they also indicate a communal and co-ordinated response to the threat of attack.

Increasing prosperity led to a steadily rising population and this in turn led to serious overcrowding within the city walls. By the end of the eighth century BC living conditions had deteriorated. The whole peninsula was covered with a chaotic and haphazard arrangement of oval, apsidal and rectilinear dwellings. Only a small area close to the northern gate, which was reserved for public use and can probably be identified as the agora, seems to have remained free of buildings. The situation at Old Smyrna was only relieved when an earthquake destroyed the town at the end of the century and the authorities completely remodelled the city to a radically new design.[25]

Zagora on the cycladic island of Andros faced similar problems (Figure 2). Founded originally some time before 800 BC the town occupied a remote but relatively flat-topped headland on the western coast of the island.[26] The steep cliffs offered adequate protection from the sea, whilst a strong defensive wall across the promontory protected the town on the landward side. Earliest habitation was scattered, beginning simultaneously at several

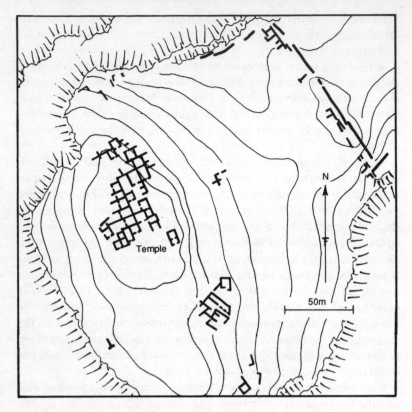

Figure 2 Zagora, Andros

points throughout the site. However, in the course of the eighth century BC an increasing population and possibly an influx of new colonists brought rapid expansion. The rectilinear shape of the houses allowed the easy abutment of new buildings and in consequence large groups of adjoining houses, often served by interconnecting courtyards, spread across the site. The regular alignments of the house walls gave a sense of order to the houses, but the regularity is deceptive and is the product of the constructional methods in which an existing house wall was employed as one of the walls of the adjoining house.[27] It does not imply, as has been suggested, that the town was laid out to an overall master plan.[28] The lack of any regularity is confirmed by the streets. The few pathways which have come to light are typically narrow and sinuous. Their widths and directions were

16

dictated by the geography of the site and the groups of houses which they served.

The provision of adequate supplies of water must have been a problem at Zagora. Today there is no convenient spring within the town and water must have been collected and stored.[29] Nor is there evidence of an open space corresponding to the agora at Old Smyrna. In the centre of the town, however, surrounded by clusters of houses, there was a small, free-standing temple. The building was presumably the shrine of the protective deity of the town and it continued in use long after the site itself was abandoned at the end of the eighth century BC.

The relatively flat terrain of the promontory of Zagora was a vital factor in the development of the township. The terrain was also influential in the development of the approximately contemporary town of Emborio on Chios, but the declivity of the slope had the opposite effect, promoting free-standing houses and necessitating heavy terracing. The town is situated at the southern end of the island on the western slopes of the hill known as Prophetes Elias, close to a good natural harbour but hidden from the sea.[30] The flat-topped summit of the hill, which was encircled by a crude defensive wall, was occupied by the chieftain's residence and, associated with this, there was initially an altar. Subsequently a temple was erected (Figure 3).

The lower town, lying below the road which led to the acropolis, was traversed by a number of irregular but approximately parallel pathways which followed the natural contours of the hill. The houses, all free standing, were arranged along these paths. The arrangement of the houses again gives the impression of regularity but this is due only to the nature of the terrain. A stone-lined well below the occupation area probably served as the only public supply of water.[31] No public meeting place has been identified with certainty, although the free space in front of the chieftain's house on the acropolis might have been so used, and commercial activity would probably have taken place around the harbour.[32] The site had been abandoned by the end of the seventh century BC in favour of a more accessible location close to the harbour.

It remains problematic whether such settlements can be regarded as cities. Nevertheless, they display features of the typical Greek city of the Classical period. The construction of the impressive series of defences at Old Smyrna and the wall at

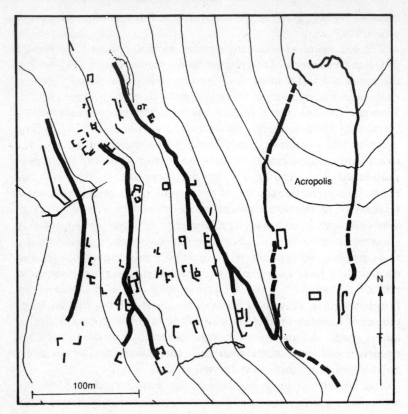

Figure 3 Emborio, Chios

Zagora indicates some degree of central co-ordination and public control. Although there are few public buildings with the exception of temples, several towns had areas specifically reserved for public use, presumably as agoras.[33] The importance of such a space is apparent at Old Smyrna, where the area close to the northern gate was maintained even in the overcrowded conditions of the later part of the eighth century BC. One of the first acts that the colonists at Megara Hyblaea undertook was to mark out and reserve an area as the town's agora.[34] Similarly an early date for the development of the agora of Dreros is suggested by the fact that the associated temple dates back to the eighth century BC.[35] Public awareness or concern is also evident in other areas of urban development. At Miletos a large, well-built drain, dating to the eighth century BC, has been found beneath one of the streets,[36] and several major roads in Athens and other cities were graded and had metalled surfaces at least as early as the seventh century.[37]

Developments continued throughout the seventh and the sixth centuries BC.[38] However, the degree of urbanisation was not uniform. Many cities remained sprawling collections of villages. Nevertheless, by the Classical period the main outlines of the Greek city were firmly established. With the spread of urban defences the acropolis, once the last place of refuge for the occupants, had become a centre of cult, especially for the city's protecting deity. The agora, on the other hand, had become the most important area of the city, attracting public buildings, residential occupation and commercial activity to its environs. The network of roads also developed as the city itself increased in size. In contrast to this the Classical city was still developing architecturally and in many there was still much free space. Even so there was little co-ordinated control or planning in these long-established cities.

Athens in the Classical and Hellenistic periods was a mixture of public buildings, private houses, temples and sacred precincts, interspersed with narrow winding streets, undeveloped plots and open spaces. Minor public buildings and shrines were to be found throughout the city, although they were concentrated on and around the Acropolis and in the vicinity of the agora. Other sanctuaries and the large but incomplete temple to Olympian Zeus were situated in the vicinity of the Ilissos stream. New buildings had to be accommodated wherever space was available.

The most vivid picture of Classical and Hellenistic Athens comes from the south-western quarter of the city, along the lower northern slopes of the Areopagus and in the valley which runs between the Areopagus and the Pnyx. Residential districts, industrial establishments, minor public buildings and shrines have come to light throughout the area (Figure 4). The major roads leading from the south-western corner of the agora were conditioned by the topography of the area. Narrow and sinuous, they hug the contours of the hills but avoid the valley bottoms which were prone to flooding. Other minor streets and alleys, in places often reduced to narrow flights of steps, led from these roads and defined irregular residential and industrial *insulae*. The whole area was interspersed with minor public buildings and shrines.[39] New buildings were added and existing houses were

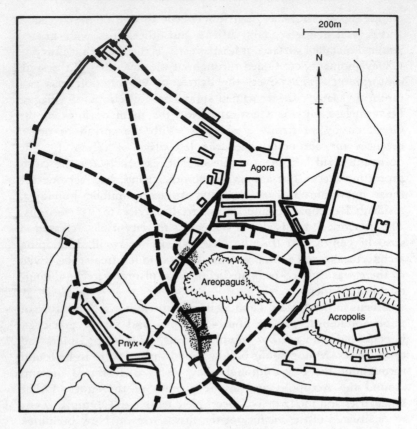

Figure 4 South-western area of Athens

remodelled as conditions changed and property owners took advantage of differing opportunities.[40] The other sides of the agora were similarly crowded with private properties and public buildings.[41]

Further away from the city centre the picture changes only slightly. Houses become more spacious, but there is little attempt at systematic development. House plots, terraced into the slope wherever necessary, continue to be irregular.[42] The streets remain narrow and winding, and on steeper ground are reduced to flights of stone steps. Even when a more systematic exploitation of the terrain was possible the opportunity was not taken and regularity remains minimal.[43] Road widths are rarely constant and building blocks vary in size, shape and configuration without reason.

Increasing urbanisation brought improvements in the provision of essential amenities. Like the tyrants of other cities, the Peisistratids at Athens took an interest in the provision of water by improving the supply to the agora with the construction of an aqueduct and fountain house. Further additions and renovations to the water supply continued throughout the Classical and the Hellenistic periods, culminating in the extensive renovations of Hadrian, which included the construction of a new aqueduct and a large holding cistern at the foot of Lycabettus.[44] The continued growth of the city brought problems of drainage, necessitating the gradual construction and extension of a system of sewers to cope with storm and waste water.

Athens was a city of contrasts. The fine temples and public buildings of the Classical and Hellenistic periods were fitted into an urban plan which had developed over several centuries and was continuing to do so. Athens only reflects on a larger scale the evolution of many cities of the Aegean. Yet the resulting cities were not the same. The geography of the site and differing historical and economic circumstances influenced the development of the towns.

Thorikos, on the southern coast of Attica in the heart of the mining district of Laureion, offers a unique glimpse of an ancient mining town. The town itself occupies a conical-shaped hill close to the sea. In post-bronze-age times evidence of industrial activity has come to light as early as the end of the tenth century BC[45] and in the Classical period, except for the years after the fortification of Decelea by the Spartans during the Peloponnesian War, it was a thriving mining town. Its arrangement, however, was totally haphazard.[46] The roads, cut from the natural rock, were conditioned by the configuration of the terrain and existing buildings. Private houses, industrial establishments, minor shrines and public buildings were constructed without any sense of order wherever convenience allowed. Even the entrances to the mine workings were located within the city. On the lower southern slopes of the hill there is a curiously irregular theatre with an elongated auditorium, resulting from later rebuilding. The re-establishment of mining activity after the Peloponnesian War did not improve conditions. Thorikos remained an amalgamation of public and private buildings and industrial establishments.[47]

Thorikos was an industrial town. Delos, on the other hand, situated on the western coast of the Cycladic island of the same name, was a port and is arguably the most impressive urban site in the Aegean, ranking in importance with Pompeii for the information which it supplies regarding urbanisation. Famed as the birthplace of Apollo and centre of the Ionian confederation formed by Athens after the defeat of the Persians, Delos was not only an important religious centre but it also developed into a thriving commercial city and trading port. Its commercial importance lasted until the first century BC when it suffered two destructive attacks as a result of the Mithridatic Wars. Furthermore, the re-establishment of Corinth and its growth as a major commercial city effectively brought to an end the island's prosperity.

The town, as it stands today, began its development in the sixth century BC, reaching a peak under the influence of the Romans in the latter part of the Hellenistic period. The city grew around the harbour, spreading northwards and eastwards as well as up the lower slopes of Mount Cynthus, the highest point on the island.[48] The sanctuary of Apollo, situated on the flat coastal plain next to the harbour, was the focal point of the town and around it the civic area developed. The successive extensions and the addition of new buildings within the sanctuary were visually harmonised but in general there was little co-ordinated planning. Public buildings, shrines and other monuments were added and renovated progressively. Because of the nature of the terrain and the limited availability of space it was found impractical to place the larger public buildings close to the city centre. Instead the theatre was situated in a natural hollow to the south, whilst a sports complex, including the site of the earlier hippodrome, the gymnasium and the stadium, lay on the relatively flat ground between Mount Cynthus and the neighbouring low hill to the north (Figure 5). In addition to the main sanctuary to Apollo close to the harbour, other sanctuaries were located on the slopes of Mount Cynthus.

The city centre and the port attracted commercial activity in the form of shops and other commercial properties. Main roads, in some cases also lined with shops, radiated outwards from the civic centre to other parts of the city.[49]

The residential districts, occupying the gently sloping ground which rises from the harbour, developed fan-like around the city centre. Two areas in particular have been investigated and offer a contrasting picture of domestic quarters in a Greek city. One, extending from the southern side of the city centre towards and

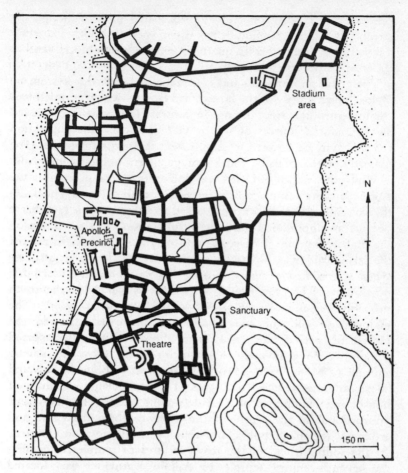

Figure 5 Delos

around the theatre, is typical of many residential areas of Greek cities. The houses are crowded together without order. The streets are narrow and tortuous and, apart from those which act as major routes of communication, serve only to divide the successive blocks of houses and give access to the individual properties.[50]

In contrast the residential area to the north of the sanctuary in the vicinity of Skardhana Bay has a much more regular appearance.[51] The streets meet approximately at right angles, and overall the *insulae* are rectangular. Even so the area was not the

23

product of a rigidly conceived and executed plan. Although the streets tend to be straight, they often vary in width like their counterparts in the 'theatre quarter', and the house blocks tend to differ in shape, size and internal arrangements.

There was an imposing and comprehensive drainage system on Delos. The majority of the houses had latrines which emptied into the underground street drains. In contrast few roads were paved and, as natural sources of water were restricted, the population relied heavily on cisterns to supplement the natural supplies. The majority of houses had a water-storage cistern in their courtyards.

Whilst the success of Delos was due to its central position in the Aegean and its commercial activity, the small town of Thera, on the volcanic island of Santorini, owed its success to the fact that it became an important Ptolemaic naval station. The town sits on the high rocky hill of Meso Vouno on the south-eastern side of the island and was obviously chosen for its defensive qualities when it was first occupied during the ninth century BC. Little now remains of the original settlement. Like Delos the town probably began its development in the sixth century BC. The majority of the surviving buildings, however, date to the Hellenistic period and to Roman times.[52] The town spread ribbon-like along the main road which ran just below the curving summit of Meso Vouno. From the main axis cobbled roads and alleys, at times reduced to flights of steps, led into the mass of houses and buildings which made up the town. The main road widened out in the centre of the town to form the agora and around it the major public and religious buildings concentrated. At the southern end of the town an area of temples, including the seventh-century temple to Apollo Karneios, was located (Figure 6).

Thera was a Dorian city. Lato and Dreros in eastern Crete were also Dorian cities. The former occupied the slopes and the intervening valley of two adjacent, steeply sloping hills. The natural defensive qualities of the location were further enhanced by the arrangement of the town itself. The houses, built on terraces, climbed the slopes in a series of irregular rings presenting to any enemy a successive series of high blank walls.[53] The dwellings, the majority of which date to the fourth century BC, were completely adapted to the terrain. They were arranged on the terraces in a linear manner with one room behind the other.[54] The agora of Lato lies in the saddle of land between the two

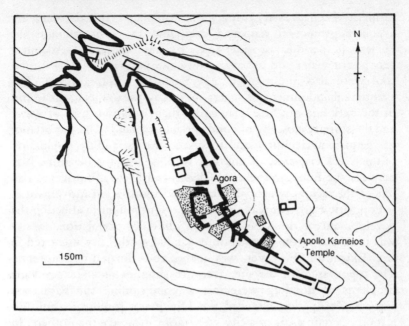

Figure 6 Thera

hills. It is small and irregular in shape and with it is associated a prytaneion, approached by a flight of steps which was probably used by spectators, a temple and other public buildings. From the agora narrow roads radiate to different points of the city.

The buildings of the agora as preserved today date no earlier than the fourth century BC. A similar civic centre was found at Dreros, to the north of Lato, which flourished between the eighth and the sixth centuries BC.[55] The agora occupies a position on the northern slopes of the valley between the two hills. Like Lato, the civic centre included the agora itself with stepped area, a prytaneion, and a temple, the remains of which date back to the eighth century BC. A public cistern was added in the third century BC.

The Greeks readily distinguished these 'old' cities from the 'new' regularly planned cities of the Greek world.[56] They are seen to reflect the spontaneity and freedom which is characteristic of the Greek way of life. The slow and piecemeal development of these cities over a long period of time was in part the result of geographical and historical circumstances. In many cases sites had primarily been chosen with a view to defence, and the need for adequate protection remained even into the Classical and the Hellenistic periods, as inter-state rivalry continued. Adequate supplies of water and the availability and potential of agricultural land were also important in governing the choice of site. The eventual abandonment of several towns in the Aegean at the end of the dark age can be explained by their isolation, lack of water and the scarcity close-by of good agricultural land. The importance of adequate agricultural land to sustain the expanding population of the Greek city-states is not only witnessed by the Lelantine War between the Euboean towns of Chalcis and Eretria, but it was also one of the factors which stimulated the colonisation movement.[57]

Population growth was also an important influence affecting the development of these early towns.[58] Initially population density was low, but as the population expanded so the city increased in size. Expansion, however, was neither co-ordinated nor uniform. The topography of the site, access to supplies of water, and the problems of flooding were factors conditioning the habitation pattern. Occupation extended along the major routes of communication. Certain areas of a city were more attractive than others. In these areas competition for space was often fierce and development haphazard and opportunistic. The civic areas of the city developed in the same uncoordinated way.

Because of the constraints of the evidence, the overall habitation density of ancient Greek cities is often difficult to estimate. Few cities were totally built up. Much of the population of Attica was accommodated within the city, the long walls and Piraeus at the start of the Peloponnesian War, although the consequent over-crowding led to serious problems and presumably facilitated the spread of the plague.[59] By the end of the Peloponnesian War the situation at Athens had changed and free land was again available. Shortly after the final defeat of Athens Xenophon recommended that the government exploit the undeveloped areas of the city by building houses and renting them out.[60] Elsewhere the picture is similar. The text of the exile decree of Alexander suggests that Tegea in the Peloponnese was a spacious, rural market town with houses interspersed with gardens and agricultural plots.[61]

The established pattern of landownership within a city must have been one of the greatest barriers to any co-ordinated redevelopment of existing cities. Few cities were given the opportunity to replan on the scale of Old Smyrna.[62] Even if opportunities did arise they were not taken. With the advance of democracy and the importance attached to landownership for political status in fifth-century Greece, such replanning, with its implicit threat of land redistribution, would have been impossible. At Athens the Solonic oath, sworn by all members of the Heliaia, included the statement that they would not allow the lands and the houses of the Athenians to be redistributed.[63] This fact together with the need to reoccupy the city quickly, because of the continued threat from the Persians, explains why Athens was not replanned after its destruction by Mardonius.[64]

The attitudes of Greek architects to the siting of public buildings and temples must also be considered a factor in the piecemeal development of Greek cities. In the early stages of urban development in Greece there were few public buildings except temples; and they were positioned to protect and overawe. Thus Greek architectural traditions emphasised the individuality of buildings not their place in a co-ordinated group, and so the construction of buildings into planned ensembles was not practised on any large scale. Public buildings were added to the townscape as necessary and as funds became available. Even the earliest evidence for Greek planning shows little or no attempt to co-ordinate the development of public buildings. Land was set aside for public use but its architectural development was often slow and piecemeal.

Although it is possible to discern the factors which contributed to the evolution of the Greek city, the question of its origins remains controversial, and the problem is exacerbated by the fact that before the eighth century BC architectural remains are few and insubstantial. For the most part direct influences from the Greek bronze age can be discounted except on Crete, where, despite destruction and abandonment, some traditions continued.

Places like Karphi, Kavousi and Prinias preserved bronze-age traditions in construction, arrangement and layout, and this fact presumably assisted the post-Mycenaean urbanisation of the island. The agglutinate arrangement of the post-Minoan settlements of Karphi, Kavousi and others, in which houses are packed together with common walls, recalls the nature of settlement around Minoan palaces. The seventh-century temples of Prinias resemble the earlier Minoan shrines.[65] The stepped areas of the agoras of Lato and Dreros have parallels in bronze-age palaces on the island; and it has even been suggested that the whole complex of temple, stepped agora and prytaneion at these cities reflects on a smaller scale the complex of palace, open space and possible town hall of the Minoan town of Mallia.[66] Elsewhere in Greece such direct links with the past are deficient. Even where former bronze-age settlements were reoccupied, the overall pattern of settlement, building design and constructional methods changed.

The Near East is one obvious area which could have influenced urbanism in Greece. Not only were cities a common feature of the near-eastern civilisations but also, as has been pointed out, it was contact with the civilisations of the Near East which laid the foundations for the emergence of Greece out of the dark age. Certain influences are direct and obvious. The technological innovations in iron working and the resumption of bronze working owe much to renewed contact with the Near East. The art of writing and the development of the Greek alphabet are also directly attributable to contact with the Near East and especially the Phoenicians. The influence of Egypt in the development of monumental stone architecture is accepted, and there is the all-pervading influence of near-eastern cultures on artistic development.[67] Certain parallels can also be observed between the Greek *polis* as a political and religious entity and the city-states of Phoenicia.[68]

Nevertheless, direct evidence of any stimulus from the civilisations of the Near East on the urbanisation of early Greece is minimal. Near-eastern cities with their high occupation density, characterised by cramped domestic quarters, which crowded around monumental palaces and other public buildings, have more in common with the arrangements of the Mycenaean town than the loose-knit, village-like development of early Greek cities. Many cities grew only slowly. Public buildings were few until the Classical period. The city was a political, religious and to a lesser extent social centre for the community, but not necessarily the main centre of habitation for the population. Even in the Classical period urban dwelling was despised.[69] Thus influence from the Near East in certain spheres of urbanisation might be acceptable but evidence of direct stimulation is lacking.

The new settlements, out of which the Greek city developed, reflect the new and changing conditions of post-Mycenaean Greece. Greek urbanisation developed in response to the changing political, social and economic conditions within the Greek world. The economic revolution of the eighth century was an important stimulus; so too was the colonisation movement. The establishment of overseas colonies involved more than merely building houses for the settlers. The settlers were effectively creating new Greek cities abroad and they had to define and delimit what constituted a city. Land had to be apportioned both to individuals and the community; and this fact, as will be seen below, provided the further impetus to regular planning.[70] The basis of the future government and administration of the community and the rights and obligations of the colonists had to be established. The position of any later influx of colonists to the colony had to be regulated. The colonisation movement not only assisted the development of regular town planning but must also have been a stimulus to the process of Greek urbanisation in general. The advances which were apparent in the urbanisation of the western colonies by the fifth century BC could not have gone unnoticed elsewhere.

If then the western colonies provided general examples, the tyrannies established both in Greece and in the west in the course of the seventh and the sixth centuries BC directly assisted in the process of urbanisation. Many of the Greek tyrants pursued an active building policy. The reasons for this policy were competition between the various tyrannies, the provision of employment, and obviously the desire to impress their fellow citizens and emphasise the benevolence of their regimes. The construction of temples and water supply systems were particularly favoured. But other public buildings were not neglected, and at Akragas the tyrant, Theron, even added a system of underground sewers.

Whatever were the exact origins of the Greek city, the Greek settlements along the western coast of Asia Minor played a crucial role in the development of Greek urbanisation. By the seventh century BC Old Smyrna, Miletos and presumably other west-coast cities were superior to their contemporaries in other parts of Greece. Later it was from the same area that new stimuli and resources came which were to transform the traditional Greek city. These developments and the factors which brought them about are the subject of a later chapter.

3

THE ORIGINS AND DEVELOPMENT OF GREEK PLANNING IN THE MEDITERRANEAN

'I can't imagine the Greeks allowing themselves to be town planned.'[1] This comment about Kalymnos in the Dodecannese comes from a C. Day Lewis detective novel. It conveys the spirit of freedom and spontaneity which is seen to be characteristic of the Greeks, and consequently for whom the idea of a rigidly ordered urban environment seems alien. It could also be argued that the Greeks were highly rational people with enquiring and fertile minds; it would therefore be wrong to maintain that they could not bring the same rational approach to town planning that they exhibited in their other achievements.

In the *Birds*, Aristophanes ridicules the mathematician, Meton, whom he portrays as planning a circular city.[2] Despite the obvious comedy in the scene and the fact that the circular plan of the city is fanciful, the audience perfectly understood the caricature of the town planner conveyed by Aristophanes. By the second half of the fifth century BC the idea of town planning was firmly rooted in Greek building tradition. Indeed the earliest evidence for town planning antedates by several centuries not only the production of the play but even the life of the supposed inventor of town planning, Hippodamos of Miletos. By the fifth century BC town planning was a firmly established science. The object of this chapter is to trace the origins of Greek town planning and to analyse its development.

The origins of Greek planning remain a source of endless debate and controversy. Those who argue that the concept of grid planning is so simple that it needs no antecedents are countered by those who point out the relative sophistication of even the earliest regularly planned towns of the Greek world, and the fact that regular planning was not exclusively practised by the Greeks. The established civilisations of the Near East are the natural place to seek the origins of Greek planning. But the whole question is complicated by suggestions of an independent Italic planning tradition, which, through the Etruscans, could have inspired the Greeks of southern Italy. Thankfully this idea can now be firmly discounted. Not only do the foundation dates of the earliest planned Greek colonies in the west antedate the earliest evidence for Etruscan planning, but also the evidence on which the argument for an independent tradition of Italic planning rested has been disproved.

Undoubtedly the Near East remains the most likely area from which the Greeks developed regular town planning. Certainly there was a long, if not widespread, tradition of regular planning there. The workers' villages of Kahun and El-Amarna, built respectively by the pharaohs Sosostris II and Akhenaten, were regularly laid out.[3] Closer to Greek practice both geographically and chronologically are the so-far unique Urartian city of Zernaki Tepe in eastern Turkey with its intersecting orthogonal axes and neat, square *insulae*,[4] and the Assyrian levels of the Palestinian city of Megiddo.[5] Further east on the Euphrates, King Nebuchadnezzar refurbished Babylon and reconstructed Borsippa.[6] Both were regularly laid out with a celestial orientation, emphasising the importance of Babylon in the field of astronomy and geometry.

Contacts between the peoples of the Near East and the Aegean can be traced back into prehistory. For a time after the collapse of Greek bronze-age civilisation there was a recession and the contacts were broken. The hiatus, however, did not last long. The renewal of intercourse with the higher civilisations of the Near East, which was one of the key factors in the re-emergence of Greek civilisation in post-bronze-age times, has already been discussed. By the eighth century BC contacts were extensive. According to Homer, the Phoenicians, who were great city-builders themselves, were trading extensively in Greek waters.[7] Slightly earlier still the Greeks had established a trading post at Al Mina at the mouth of the River Orontes.[8] Greek mercenaries were serving in Egypt. It would thus have been easy for new planning ideas to be transmitted during this renewed period of intercourse. It was not, however, in Greece proper but along the western coast of Asia Minor that the earliest steps in regular planning in the Aegean were taken.

Greek colonisation of the eastern seaboard of the Aegean began as early as the eleventh century BC, and by the eighth century BC many thriving communities had been established.[9] The uncertainty of the times, which had forced the colonists to seek rocky, naturally defensible sites, reduced the need for a planned environment. Nevertheless, two of these towns, Old Smyrna and Miletos, have produced the earliest evidence for a new approach to town planning in the Aegean.

The deterioration of living conditions at Old Smyrna in the course of the eighth century BC has already been noted.[10] The town was destroyed by an earthquake at the end of the century and this disaster gave the authorities an opportunity to replan completely.[11] The new layout was simple in its concept but radical in its effects. The peninsula was divided into a series of building strips by a system of parallel streets. Few cross streets came to light in the excavations but communications within the *insulae* were probably facilitated by the provision of lanes and private arrangements for access between properties.[12] The development of the houses within the *insulae* was orderly but not rigidly controlled. Houses were free-standing and tended to be orientated in the same direction. Although rectilinear dwellings appeared and came to dominate, the curvilinear huts typical of the eighth-century city continued to be built for a time.[13] The new arrangements reduced the availability of living space on the peninsula itself and necessitated the expansion of the city on to the adjoining mainland.

The existing public area on the northern side of the town close to the north gate was enlarged and a temple was erected, thus creating a religious and civic zone. The new town plan was completed by the construction of a fountain house, formalising an existing freshwater spring in the ruins of the earlier city wall.[14] Finally towards the end of the seventh century BC, just before the town was sacked by Alyattes, new fortifications were built.[15]

It remains disputed whether the reconstruction of Old Smyrna is a true example of regular planning.[16] Certainly its final form just before its destruction was the product of a century of growth. Nevertheless, the new layout was a great improvement over the conditions which prevailed at Old Smyrna at the end of the eighth century BC. It brought order out of the chaos of the earlier town and offered the inhabitants a sense of spaciousness and freedom within an orderly urban environment.

The town was destroyed again at the end of the seventh century

BC by Alyattes and then rebuilt. Although not as grand as the seventh-century city it was still regularly laid out. The streets were realigned, paved with cobbles and provided with drains.[17]

The foremost city of Ionia throughout the seventh and the sixth centuries BC was undoubtedly Miletos until its destruction by the Persians in 494 BC during the Ionian revolt. Situated on a peninsula at the mouth of the River Maeander, the prosperity of Miletos rested on its rich, fertile territory and its extensive commercial and trading interests, which, according to tradition, led to the establishment of no less than ninety colonies.

The size of the Archaic town is impressive, reflecting its importance. It covers a large part of the peninsula, stretching from Lion bay in the north to the acropolis of Kalbaktepe to the south.[18] Unfortunately, detailed knowledge of the city before the Persian attack is tantalisingly incomplete. The city centre lay in the vicinity of the Athena temple between the two harbours of Theatre bay and Athena bay. Moreover, it is now firmly established that parts of the Archaic town were regularly laid out, although the orientation of the streets of different districts was not uniform. As some of the districts were aligned in the same direction of the new fifth-century town, the earlier network of streets was undoubtedly a factor in the development of Classical Miletos.[19]

Because of the scarcity of evidence, the reasons for the new phase of urban development and the date at which it took place remain conjectural. It is, however, possible that the changes were already under way by the end of the eighth century BC. First, there were changes in domestic architecture. About this time, two oval huts, situated to the west of the Athena temple and similar in design and construction to the eighth-century huts at Old Smyrna, went out of use. They were replaced by a series of more substantial rectilinear buildings which were altered and renovated several times throughout the seventh century BC. Despite the remodelling the buildings maintained the same orientation.[20] Secondly, in the same area a stone-built drain has come to light. It lay just to the west of a house of the geometric period and ran in a northerly direction to the sea. Its associated pottery dates the drain to the eighth century BC.[21] Cumulatively this evidence is meagre but it, nonetheless, suggests that a new phase in the urban development of Miletos had already begun by the end of the eighth century BC, approximately contemporary with or even slightly earlier than alterations at Old Smyrna.

Old Smyrna and Miletos remain isolated examples in the Aegean of a more formal approach to the problems of urban development. However, they indicate the practical expertise in urban planning which was available to the Greeks by the end of the eighth century BC and what could be achieved when the opportunity arose. Although the reorganisation of Old Smyrna resulted from the destruction of the city, it required a measure of strong, centralised control to effect the changes and the acceptance by the population not only of the destruction of existing property boundaries but also the removal of a proportion of the inhabitants from the peninsula to the adjoining mainland. In many of the existing towns of the Aegean such opportunities were either limited or could not be exploited. In contrast the colonisation movement provided both the impetus and the opportunities to experiment with regular town planning.

Inspired by the quest for land, seeking new markets and raw materials, or merely due to disillusionment with conditions at home, the Greeks established new, permanent settlements throughout the Mediterranean and along the Black Sea coast from the eighth century BC onwards. In their new homes the colonists were faced with the practical difficulties of creating new cities. Provision of land for houses and cultivation had to be made for the colonists. Space had to be reserved for the deities which the colonists brought with them from their native home, and for the communal use of the nascent city. Future expansion of the population and the possibility of a new influx of colonists had to be taken into account.[22]

The establishment of the new cities could be achieved without the problems which restricted a more methodical approach to development in the towns from which the colonists had come. The flat coastal sites of Sicily and southern Italy, which were often chosen, were more conducive to regular planning. Sometimes the colonies were planted on virgin land. On the other hand, if the chosen site was already occupied, the natives were often forcibly ejected.[23] In either case the settlement of the new city could be achieved without having to take into account pre-existing conditions. It is, therefore, not surprising that the colonisation movement fostered a more formal approach to urban development and in planting colonies the Greeks took the opportunity to experiment with town planning.[24]

Not every Greek colony throughout the Mediterranean and the Black Sea was regularly planned. The evidence from the early Greek colonies suggests two distinct but related developments. Whilst some sites show a clear tendency towards an orderly arrangement but cannot be considered regularly planned, others are obviously laid out to a preconceived, regular pattern.

The former group share several common features. They include the basic zoning of areas, and the use of one and sometimes two main axes which ran across the site and conditioned the alignment of the buildings. The earliest phase of the Spartan colony of Tarentum is so laid out. Situated on the promontory on the Gulf of Taranto the buildings were aligned with a major road which traversed the site.[25] Akrai and Heloros, two colonies established by Syracuse to guard her territory, were similarly arranged. Heloros was founded in *c.* 700 BC on a hill overlooking the southern approaches to Syracusan territory.[26] The layout resembles that of Tarentum. One main artery, following a slightly sinuous course, crossed the town in a north to south direction. Other equally sinuous streets intersected with this road at intervals of approximately 28 m. The location of the agora along the main road has also been found. Akrai, planted inland of Syracuse, had a similar but slightly more regular arrangement than Heloros.[27] Again it is situated on a hill and is traversed by one major artery which was paved in Hellenistic times. A series of regular side streets ran across the road at an oblique angle, creating sub-rectangular residential *insulae*.

It might be expected that these towns are the first step in the development of regular planning and as such they precede more formal planning methods. This is not so. Elea in Italy and Olbia in the Crimea, both established only during the sixth century BC,[28] were similarly arranged.

Olbia probably best illustrates the tendency towards regularity which certain colonies had, and how such a tendency can be misinterpreted. The colony was established by colonists from Miletos and other Greek cities in the course of the sixth century BC on a large triangular piece of land on the eastern bank of the River Dniepr close to its confluence with the River Bug. It was perfectly situated for trade with the hinterland and for the exploitation of the natural resources of the region. In fact it replaced an earlier trading post established on the island of Berezan in the river. The city lies on two terraces and by the end

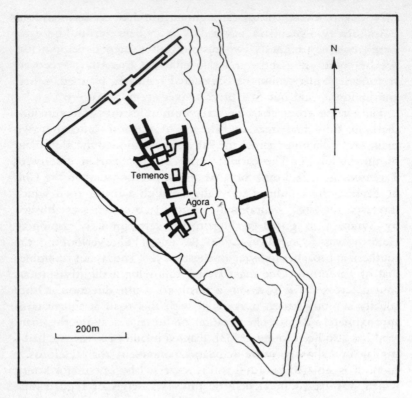

Figure 7 Olbia

of the sixth century BC the upper terrace was being systematically developed (Figure 7). Here space was reserved for the town's agora and associated with it was a triangular-shaped temenos. The rest of the terrace like the lower terrace was given over to private development.[29] A wide arterial road bounding the western side of the agora ran the full length of the city. Two other roads ran approximately parallel to this to the east of the temenos. The residential areas were developed as approximately rectangular *insulae* around the agora and temenos and on the lower terrace. In common with many early colonies the city walls were only constructed later.

The town plan of Olbia has for a long time been interpreted as a strictly orthogonal arrangement, based on two intersecting axes with a celestial orientation.[30] Careful study of the plan reveals no such arrangement. The orthogonal intersection is non-existent. Indeed the two streets leading northwards from the agora are not even exactly parallel but diverge slightly from each other. Although the residential *insulae* were usually rectangular, they were not regular and they differ from each other in area, shape and configuration. The alignment of some of the streets to the points of the compass is best explained not as evidence of the application of theoretical concepts of celestial orientation, but as being merely coincidental in order to make the best possible use of the site. Thus Olbia, far from being rigidly planned, conforms to the arrangement found in several colonies in the western Mediterranean.

The orderly arrangement of these and other towns is clear.[31] The recurring feature of them was the main road which traversed the site. This road conditioned the general orientation of the buildings and other streets. Initially houses and other buildings tended to concentrate along it. The regularity is deceptive. The roads were not always straight and the cross streets were not always strictly perpendicular. The resulting domestic *insulae* were consequently not uniform.

The geography of the locations was one determining factor in the development of these towns. In the majority of cases they occupy rocky hills or promontories with good natural harbours. The emphasis was clearly on defence and the exploitation of the natural features of the site for protection. Another probable influence is the fact that all, with the exception of the satellite colonies of Syracuse, were primarily established for trade and commercial exploitation. In such towns, unlike in agricultural colonies, a more systematic division of land was not required.

One would like to know more about the arrangements of other early Greek colonies, but in many cases the evidence remains elusive. Certainly it appears that the island of Ortygia, the earliest part of Syracuse to be settled, had an orderly if not strictly regular arrangement. Several parallel east-west streets, along which lay simple one-roomed houses, have come to light in excavations, and a major north-south thoroughfare has possibly been found to the east of the temple of Apollo.[32] When the city later expanded on to the mainland itself it was regularly laid out.

Similarly the new residential quarter of Naxos, which was added to the original eighth-century colony in the course of the seventh century BC, was regularly laid out. Traces of a regular

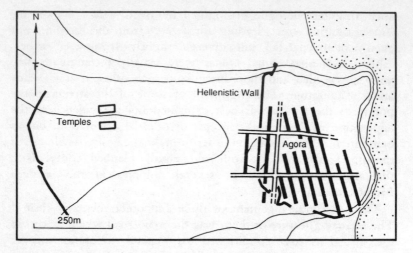

Figure 8 Megara Hyblaea

street grid have come to light, and as they are aligned to the temple of Aphrodite on the south-western side of the town it suggests that the whole of the seventh-century city followed the same orientation.[33] There is also a policy of zoning at Naxos. The temple stands on the edge of the city, clearly segregated from the residential areas. The commercial and industrial areas of Naxos were also specifically segregated from other areas of the town.[34]

The evidence from many of the early colonies in the west is often deficient; this fact makes Megara Hyblaea, the last of the eighth-century colonies to be planted in Sicily, all the more important. Situated between the earlier colonies of Leontini and Syracuse, the colony was established in the second half of the eighth century BC on two slightly raised plateaux to exploit the rich agricultural land of the coastal plain.[35] The general features of the layout include the separation of land for different uses and the development of several differently aligned street grids (Figure 8).

The date at which the town was formally laid out remains disputed. However, the fact that the earliest eighth-century houses were aligned with the streets, and the fact that early structures were found neither on the streets nor in the agora suggests that the laying out of both the streets and the agora was contemporary with the foundation of the city.[36] The whole town plan, however, was not laid out at the same time. The agora and the residential

38

area to the east were the first stage in the development of the city. The residential area to the west of the agora with its different alignment was a later addition, although the presence of eighth-century structures in the area suggests that the time difference between the first and the second stage of development was not long. The latter took its orientation from the major road bounding the western side of the public square. Subsequently no less than five residential districts grew, all with differently orientated street systems, either as the city expanded or there were new influxes of colonists.[37]

Communications between the agora and the district to the west of the city, which included the two suburban temples, were maintained by the two major avenues, following slightly sinuous courses, which bounded the northern and southern sides of the agora.[38] The resulting *insulae* formed by the intersection of these roads with the streets of the residential districts around the agora are elongated and trapezoidal in shape. The *insulae* were divided longitudinally by axial walls and their perimeters were clearly defined by low stone curbs, which separated them from the public streets.[39] As stated above, two temples stood at the western extremity of the city and two cemeteries developed outside its north-western and southern bounds.

The seventh century BC witnessed a great increase in both the size and the prosperity of the colony. More residential quarters were added, there was an increase in the size of the houses, and the architectural development of the agora was begun. The amount of land allocated for the agora in the original layout was found to be inadequate for the needs of the expanding town. Consequently parts of adjacent residential *insulae* were taken over for the construction of public buildings. As in other parts of the *insulae*, cross walls clearly segregated the public buildings from the residential structures of the *insulae*. Finally towards the end of the sixth century BC the city wall was added.

Megara Hyblaea lacks an overall master plan. It developed in response to a changing situation over a period of time and to the practical considerations of the site itself. Nevertheless, its overall layout is coherent, combining the public, religious and private requirements of the colony into a cohesive entity. Moreover, from the initial implantation of the colony certain principles were laid down. Areas were specifically designated for different uses, and even the lines of the streets were laid out from the initial

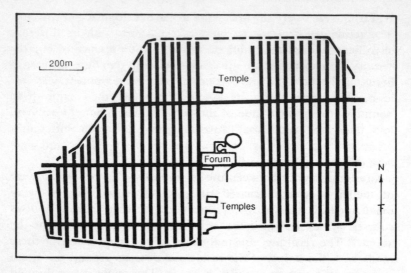

Figure 9 Poseidonia/Paestum

foundation. The plan used a system of major arteries and numerous minor streets to create elongated *insulae*. The principles of the town plan of Megara Hyblaea were refined into a standard urban design in the subsequent centuries in Greek colonies throughout the Mediterranean and the Black Sea.

The pattern was already firmly established by the time that settlers from Sybaris established Poseidonia, later to become the Roman colony of Paestum, on the coast of Campania. The town consisted of two regularly laid out residential areas which were separated by a large strip of land allocated for public use.[40] The layout is typical (Figure 9). The residential districts were divided into parallel strips of land by three widely spaced avenues which ran across the site from east to west. One lay immediately to the south of the later forum. Another was situated midway between this road and the northern city wall, and the third, found only in the western residential area, was situated at an equal distance from the central avenue to the south. More than thirty cross streets have been identified by aerial photography and excavation, and they created elongated rectangular *insulae* measuring 35 × 300 m. Whereas a few of these north–south streets might have been major arteries in their own right, the majority of the cross streets served merely to divide up the *insulae* and give access to the houses.

The area designated for the town's temples and public buildings originally lay adjacent to the western residential district and it only assumed its central position when the eastern residential area was added later. Here all the city's major civic and religious buildings were accommodated. The public buildings were developed independently of the street system and, curiously, the temples of the original Greek city together with the other public buildings were aligned slightly differently from the street system.

As recovered, the layout of Poseidonia is simple. Nonetheless, several features of the plan remain problematical. The date of the actual development of the plan is disputed, although it is now generally accepted to have been laid out towards the end of the sixth century BC. Another difficulty arises in dating the walls, which, in common with many Greek cities, were only added later. The most puzzling aspect of the plan is the slight but obvious misalignment between the residential districts and the temples. It has been suggested that this misalignment reflects an earlier 'pre-planning' stage in the development of the city when the general orientation of the colony was drawn up but the streets were not precisely laid out.[41] Indeed the colony was first established in the seventh century BC and the earliest temples at Poseidonia almost certainly antedate the accepted date for the development of the street system towards the end of the sixth century BC.

There is another possible explanation for the discrepancy. The long axes of the temples follow the normal east-west orientation of temples. The city, however, is built on an outcrop of limestone, the edges of which are followed by the city wall and dictate the shape of the perimeter. It is thus possible that the roads were aligned differently from the temples in order to reduce the number of oddly shaped plots within the city. Furthermore the district around Poseidonia was swampy and consequently liable to flooding. It is again feasible that the line of the streets, following the slope of the ground, was chosen to assist the drainage of the site.[42] Consequently, the differences in orientation between the streets and the temples could be the result of a combination of religious scruple and the practical utilisation of the topography of the site.

The layout of Poseidonia is characteristic of many of the colonies in the west. In Italy the design was repeated at Naples, where a new colony was established in the fifth century BC a short distance away from the original town.[43] The gridded plans of Croton[44] and Locri[45] seem probably to have had the same layout, whilst Metapontum, near to Taranto in southern Italy, is remarkably similar to the arrangement of Poseidonia. The city contained two residential districts which were separated by a large strip of land reserved for public use. The northern residential district was constructed first and was clearly segregated from the agora and temple of Apollo Lykeios, which lay to the south-east, by a road. Only as the city expanded was the second residential district laid out to the south of the agora and temple. The street grid of the colony created typical elongated rectangular *insulae* which measured 190 × 35 m.[46] The main avenues, some of which attained a width of 12 m, ran east to west. The north-south streets were narrower although, like Poseidonia, at least two of them were major thoroughfares in their own right (Figure 10).

Besides the town plan important research on the organisation of the territory around the colony of Metapontum has also taken place. The territory was systematically divided into regular parcels of land which were defined by drainage ditches. The areas were approximately 205 m in width, whilst the transverse divisions seem to have been 323 m apart. There is also evidence that the tracts of land so defined were further subdivided into smaller units for distribution to individual colonists. Although the present visible remains date to the early decades of the fifth century BC, they perpetuate an earlier system which dates back into the sixth century BC and can probably be associated with the foundation of the colony.[47] Like Metapontum, the neighbouring colony of Herakleia, planted in *c.* 433–432 BC, offers further evidence of the division of its surrounding territory. In other parts of the Greek world the possible influences of rural land division on town planning are slowly beginning to emerge.[48] At Metapontum and Herakleia the exact relationship is still difficult to substantiate. Nevertheless, the association of a regularly laid out town with the systematic development of the neighbouring *chora* at both Metapontum and Herakleia cannot be fortuitous and emphasises the importance of agricultural land division in the development of Greek town planning.

Gridded layouts similar to those of southern Italy are found in Greek colonies throughout the Mediterranean. In Sicily they include Himera, Naxos and the Syracusan colony of Kamarina.[49] At both Himera and Naxos the town plans of the original colonies

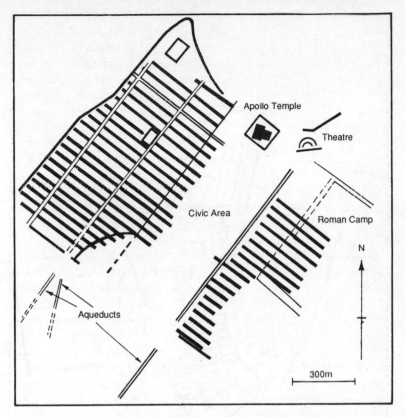

Figure 10 Metapontum

were swept aside in the fifth century BC and new street grids with a different orientation were imposed.[50] The Greek colonies at Cyrene and Eusperides on the northern coast of Africa follow the same general arrangement,[51] although at Eusperides the alignment of the streets is neither consistent nor are the *insulae* uniform in size.

Many of the Greek colonies in the west prospered greatly as a result of their extensive agricultural and commercial interests and far outgrew their founding cities. The two Sicilian colonies of Selinus and Akragas were particularly important and influential in the region, a fact reflected in the towns themselves. Their layouts, whilst based on the gridded network of streets typical of the western colonies, were conceived and executed in a monumental

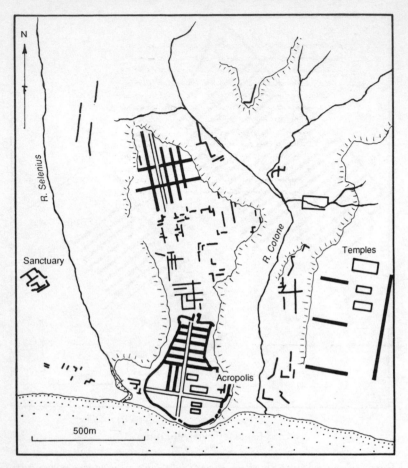

Figure 11 Selinus – general plan

fashion, combining impressive locations with fine public buildings.

Selinus, which occupies a promontory site between two rivers on the southern coast of Sicily, is one of the most beautiful and impressive sites on the island, and became one of the strongest cities on the south coast until it was destroyed by the Carthaginians in 409 BC. The original Greek city was vast. It encompassed not only the urban centre with extensive residential areas and the acropolis overlooking the surrounding fertile plain, but also included two harbours and two large, suburban religious precincts (Figure 11). In addition there were also extensive

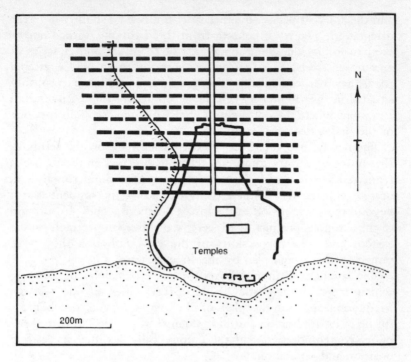

Figure 12 Selinus – Archaic/Classical acropolis

cemeteries and quarries in the vicinity.

The significance of Selinus in the history of town planning has been much debated. The intersecting axial roads of the acropolis in particular have caused much discussion and controversy.[52] Recent investigations not only confirm the importance of Selinus in the sixth century BC but have also radically altered the accepted interpretation of the town plan.[53] It now seems certain that the orthogonal arrangement on the acropolis was the result of replanning in the fourth century BC after the destruction of the city in 409 BC. The earlier town followed a different arrangement.

The acropolis was divided into two distinct areas by a newly discovered east-west road. To the south of the road lay the acropolis temples, whilst to the north of it there was a regularly laid out residential area. The latter extended for approximately six blocks beyond the end of the acropolis on to the saddle between the acropolis and the adjoining Manuzza hill to the north (Figure 12). The rest of the city, encompassing the slopes of Manuzza hill

45

and the adjacent plains on either side, followed a slightly different orientation. The road, coming from the acropolis, turned north-west to follow the longitudinal axis of Manuzza hill. A series of narrower streets, interspersed occasionally with wider arterial roads, lay perpendicular to this road. The agora was probably situated in the saddle between the acropolis and the Manuzza hill at a point where the north-south road from the acropolis met one of the major east-west avenues.

The newly discovered east-west thoroughfare on the acropolis clearly segregated the important religious precinct on the acropolis from residential *insulae*. Yet at the same time the acropolis was united with the rest of the city by extending the residential area beyond the acropolis on to the lower northern slopes. In addition to the acropolis precinct there were two suburban precincts on the eastern and western outskirts of the city, although they were united to the overall plan by the street system.

The layout of Selinus follows the same principles of planning which were characteristic of the Greek cities of the western Mediterranean. But the plan of the whole city is much more subtle in its application and monumental in its concept than those of its contemporaries, and the colony fully justified its leading position and reputation.

From Selinus we turn to Akragas, the last of the major Greek colonies to be established in Sicily.[54] The city was founded in 580 BC as a joint venture from Gela and Rhodes and occupied a theatre-like depression surrounded on three sides by hills. Under a succession of tyrants it rapidly grew and became the bastion of the Greek way of life in the face of Carthaginian influence on the western side of the island. Settlement probably first began on the northern side of the town underneath the acropolis where a scatter of irregularly planned structures has come to light. The gridded system which developed in the hollow between the hills produced typically elongated *insulae* approximately 35 × 200 m. The street grid was based on at least six parallel arteries which were traversed by many cross streets. The house blocks were divided longitudinally by narrow alleys and there is also evidence for other narrow passages to facilitate circulation within the *insulae*.[55] Akragas underwent a great period of prosperity and aggrandisement after the defeat of the Carthaginians at the battle of Himera in 479 BC, prompting the comment from Empedokles, the city's philosopher and democratic reformer, that his fellow citizens 'eat

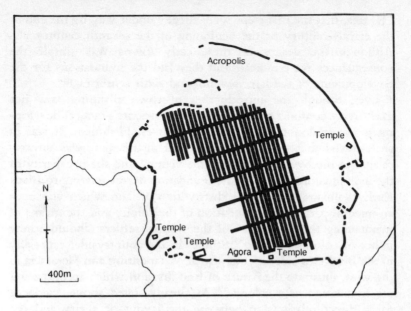

Figure 13 Akragas

as if they were to die tomorrow, and build as if they were never to die.'[56] Temples and other public buildings were constructed, the majority occupying prominent positions on the heights which surround the town. The city wall was added, a system of underground channels brought piped water into the city, and drains were constructed.[57] These works transformed the city into a model of Archaic planning (Figure 13).

The city of Akragas has become increasingly important for the history of town planning. Its plan, like that of Selinus, was conceived on a grand scale, and the functional layout of the streets was expertly combined with a sense of spaciousness and the monumental design of its public buildings. The simplicity of the regularly laid out residential areas contrasted with the imposing, aesthetically pleasing temples which dominated the heights, and with the addition of piped water and underground drainage, Akragas offered a degree of luxury not often found in contemporary cities of the Greek world.

The introduction of regular town planning marks an important step in the history and development of the Greek city and it seems likely, on the evidence from Miletos, Old Smyrna and Megara

Hyblaea, that the first steps were already under way by the end of the eighth century or the beginning of the seventh century BC. Although the design of these early towns was simple the consequences were radical, and they laid the foundations for the developments of the later seventh and sixth centuries BC.

Even though the introduction of town planning was not exclusively confined to agricultural colonies, its practical development was undoubtedly assisted by their establishment. It was in such towns that the question of land distribution was directly related to the overall success of the venture and the prosperity of the individual inhabitants. The foundation decree relating to Black Kerkyra illustrates the clear distribution of land which was both an integral part of the foundation of the colony and the means of maintaining the supremacy of the original settlers, should a new influx of colonists arrive.[58] Studies in the countryside, especially in the Black Sea colonies but also at Metapontum and Herakleia in the west, illustrate the nature of land division which accompanied the foundation of a colony.[59] As already stated above, evidence for a direct relationship between the layout of a city and the division of the agricultural land remains meagre, but the planimetric nature of early Greek planning emphasises the importance of the land surveyors, who presumably accompanied the ventures. Their practical experience in dividing and distributing land is reflected in the division of these early colonies.

The policy of zoning and the laying out of a regular grid of streets were the two most important features of early Greek planning. Land was specifically reserved for public, private and sacred use. Often the different areas adjoin, but in reality remain mutually distinct. In several towns temples were allocated suburban locations. In some cities economic activity was specifically segregated.[60] Zoning allowed each district, if necessary, to develop independently of the others and even permitted differences in orientation. At the same time it introduced a judicial element to the planning of a city. Different areas were clearly defined, as has already been seen in the case of Megara Hyblaea.

The street grid, with its characteristic network of intersecting wide avenues and narrow streets, was the modulating factor in the development of the residential quarters, creating long, rectangular house blocks for private development. Within the *insulae* themselves development was not uniform. Unlike town planning in the Classical period, where house plots were often regular, the distribution of land within the *insula* did not necessarily aim at equality. The inscription from Black Kekyra makes a distinction between the initial colonists and those who came later, and studies in land holding in some of the early Greek colonies in the west confirm the fact that building plots differed in size.[61] In such elongated house blocks there must have been problems of rights of access which in several cases were alleviated by private arrangements allowing passage.[62]

Early Greek planning remained essentially practical. Thus the topography and the geography of the site were important determinants in the evolution of the town. Streets were orientated to make the most efficient use of the terrain, to reduce the number of oddly shaped plots, or to assist with such practical considerations as drainage. Natural features were taken into account to enhance and to beautify the towns. Nevertheless, in general, early Greek planning displays an air of artificiality. Often the town plan seems imposed upon the site regardless of other considerations. In the same way new extensions were added or existing towns swept aside and a completely new grid imposed with only a minimal attempt to co-ordinate any remaining elements.

As was observed at the beginning of the chapter, Greek town planning did not develop in a vacuum. Renewed contacts with the Near East brought technical expertise in such areas as geometry, stone architecture and concepts of monumentality. In Italy and Sicily the Greeks came into direct contact with the Carthaginians and the Etruscans; and merely because it is now certain that the Greeks introduced grid planning into Italy and Sicily it is not necessary to maintain that the dissemination of all ideas was one way. Even so the Greeks made a unique contribution to the history and development of town planning in Europe and the Mediterranean. As J. B. Ward-Perkins observed, 'the city was the formal planning unit and within it individual buildings had to find their appropriate place'.[63]

Direct antecedents of such an approach to urban planning are difficult to substantiate. The majority of the cities of the Near East follow a radically different pattern from Greek cities. In the long-established cities of the Near East there was little order. Houses and other buildings were tightly packed together, and the streets were narrow and tortuous. Even the few regularly planned cities which have been found differ markedly from those of the Greeks. The plans show a preference for an axial arrangement, occasionally with a celestial orientation, but these features are neither clear nor consistently applied.[64] Within the towns themselves, emphasis is placed on the public buildings; the domestic areas often continued to develop in the time-honoured way without any order, even when there was a regular street grid.[65]

The majority of the towns in the Near East were the product of strong, centralised and autocratic political systems. Phoenicia is an exception. Phoenician cities share several features in common with the Greek *polis*.[66] They were politically independent. Each city controlled its own surrounding territory.[67] They traded and established colonies throughout the Mediterranean, even penetrating into Greek waters. But Phoenician cities still differ from their Greek counterparts. They were small and crowded together in typical near-eastern fashion. They were protected by strong defensive walls, and with the exception of Megiddo II, which was built under Assyrian domination, none was regularly planned.[68] In contrast, although Greek cities are small, the actual area covered is often extensive. Occupation is consequently scattered. Frequently city walls were not the first feature of the city to be built even in potentially hostile territory and, with the exception of temples, public buildings were few.

Greek town planning originated as a practical response to the problems of establishing new towns or occasionally, if the opportunity arose, redesigning an existing community. It cannot be totally fortuitous, however, that the beginning of regular planning coincides virtually with the formative period in the evolution of the *polis* as a political, social and religious institution. The nature of early Greek planning both reflects and caters for the incipient *polis* by clearly defining and allocating land for its component parts. At its simplest, early Greek planning was a rationalisation of the already emerging cities of Greece. The regular arrangement offered the nascent city space to develop and at the same time allowed freedom, both to the individual and the community in general, within an orderly framework.

4

PLANNING IN THE CLASSICAL PERIOD

Hippodamos of Miletos not only dominates the history of Classical town planning but, as the first recorded town planner of antiquity, he is the source of endless debate and confusion.[1] His career as a town planner is controversial. His name is specifically associated with the cities of Piraeus, Thourioi and Rhodes, but his involvement with Piraeus, planned at some time during the first half of the fifth century BC, and Rhodes, built in 408 BC, creates obvious chronological difficulties. More problematic is the place that Hippodamos occupies in the history of town planning. Regarded as the father of town planning, it was at one time claimed that he invented the system of regular planning with which his name is associated.[2] That he did not invent town planning is now clear from the extensive evidence from the Greek colonies of the west, from Old Smyrna, and even from his own home town of Miletos; and the alternative suggestions which are advanced to account for his reputation, such as that he codified existing practice, are conjectural and spurious. The fact is that, despite his reputation, Hippodamos remains an elusive and controversial figure.

The city-state, with its urban centre and surrounding territory, is seen as the dominant political form in Greece in the Classical period. Whilst it is true that the history of Classical Greece is dominated by the relations between the major *poleis*, it is often forgotten that in reality the *polis* was confined for the most part to areas of central and southern Greece, the islands of the Aegean and those regions of coastal Asia Minor which had been colonised by the Greeks. In other parts of the Greek peninsula there were other political forms and social structures which were not based upon the concept of the city-state, and in consequence large parts of the

Balkans remained unurbanised. Furthermore, a clear distinction must be made between the development of the *polis* as a political and social institution, and the development of its associated urban centre. The urban centre, the *asty* in Greek, whilst its main outlines were clearly defined by the Classical period, was for the most part still developing architecturally. Thus opportunities for town planning were extensive throughout the Aegean. New cities arose through the synoecism of local communities into larger towns, existing cities were moved to new, more favourable locations, and the Greek urban way of life was spread to the less Hellenised parts of the Aegean and the Balkans, sometimes in the face of local opposition.[3] In addition the cities destroyed or damaged by the Persians had to be renovated or rebuilt.

Sometimes the opportunity to replan was not taken. Athens is one case where, after its destruction by the Persians, the city was merely rebuilt to its former irregular pattern. The reasons for this – the need for speed because of the continued Persian threat, and the established pattern of land holding within the city – have already been discussed.[4] The situation at Miletos was different. The town had been destroyed during the Ionian revolt almost fifteen years prior to the eventual defeat of the Persians, and it had not been extensively reoccupied until Ionia had been freed from Persian domination after the battle of Mycale. Moreover, the basis of a regular street plan in some districts had already been laid in the pre-Persian city, and the old street plans would only have had to be redrawn.[5]

This fact should not, however, detract from the ambitious design of the new Classical city. The plan, embracing harbours, commercial districts, public areas and residential zones, not only controlled the development of the city but also laid the foundations of its future expansion into Hellenistic and Roman times.[6] As an integral feature of the new city plan the old city centre was greatly extended (Figure 14). A large L-shaped tract of land in the middle of the peninsula, situated between the two main harbours of Miletos, was reserved for public use. Here the administrative, political, commercial, sacred and public buildings of the city developed. The civic buildings were so sited in a loose but unified relationship that it is difficult to believe that their planning and construction was not achieved at one time. In fact the civic centre was the product of centuries of development,

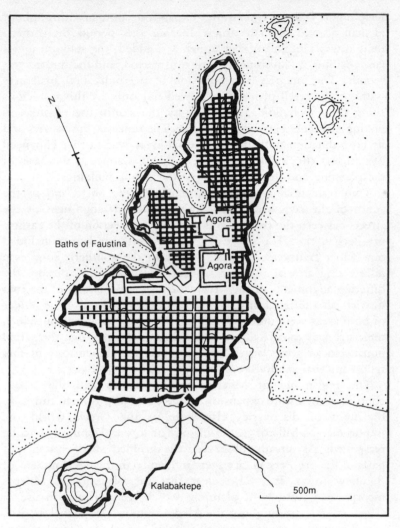

Figure 14 Miletos

entailing the redesigning of existing buildings as well as the addition of new structures.

Between the fifth and the first centuries BC a complex of public, administrative, commercial and religious buildings was constructed. They included two markets, a bouleuterion, a new

53

Delphinion and a gymnasium. Expansion continued throughout Hellenistic and Roman times. During this period the Athena temple was rebuilt, another agora was added, the stadium and a large bathing establishment were constructed, and the theatre was rebuilt. The integrity and cohesion of the individual structures within the overall plan was achieved not only by the auspicious siting of new buildings but also by the skilful use of stoas as linking elements between buildings. The unity of the district and its co-ordination with the residential areas was further enhanced by utilising the *insula*-unit of the residential zones as the basis of the planning and the laying out of the public buildings.

Two residential areas were laid out to the north and to the south of the civic area. The slightly different alignment of the streets between the two areas is possibly a reflection of the earlier, pre-Persian city. The street grid of the northern district included one wider transverse avenue, whilst in the southern zone two intersecting arterial routes assisted communications. Besides the differing alignments of the streets the residential *insulae* of the two districts also differed in size. Indeed the dimensions of the *insulae* of both areas were unusually small. But as the evidence on which their size was calculated was limited, it is possible that the actual house blocks were larger and the recorded dimensions in fact reflect internal subdivisions of larger residential *insulae*.[7]

The replanning of Miletos was a success and the layout controlled the future expansion of the town into Roman times. In the light of discoveries elsewhere in the Greek world the importance of Miletos in the history of town planning has to be reassessed. As already observed, the gridded street systems of parts of the pre-Persian city were influential in the development of the new town. It is also clear that the planning of Miletos incorporated features of planning which were already in use in Greek colonies throughout the Mediterranean. Nevertheless, it is equally apparent that Miletos also included new ideas in planning. Most obvious is the use of the *insula*-unit, not the streets, as the modulating factor in the development of the town.[8] The residential zones were laid out as a repetitive series of *insulae*. The public buildings, although not fully incorporated into the street grids, were similarly designed and constructed as multiples of the standard unit.

Discussion of Miletos leads on naturally to the work of Hippodamos and his role in the history of planning. Aristotle is our fullest source of information about Hippodamos. He presents him as an eccentric and a social and political theorist who speculated about the nature of the ideal city. Of his planning activities Aristotle further states that he invented the division of cities and planned Piraeus.[9] It is also accepted that he participated in the pan-Hellenic colony of Thourioi, and the planning of Rhodes is also ascribed to him. Elsewhere he is described as a *meteorologos*.[10] As a practising town planner he would undoubtedly have had an interest in, and presumably intimate knowledge of, the layout of Miletos, but it is only conjecture to maintain, as some writers do, that he also had been involved in its actual design. Indeed Hippodamos can be associated with only three cities – Piraeus, Thourioi and Rhodes – and so any assessment of Hippodamos' place in the history of town planning has to come from the evidence of the towns on which he actually worked.

The only city directly attributable to Hippodamos is Piraeus, the port of Athens. Aristotle states specifically that Hippodamos planned Piraeus. The date at which the city of Piraeus was laid out remains disputed. Themistocles, who chose Piraeus in place of Phaleron as the anchorage for the Athenian navy, fortified the site before Xerxes' invasion of Greece.[11] It can, therefore, be plausibly argued that the town itself was also laid out at the same time. Yet a date closer to the middle of the fifth century BC for the planning of the town is suggested by the style of lettering on a series of boundary markers which were found in the city, and which relate to the town plan.[12]

It is possible to reconcile this chronological discrepancy if it is accepted that the evidence represents two distinct stages of development. The first involved the construction of the naval facilities under Themistocles; and then, later in the century, the development of the civilian town and its commercial facilities took place. Whilst not conclusive, the known evidence for the history of the city at least permits such an explanation. On the one hand, Thucydides' account of Themistocles' work on Piraeus indicates that his main efforts concerned the construction of the naval installations and the fortification of the site. He details at length the construction of the walls but mentions neither the laying out of the town nor Hippodamos' association with it. Admittedly Thucydides is primarily concerned to understand and account for Athenian imperialism. The construction of the naval and military installations at Piraeus was an important aspect of the growth of Athenian power, whereas the development of the civilian town was not. However, even accepting that the silence of Thucydides on the subject is not conclusive proof, it can be plausibly argued that if the town plan was laid out in the Themistoclean era, Thucydides would have mentioned the fact, not only because of the subsequent reputation of the planner involved, but also because such a notable event in the early years of the fifth century BC would have provoked comment. On the other hand, a date towards the middle of the century for the planning of the port is not only more appropriate to the expansion of Piraeus as a commercial town, an aspect of development in which Hippodamos might have had special interest since the main commercial agora was named after him,[13] but it is also contemporary with the building of the long walls between Athens and her harbour town. Furthermore, a date later in the century for the planning of the city to some extent alleviates the chronological difficulties involved in accepting Hippodamos' involvement in the planning of Rhodes at the end of the fifth century BC.

Whatever is the actual date for the planning of Piraeus, little of the Classical city remains today because it lies below the bustling modern port. Even so the limited archaeological investigations which have taken place in the modern city shed some light on the ancient town plan. As far as the evidence allows interpretation, the planning of Piraeus integrated the existing harbour facilities with the newly laid out public areas, buildings and residential districts. The few streets which have been excavated, one of which attained a width of over 14 m, suggest that not one but several differently aligned street systems were in use in different parts of the city, athough the unity of the town plan was maintained.[14]

Of more significance for the reconstruction of the town plan is the series of boundary markers which have come to light. The markers separated public and private land, divided the city into different districts including, where necessary, a differently orientated grid of streets, reserved areas for public use and even defined the limits of the public buildings.[15] Thus the layout of Piraeus was a comprehensive and integrated design, embracing the commercial and military installations around the harbours as well as public and private districts, and controlling present and future expansion.

Hippodamos' association with the planning of Thourioi remains conjectural. Several eminent fifth-century figures, including

Herodotus and Lysias, accompanied the venture and a Hippodamos is also known at Thourioi. He is assumed to have been the town planner. Although this identification is not indisputable, it could be argued that such a pan-Hellenic venture might have appealed to the Milesian's social and political interests, and with all its potential difficulties and problems in attempting to unite the different Greek contingents into a single community, it offered a challenge to his concepts of how to create and plan the ideal state. If the Hippodamos known at Thourioi was the town planner, it is reasonable to suppose that as the only known town planner on the expedition, who had already planned the port of Athens, he would have been intimately involved in the design of this Athenian-inspired colony.

Diodorus' account of the planning of the colony still remains the most informative.[16] The site was chosen because of a nearby spring which assured a good supply of water. Of the construction of the town itself, the line of the walls was first defined and the walls themselves were built. Then the interior of the town was laid out. The area inside the walls was divided up into large sectors by seven avenues, four running in one direction and three in the other. The resulting areas were then filled out with narrower streets to create regular housing blocks.

The description is unfortunately brief and excavations on the site have so far only succeeded in elucidating the levels of the later Roman colony of Copia, which partially overlaid the Greek city.[17] Despite the brevity of Diodorus' account, the plan of Thourioi bears a general resemblance to Piraeus. The similarities include the use of major streets to define the different areas of the city, the adoption of a rectangular grid of streets within each area, and the overall unity of the design.

The last city with which the name of Hippodamos is associated is Rhodes. Strabo records the popular belief, current in his day, that the city of Rhodes was planned by the same man who laid out Piraeus.[18] Despite the chronological difficulties, the characteristics of the town plan of Rhodes have affinities both with Piraeus and Thourioi, and support the idea that Hippodamos was in some way involved in its planning.

The city of Rhodes was admired in antiquity. Strabo considered it to be superior to all other cities in harbours, roads and other amenities.[19] The town itself was founded on the northern tip of the island in 408 BC by the synoecism of three neighbouring

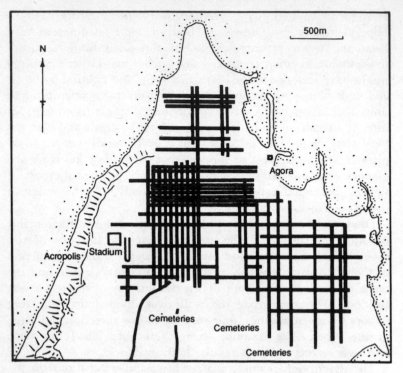

Figure 15 Rhodes

communities. Diodorus' description of the city as 'theatre-like' has in the past caused problems. However, it has now become clear that the description refers to the nature of the terrain and not to any fan-like arrangement of the streets.[20]

The town plan, recovered from aerial photographs and confirmed by excavations, was precisely drawn up and comprised a rectangular grid of streets which embraced the whole of the site.[21] The basis of the layout was a series of large squares, approximately 201 m in length, which were defined by a network of major arterial thoroughfares.[22] The larger squares were then divided into smaller, rectangular housing blocks by narrower streets. The grid has been reconstructed with a fair amount of accuracy although difficulties remain (Figure 15). For instance, as at Miletos, the residential *insulae* are especially small and suggest that some of the streets were in fact internal subdivisions of larger housing blocks.[23]

Other features of the town plan are also apparent. Little of the town centre remains, although the sites of several temples are known and it is probable that the large area of land situated close to the main bay and apparently devoid of ancient buildings and roads, was in fact the location of the original agora.[24] It is also possible that the area around the stadium and the temple to Apollo at the foot of the acropolis was reserved in the original plan for cultural and leisure activities, because a gymnasium and an odeion have been located in the immediate vicinity.[25]

The planning of Rhodes involved more than drawing up the street grid. Its layout was conceived and executed on a monumental and unified scale. The extensive use of terracing exploited the visual advantages of the sloping terrain and gave commanding views across the bays. Indeed, when Demetrius attacked Rhodes in 305 BC the old men and women of the city had a perfect view of the invasion fleet from their houses.[26] It would appear that the city fully justified Diodorus' description.

The theatre-like topography of the site, however, also created problems of flooding. There was the danger in severe weather that water, running down from the slopes of the surrounding hills, would inundate the lower areas of the city. Diodorus Siculus records that the city was seriously flooded on three occasions.[27] The first caused little damage because it occurred shortly after the city had been built and there was much open space. The second was more destructive. The third, coming at the beginning of the spring of 316 BC, when it was thought that the rainy season was over and consequently the drains had been neglected, caused extensive destruction and loss of life. The lower areas of the city, including the market and the Dionysion, were completely inundated and the water even threatened to destroy the temple of Asclepius. Further damage and destruction were avoided only when the walls, unable to sustain the weight of the water, collapsed and the flood water poured into the sea.

The original planner of Rhodes had realised the potential difficulties of the site and had included a drainage system as part of the original design.[28] In fact Diodorus blames the neglect of the drainage system as the prime reason for the scale of the disaster of 316 BC. Excavations have revealed three sewerage systems. The earliest, dating to the Classical period, is probably associated with the initial foundation of the city and must therefore be considered one of the earliest complete drainage systems in Greece. This was subsequently replaced in the Hellenistic and Roman periods by two other systems. The sewerage system was impressive. Smaller-sized drains leading from houses and other buildings fed larger street drains which in turn emptied into major sewers, sufficiently large to allow maintenance gangs to pass through.

Despite the differences between the towns and the problems of ascribing Piraeus, Thourioi and Rhodes to the work of Hippodamos, the three cities display certain common characteristics. They include the division of the land into large areas and the demarcation of these areas by wide arterial roads. Within each area there was a gridded system of streets. At Piraeus the grids of the different parts of the city were aligned differently; at Rhodes and probably also at Thourioi the street grids were completely unified.

Some of the characteristics of Hippodamian methods, like the division of the city into different areas and the clear demarcation of those areas, are not unique; they are found in Greek planning methods throughout the Aegean and the Mediterranean. But the overall concept of Hippodamos' design differs from the regularly planned colonies of the west and even from his home town of Miletos. First, it aimed at the total integration of the different parts of the city. According to Aristotle, Hippodamian ideas on both the nature of the ideal city-state and its layout were based on the division of the population and its territory; thus he divided his ideal town into three classes, and he separated urban land into three types. Aristotle even uses the verb 'cut up' in reference to the planning of the Piraeus. But the purpose of Hippodamian planning was to achieve the ideal state, totally balanced and fully integrated. In laying out Piraeus, Thourioi and Rhodes attempts were made to achieve this. All three show a degree of unity and cohesion between the different elements of the cities which had hitherto not been apparent in town planning.

The *scholion* of Aristophanes' *Knights* 328 makes both an illuminating and relevant comment regarding the planning of Piraeus. The text mentions a certain Archeptolemos, whom the commentator identified as the son of Hippodamos of Miletos. Although this identification is disputed,[29] the comments which he makes about Hippodamos, whom he believed to be the town planner, are significant for understanding Hippodamos' work in Piraeus. He described Hippodamos as the man who 'pulled Piraeus together'. The significance of the verb is clear. It emphasises the unity and integration of the town plan, which are reflected in the known details of the port and, indeed, the other two cities accredited to Hippodamos. Aelius Aristides' description of Rhodes similarly emphasises the overall unity and cohesion of the town plan.[30] He states that the city was well arranged with no part in excess of any other, and goes on to compare the plan with that of a house rather than a city. The analogy between the unity of a house and the diverse elements which make up a city is an obvious reflection of the cohesion of the original layout.

Secondly, Hippodamos' is described as a *meteorologos* and the design at Rhodes at least, and probably also at Thourioi, seems to have been based on theoretical and mathematical principles.[31] The use of larger squares of land of predetermined size to subdivide the city initially is not unique. The technique was possibly derived from rural land division but the precise, geometrical arrangement of Rhodes goes far beyond the simple arrangements of land subdivision which were employed elsewhere.[32]

Thirdly, public buildings were grouped in a clear functional relationship to each other, as is suggested by the relationship between the harbour and the agora at Piraeus and the stadium, gymnasium and odeion at Rhodes. Moreover, the public buildings were clearly defined and fully incorporated into the street system. The addition of a complete drainage system at Rhodes as part of the town plan is in keeping with Hippodamos' social concerns and indeed might have been inspired by his visit to southern Italy.[33]

Fourthly, the layout of Rhodes in particular has a planned monumentality. Its design involved the systematic exploitation of the sloping terrain for visual effect by the extensive use of terracing and landscaping. The result was a visually pleasing ensemble, offering commanding views across the shore and the harbours, which is aptly reflected in Diodorus' epithet, 'theatre-like'.

The immediate relevance of Hippodamos to the history of fifth-century planning lies in the fact that he introduced a specific system of planning which differed in both detail and overall design from contemporary practice. The effect of Hippodamian methods on the subsequent history of town planning remains problematic and judgement must be postponed until the analysis of Classical planning is complete.

The changing political, military and economic fortunes of the Greek city-states in the Classical period provided continuing opportunities for the town planner. New towns were created for political expediency, military domination, or because of changing economic fortunes. Furthermore, colonisation in the west and the north continued. In the majority of cases regular grid planning conformed to standard principles. It involved the development of a gridded network of streets by the successive extension of regular *insulae* across the site. All aspects of the town plan were governed by the size of the basic house block or multiples of it.[34] Even the public buildings, which were fully incorporated into the network of the streets, were constructed as multiples of the basic *insula*-unit. Indeed this fact might also explain the origin of Pausanias' so-called 'Ionian' agora, the regularity of which would fit perfectly the rectangular street system.[35]

Olynthos, destroyed by Philip II of Macedon in 348 BC, is typical of fifth-century grid planning. The original town, occupying the southernmost of two adjacent, flat-topped hills, was small and irregular. With the revolt of the Chalcidice from Athenian domination in *c*. 432 BC the town was chosen as the capital of the newly formed Chalcidic League. As a result of the synoecism of surrounding communities, the city was greatly increased in size. A new, regularly laid-out residential area was added to the northern hill and on to the plain below.[36] The street grid framed a series of identical rectangular *insulae*, ideally 300 × 120 Greek feet (86.34 × 35.00 m) in area, although the dimensions were reduced at the edges of the hill where the ground became irregular. The streets were originally planned to be the same width but, after the start of the construction of the city, the main avenue leading from the northern gate was increased in size by reducing the size of the adjacent house plots. The change in plan created a major north-south arterial road which united the northern gate with the agora at the southern end of the hill. There were also other changes to the town plan. The size of the house blocks on the eastern side of the hill was reduced because of the terrain and a transverse avenue, which probably led to the port of Olynthos at Mecyberna, was included (Figure 16).

The public buildings lay at the southern end of the northern hill and extended on to the saddle of land between the two hills. The only part of the civic area to be extensively investigated was part of the agora.[37] It occupied a position at the southern end on the northern hill, immediately to the west of the main north-south road. It was bounded on its northern side by a stoa, the width of which was equivalent to the size of a residential house block, and

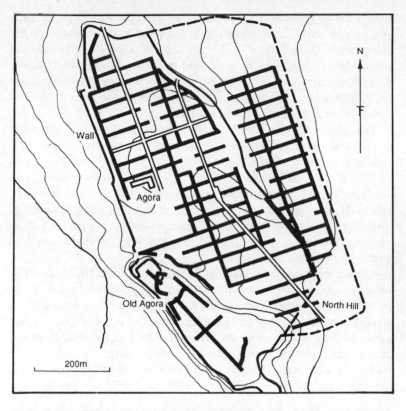

Figure 16 Olynthos

on its eastern side there was a fountain house. The residential *insulae* were divided into two rows of five houses of equal dimensions. Such an arrangement, based on the idea of the equality of plots, was widespread in the planning of the Classical and Hellenistic periods. Not only did it facilitate the construction of the house blocks but it also implies a democratic element in both the concept and the execution of the plan, a fact which would in part assist the integration of the new elements of the population, if the synoecism proved to be unpopular with those who were forced to abandon their own homes.[38]

Essential amenities were also provided. There were at least two fountain houses supplying running water.[39] One, as stated, lay on the eastern side of the agora alongside the main road from the northern gate. The other was located at the gate on the southern hill, and was obviously intended to refresh travellers as they entered the city.[40] The water was brought from sources over 7 miles away from the city by means of a pipeline of jointed terracotta sections which were laid in an underground channel. The street surfaces were cobbled in places and there was evidence for the provision of drains, although neither the streets nor the drains were extensively investigated.[41]

The planning of Olynthos and the alterations, which were introduced after the start of construction, were a practical response to the conditions which the planners and builders found on the site as the work progressed. Despite lacking visual and aesthetic appeal, the planning of Olynthos was facilitated by the relatively flat terrain on which it was built. Grid planning, however, was also applied to exceptionally steep sites with varying degrees of success, as Priene, Knidos, Astypalaia on Cos and Soluntum in Sicily reveal.

Knidos is the most spectacular.[42] Removed from its original site to a point half-way along the Knidian peninsula around the middle of the fourth century BC, the town embraced not only the steep coastline but also an adjoining island. The plan comprises a series of four parallel avenues which ran in an east-west direction across the steeply rising ground overlooking the city's two harbours. The main avenue of the town united the eastern gate of the city with the civic area on the western side of the town. From

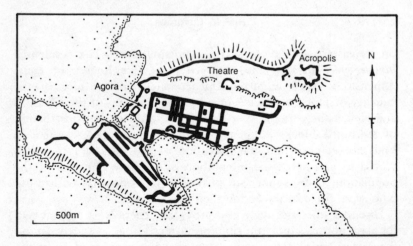

Figure 17 Knidos

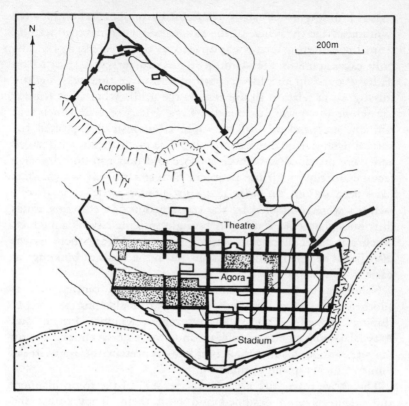

Figure 18 Priene

this road the public buildings ran down towards the coast as a series of stepped terraces in much the same manner as Rhodes. The north-south roads, which climb the slope and intersect the avenues, were particularly steep and were often reduced to flights of steps (Figure 17).

Priene reflects Knidos on a smaller scale (Figure 18). The abandonment of the original site and the relocation of the town on a rocky, steeply sloping spur of Mt Mycale during the reign of Alexander of Macedon was necessitated by the progressive silting up of the River Maeander.[43] Like Knidos four parallel avenues ran across the site in an east-west direction.[44] The road leading from the eastern gate was the town's main artery and was wider than the other streets. The city itself was divided up into rectangular *insulae* by narrower, transverse streets which in places were

65

reduced to flights of steps. The main public buildings were concentrated in the centre of the town along the main road leading from the eastern gate and conformed to the street network. The only exception was the stadium. This structure was situated on flatter ground in the lower part of the town and was slightly misaligned in relation to the rest of the grid. Again as at Knidos the whole town was surrounded by a defensive wall which was laid out independently of the streets but instead exploited the natural defensive qualities of the site. The main streets were paved and were provided with both surface and underground drainage facilities to cope with the problem of water run-off which must have been serious on such a steeply sloping site.[45] The town's facilities were completed by the construction of a complex water distribution system. Water was brought into the city by aqueduct, whence it was collected in settling tanks, and from them it was distributed to small stone fountains set in the walls of buildings at various points throughout the city.

Soluntum in Sicily, replanned in the fourth century BC, is another example of the application of grid planning to steeply sloping ground.[46] The plan resembles Knidos, Priene and Astypalaia with one main avenue and two lesser avenues crossing the site, although individual buildings represent the non-Greek, Punic elements in the population.

The above towns are a credit to the skill of the town planners and architects who designed and built them. They utilise the ground as best as they can but the terrain is not really suited to such rigid planning. Communications were restricted and the streets which climbed the slopes were often no more than steep flights of steps. Whilst a certain amount of scenic landscaping is achieved through the terracing of public buildings and residential areas, the natural advantages of the locations are not fully exploited, a fact which reinforces the view that grid planning was better adapted to level terrain.[47]

Many of the new towns of Greece in the Classical period were laid out in much the same way, although the actual size of the grids varied. Such towns include Pella,[48] Elean Pylos,[49] the Corinthian colony of Ambracia on the Gulf of Arta,[50] and Abdera.[51] In the west a similar layout was employed at Herakleia Lucania, although here the acropolis with its public buildings remained independent of the residential grid.[52]

The common feature of the above towns is the recurring use of

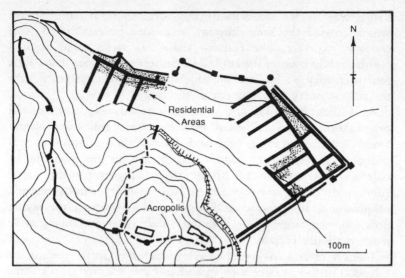

Figure 19 Halieis

the house blocks as the mode of expansion of the town. At Halieis and probably also Mantinea a different method of planning was used in which the city was divided into larger areas before the housing blocks were developed (Figure 19). The system is clear at Halieis. The town was situated on a hill overlooking the sea on the south coast of the Argolid. The public buildings were situated on the upper slopes of the hill. Below and uncoordinated with the public area were two differently orientated residential areas. The larger zone to the east was laid out as a 221 m square, which was then subdivided into strips of approximately rectangular *insulae*. The western zone, similarly divided into rectangular *insulae*, covered half the area of the eastern square.[53] The existing plan dates to the fourth century BC but, as the earlier street system of the town seems to correspond to the later streets, it probably reflects the original layout of the town in the sixth century BC.

It is possible that a similar system of planning was employed at Mantinea. The town, which was synoecised from five surrounding villages, was destroyed by the Spartans in 385 BC and reconstituted after the battle of Leuctra in 371 BC. It occupies an oval-shaped hill on the plain of Tripolis and was defended by a strong city wall, which is its most impressive remains today. Although the interior of the city has not been extensively investigated it appears that it was divided into a number of areas by a system of streets which crossed the site, although it cannot be established with certainty whether, like Halieis, the areas were based upon a regular subdivision of the land. The preserved remains date to the fourth century BC but it is possible that the street system reflects the sixth-century development of the city.[54]

At Halieis certainly, and at Mantinea possibly, the general organisation of the residential areas into large zones was clearly based upon a system of rural land division; and this in turn was probably influenced by Greek experience in the planting of colonies. The system of using larger squares for the initial subdivision of the city formed the basis of Hippodamos' method of planning. In the case of Hippodamos, however, the laying down of the larger areas and the subdivision are much more mathematically precise.

The career and conquests of Alexander the Great brought the Classical period of Greece to an end and transformed the Hellenic world. Alexander himself was a prolific builder of cities. He realised their advantages in political, military and economic terms for the control and exploitation of his vast empire. He also realised their potential for self-glorification and the aggrandisement of his reign. Consequently he founded many towns, many of which in turn bore his name. His greatest foundation was Alexandria in Egypt and it is possibly fitting that discussion of Classical planning should end there. Its plan, conceived and executed by Deinocrates, but with the personal involvement of Alexander himself, is rooted in Classical planning traditions. At the same time it looks forward to the great achievements of the Hellenistic world. It reflects the impact that the conquest of the Near East was to have on Greek urban architecture and planning, and the importance which the city was to gain as a medium of self-aggrandisement.

Alexandria, as far as can be determined from the surviving archaeological and literary evidence, was both monumental in scale and grandiose in construction. Regularly laid out, its rectangular street grid was governed by a central axial road, which according to Diodorus was 100 ft in width.[55] Other major roads ran parallel to this and at least one major avenue intersected it at right angles.[56] Within the layout, provision was made for public buildings, palaces, parks and other amenities. These, according to Strabo's account, were arranged in a completely unified scheme. Strabo's description of the different areas of the city not only suggests a completely unified scheme of design, but also, in quoting Homer, hints at scenographic planning for visual appeal. The palaces and civic buildings of the city were connected both to each other and to the public buildings around the main harbour. The royal palaces also included a grandiose museum and an enclosure called the 'Sema', where the kings were buried. The palaces around the main harbour were connected to those on the promontory of Lochias, whilst a series of public buildings, including the theatre and the Poseidium, rose above the artificial harbour. The magnificent gymnasium with its long porticoes was associated with lawcourts and groves. The whole city was dominated by the temple to Pan. This building, in near-eastern tradition, was raised on an artificial podium, giving commanding views across the city, and was approached by means of a spiral road.[57] The description of Alexandria by Strabo together with the surviving archaeological evidence suggests a combination of Greek and Egyptian architectural traditions, thus emphasising the cosmopolitan nature of the city and reflecting Alexander's ideas of cultural fusion.

It is unfortunate that more of the city of Alexandria, as described by Strabo, cannot be confirmed through excavation. Its layout is firmly rooted in Greek planning traditions and the monumentality of its design recalls the work of Hippodamos. Its concept and execution, however, transcends purely Hellenic attitudes.[58] The arrangement of its buildings into interconnecting complexes and ensembles looks forward to the great capital cities and urban centres of the Hellenised and Romanised east and is a lasting tribute to the original design of Deinocrates.

Alexander the Great was not the first person to realise the potential of the city as a means of propaganda and self-glorification. It is to a certain degree foreshadowed in the Periclean building programme at Athens. It was also realised by Mausolus, the independent and powerful satrap of Caria. During his reign Mausolus relocated and aggrandised several of the cities of his kingdom.[59] His most famous and probably his most spectacular achievement was the rebuilding of Halicarnassus, which he had chosen as his new capital (Figure 20).

The site was ideal, its theatre-like shape combining good harbour facilities with natural defences and the potential for the scenic exploitation of the landscape. Vitruvius gave a detailed

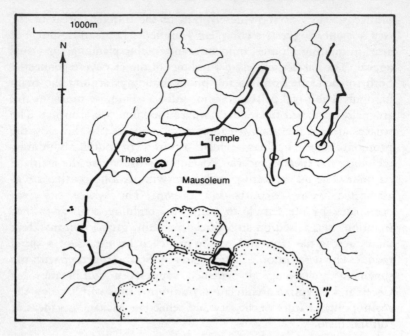

Figure 20 Halicarnassus

account of Halicarnassus and remains the chief source of evidence for the city.[60] The whole site, forming a natural depression towards the sea, necessitated extensive terracing. The agora was situated on the coast, close to the harbour. A wide avenue ran around the middle of the city and situated at the centre of this was the king's own tomb, the Mausoleum, whilst a temple to Mars overlooked the city from its position on the acropolis.

Vitruvius' account of the city of Halicarnassus is not complete. Nevertheless, from his description and the limited archaeological work at Halicarnassus itself, several important observations can be made. First, although the town was regularly planned, the design sought to utilise the natural advantages of the site. Secondly, the plan aimed to bring together the different elements of the town into a united ensemble. Thirdly, the focal point of the town was the Mausoleum, which could be seen from all the important vantage points throughout the city. The significance of the planning of Halicarnassus and its place in the history of planning will be discussed later.[61] For the present it serves to illustrate the importance of the city as a medium of self-glorification and propaganda, and it acts as an indication of the new ideas which were emanating from the semi-barbarised kingdoms of the eastern Aegean, where Greek cities and Greek urban buildings were combined with strong, centralised and authoritarian rule.

Grid planning in the Classical period remained essentially functional and Hippodamian methods seem to have had little direct influence on the development of other Classical towns. Olynthos, Priene and the other regularly planned towns of Greece display much unity, but it is difficult to establish with certainty whether this was due to the influence of Hippodamos. Certainly the use of the *insula*-unit rather than the street system to govern the laying out and subsequent development of the town achieved a far greater sense of unity and cohesion between the different elements of the town. It also had other advantages in allowing greater flexibility.

Experimentation in scenic landscaping was another feature of Classical planning. Here is possibly an area of planning in which Hippodamos might have been influential. The terrain was exploited for scenic effect. Public buildings were not merely located in commanding positions but they were so placed as to create a visually pleasing urban landscape. The sloping terrain fulfils a crucial function in this aspect of planning in that not only does it allow individual buildings to be seen because they climb one behind the other on a series of terraces up the slope, but it also gives the impression that they are interconnected. It is in the field of monumentality and visual exploitation of the site that any long-term influence of Hippodamos must lie.

The fifth and the fourth centuries witnessed a great expansion of urban life and an increase in the number of regularly planned cities in Greece. Town planning was not confined to one particular system. Planning was adapted to the situation. The layout of Miletos differs from the cities of Hippodamos which in turn differ from such places as Olynthos, Priene, Halieis and Alexandria. Just as history records the names of urban planners like Hippodamos and Deinocrates, so the individual characteristics of their methods are beginning to emerge.

Classical planning was not confined merely to the regular arrangement of the town. Social, political and juridical factors were also influential in town planning. Town planners became increasingly aware of the social problems of expanding urban life. Moreover, like the Greek tyrants, politicians of the Classical period realised the importance of providing amenities which would beautify the city, ameliorate urban life, and assist their own public careers. Thus, for example, Cimon adorned the city of Athens with, in the words of Plutarch, 'spacious and elegant places of public resort'.[62] His public works included the planting of trees and the arrangement of paths in the agora and the Academy, as well as the provision of water to the latter. The supply of adequate amounts of water, and the provision of facilities to cope with the problems of drainage and sanitation, were matters which 'needed attention. There was no common response to these problems. Each city reacted in a different way, sometimes by providing facilities and sometimes through legislation.

A democratic element in planning is observable in the arrangement of houses within *insulae*. Initially at least, the house plots were of equal size and were so arranged in two parallel rows that every house faced on to a street.[63]

A juridical element in urban planning continues to be seen in the use of streets to define different areas or buildings. But legislation in general became an increasingly important aspect of urban planning both in new cities and in existing ones as the population increased. The dumping of waste, the digging of open drains or cesspits in public places, the blocking of public highways, and regulating the individual's relationship to his next-door neighbour, are just some of the many topics which were the object of legislation. Cities appointed specific officials charged with the general maintenance of the city.[64] Their tasks seem to have been supervisory for the most part, ensuring individual citizens obeyed the laws, and, if they did not comply, fining the offenders and ensuring the work was carried out. The total effectiveness of such legislation has to be doubted. Officials could not hope to deal with every transgression, and laws at times had to be re-enacted.

Although at a practical level town planning in the Classical period remained essentially functional, there were, nonetheless, important developments. The vibrant intellectual atmosphere of the fifth century BC led to speculation concerning the ideal city. Most of the time the thought was never transferred into practice wholesale. But at the same time it must have helped to stimulate planners to think about the arrangement of the city and what facilities were essential. With the conquests of Alexander a new phase of urban planning begins. This is the subject of the next chapter.

5

TOWN PLANNING IN THE HELLENISTIC WORLD

The conquests of Alexander the Great transformed the Greek and Asiatic world. The new political, social and economic conditions resulting from his victories and the emergence of the Macedonian kingdoms, the admixture of Greek and Asiatic elements within the new kingdoms, and the tastes of the Hellenistic kings for self-aggrandisement profoundly affected the Greek city. The city not only remained the one accepted method of spreading the Greek way of life and maintaining Greek supremacy in the newly formed kingdoms which grew out of Alexander's empire, it also became an important means of propaganda. At the same time the Greek cities were influenced by the traditions of native life which were encountered throughout the conquered territories.

Throughout the Hellenistic world the cities had to adapt to and accept the changed political circumstances which Alexander's conquests and the formation of the kingdoms of his successors brought about. Although the Greek cities in reality lost their overall freedom of action, they benefited in other ways. The kings and native dynasts of the conquered territories were found to be wealthy and willing benefactors. By means of an expansive programme of urban building and city construction, the Hellenistic dynasts proclaimed the greatness and stability of their power and the glory of their reigns. These factors affected urbanisation and town planning in different ways.[1]

In the first place grid planning remained both the most convenient and the quickest method of establishing a new city in potentially hostile territory. However, the barrack-like uniformity of many of the Greek colonies of the Hellenistic east emphasised the essentially military nature of many of the new foundations. Many of the new towns achieved an extremely standardised plan,

74

often with simple mathematical ratios as the basis of their design. The repetitive uniformity of such towns must have been a stark reminder of the new political conditions which prevailed.

Secondly, the new rulers of the Hellenistic world found the city to be a suitable and enduring medium of propaganda as well as control and Hellenisation. Not only were new cities built but existing cities were also transformed. Urban architecture and civic design were profoundly affected. Monumentality in the construction of individual buildings was complemented by monumentality in the design and scenic composition of the cities themselves. Planners realised that even steeply sloping and irregular terrain, the typical locality of the majority of the established Greek cities, could be advantageously exploited in a natural way to create stunning visual townscapes. The Greek and semi-Greek kingdoms of western Asia Minor in particular were at the forefront of these developments. It was here that Greek and barbarian had lived in close proximity for centuries. Consequently, it was in this same area, amongst the strong, autocratic dynasts of coastal Asia Minor, that monumentality and grandiosity could best be fused with existing Greek architectural and urban traditions. Moreover, the rulers had both the power and the financial resources to carry through these extensive building programmes. Some of the ideas were not new but continued the traditions of the Classical period. The work of Hippodamos of Miletos at Rhodes, Deinocrates at Alexandria, and Mausolus at Halicarnassus was undoubtedly influential and laid the foundations for the achievements of the Hellenistic period. The results, however, are no less startling.

With few exceptions, the regularly planned cities of the Macedonian and Hellenistic eras reflect the military and strategic role which they had to fulfil, either as a means of control or, as in the hinterland of the Balkans, the means by which urban life was conveyed to the mountain tribes of the region. Strong defensive walls and barrack-like regularity in the planning of the residential areas were the norm, and were an indication of the fierce opposition which was often encountered in establishing these cities.

Kassopeia, north of the Gulf of Arta on the western side of the Greek peninsula, is indicative of the efforts made to bring settled urban life to the mountainous districts of Epirus. The city was founded in the third century BC on a high, sloping plateau which offered commanding views across the Gulf of Arta to Acarnania

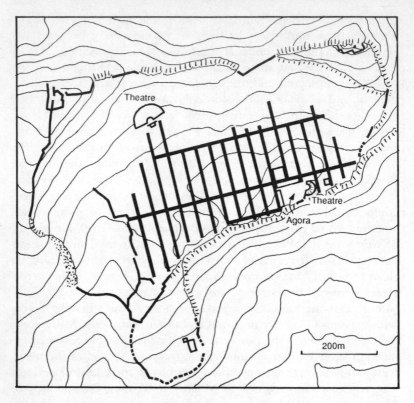

Figure 21 Kassopeia

beyond.[2] The site was obviously chosen for its defensive qualities with its strong, urban walls enclosing not only the town but also the towering crags of the mountain above. Much of the area within the walls was given over to residential occupation (Figure 21). The gridded network of streets produced elongated rectangular *insulae* which were divided into two rows of houses. With the exception of the large theatre which occupied a natural hollow on the northern side of the town, the majority of the city's public buildings were situated in a restricted area on the southern side of the town. They include a small agora with stoas, an odeion and a public guest house.

The layout of Kassopeia was completely utilitarian. No attempt was made to exploit the advantages of the site. The public buildings were reduced to the mininum required for the

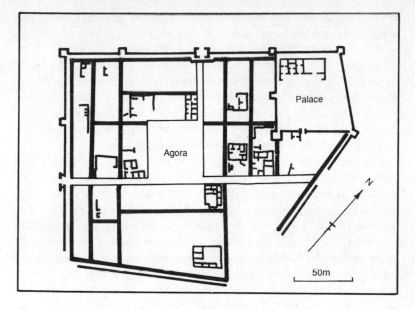

Figure 22 Seuthopolis

functioning of the city. Just as the city itself clings to the hillside so the impression persists that urbanised life on the Greek model was only precariously maintained in such mountainous and inhospitable regions.

Ammotopos in the territory of the Molossoi and Seuthopolis in Thrace were equally influenced by the needs for defence. The former, strongly fortified, was regularly laid out and included a central east-west axis which bisected the town.[3]

Seuthopolis was chosen by Seuthes III as his capital and occupied an easily defensible spur of land on a bend in the River Tundja.[4] The town was obviously Greek-inspired, with Greek-type houses and buildings. The layout itself was also typically Greek, although it was adapted to the location. Because the town was surrounded on three sides by the River Tundja there were only two gateways, in the south-western and north-western walls. The two roads passing through these gates were wider than the other streets and intersected at the centre of the town (Figure 22). At the junction there was a small paved agora. The majority of the streets were paved and provided with underground drains. Apart from the agora and the area around the king's palace, which was situated on the north-western side of the city and was separated from the lower town by a cross wall, the rest of the area within the walls was divided up into rectangular *insulae*.

Despite the fact that Seuthopolis was a capital city it is grandiose neither in design nor construction. Its houses, buildings and other facilities were comfortable rather than elaborate, and reflect Greek influences and tastes. The layout, however, remains functional and is adapted to the particular circumstances of the site and the needs of a semi-Hellenised Thracian king.

The success of grid planning lay in its essential simplicity and utilitarian nature. These very qualities, however, have potential dangers. It is a short step from simplicity to repetitive monotony, especially when a number of cities have to be built quickly. The narrow dividing line can be seen by contrasting the Thessalian towns of Goritza and Demetrias. Both were planted to control the inner end of the Gulf of Pagasai. Both were regularly planned and their grids were completely functional. But whereas the former was adapted to the topographical conditions of the site, the latter,

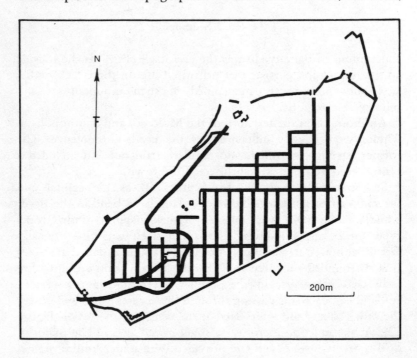

Figure 23 Goritza

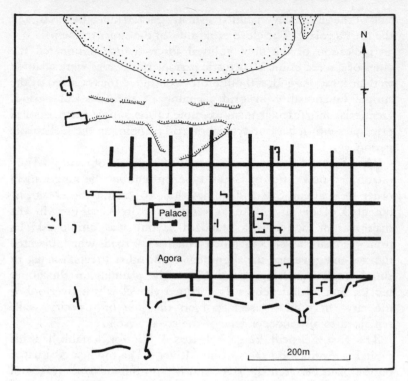

Figure 24 Demetrias

because of the relative flatness of its coastal situation, was reduced
effectively to a series of regular *insulae* of simple mathematical
proportions.

Goritza, probably to be identified with ancient Orminion, sits
on a ridge which controls the road from Thessaly to central
Greece. The overall plan was rectangular, but the *insulae* were
neither consistently orientated nor of uniform size.[5] Despite its
obvious strategic location, as in so many Greek cities the streets
remained essentially uncoordinated with the walls, gates and
towers (Figure 23).

Demetrias, on the other hand, lies on the coast of the Gulf of
Pagasai. The layout is again simple (Figure 24). The network of
streets was completely uniform and the resulting *insulae* have a
simple mathematical ratio of 2 : 1.[6] The public buildings were
fully adapted to the street grid, and were grouped on the eastern

side of the city. They included a small agora, flanked by stoas, and the ruler's palace. The close proximity of the agora to the palace is an indication of the new political forces which dominated the cities of Greece in the Hellenistic period. Both cities were adapted to their locations and, although they continued the tradition of the simple functionality of grid planning of the Classical period, Demetrias in particular is an example of the simple mathematical principles which became typical of grid planning in the Hellenistic period.

The Seleucid kings were prolific builders of cities. They established new cities of Greek type throughout the kingdom in order to maintain Seleucid domination, to exploit the economic potential of the area, and as centres of Greek culture. In the majority of the cities a standard layout was employed. Its principle characteristics included a main axial road, which bisected the city and governed the alignment of the other streets, the use of simple mathematical proportions for the planning of the house blocks, and an independently fortified citadel which overlooked the city. In typical Greek fashion the line of the city walls remained totally independent of the street system.

The first Seleucid king, Seleucus I Nicator, established his capital at Antioch on the Orontes River.[7] The town was situated on the plain between the river and Mount Silpius to the east and was dominated by the Amanus ridge. The original Hellenistic city was confined to the eastern bank of the River Orontes, but was progressively enlarged by the successors of Seleucus I and the Romans. Eventually Antioch came to occupy most of the plain and even extended on to an island in the middle of the river. Under the Romans, Antioch became one of the four greatest cities of the Empire. The original town plan of the city embraced the whole of the area which was later occupied by the city and was strictly maintained as the city developed (Figure 25).

The street system was rectangular but was not orientated to the points of the compass. It included at least five long avenues and numerous, intersecting cross streets. The resulting housing blocks measured uniformly 112 × 58 m. The long central avenue, which in the Roman period was transformed into a magnificent colonnaded thoroughfare 27 m in width, ran through the city for approximately 3 km. The city walls followed an irregular course around the perimeter, joining up with the independently fortified citadel on the eastern side. Under the streets an extensive system

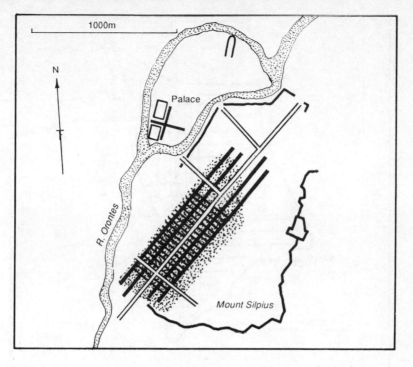

Figure 25 Antioch-on-the-Orontes

of drains and water conduits has come to light. Unfortunately, although the original Hellenistic layout has been preserved, the renovations of the Roman period have virtually removed all traces of the Seleucid city.

Other Seleucid foundations such as Beroia[8] and Apamea,[9] which became the second most important city after Antioch, further illustrate Seleucid urbanisation. Both cities were laid out in the same way as Antioch. Both have a single central avenue which attained a width of *c.* 20–25 m. The street system was rectangular and was orientated to the points of the compass. The resulting *insulae* measured 48 × 127 m and 58 × 122 m. Both were fortified and included a walled citadel which dominated one side of the town. An important aspect of these cities was the provision of adequate supplies of water and drainage. Certainly at Beroia water was brought into the city from a source over 7 miles away.

The town plan of Laodicea-by-the-sea, the port of Apamea,

81

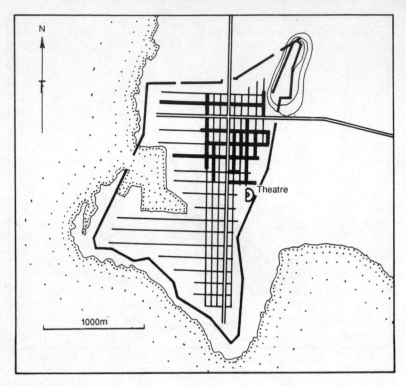

Figure 26 Laodicea-by-the-sea

conforms to the general outlines of Seleucid planning but differs in detail.[10] As with many other towns the preserved remains are Roman but the town plan was laid out in the Hellenistic period (Figure 26). Laodicea was established on a promontory and was protected to the east by two hills. The layout was based on one axial north-south avenue but, unlike other cities, there were also three transverse avenues at right angles. The residential *insulae* measured 110–20 × 57 m, the proportions being the same as those of other Seleucid cities. An area of gardens adjoined the residential district with the plots laid out in the same regular way. The urban defences, encompassing the harbour, followed an irregular course around the city.

Seleucia-on-the-Tigris had the same central avenue with the dimensions of the residential *insulae* in the ratio of 2 : 1. The simple, mathematical formula which formed the basis of the planning of these Seleucid cities is nowhere more apparent than at Doura-Europos. The colony, planted in *c.* 300 BC, was strategically located on the banks of the upper Euphrates for reasons of military security and to exploit the long-distance caravan routes across the desert.[11] The town was founded on a flat eminence overlooking the western bank of the River Euphrates. The layout was regular. Twelve roads ran in a north-south direction and nine roads, including the main central axis between the two main gates, ran in an east-west direction. All the streets were 6.35 m in width except the central axis which attained a width of 12.65 m, and the fourth and the eighth cross streets which ran either side of the agora and were 8.45 m in width. The house blocks measured 35 × 70 m. Immediately to the north of the main east-west route an area covering the equivalent of eight house blocks was reserved for the agora. As elsewhere, the city walls were constructed independently of the street system.

The planning and construction of many of the Seleucid colonies was facilitated by the fact that they were founded on virgin sites or, as in the case of Beroia, they supplanted existing native settlements. Damascus, on the other hand, was already an important native town when the Seleucid kingdom was established, and so here the planners had to contend with the problem of uniting the new Seleucid extension with the existing settlement.[12] The basis of the enlarged city was a wide east-west axial route, possibly to be identified with the street called 'straight' mentioned in the Acts of the Apostles,[13] which united the old and the new quarters (Figure 27). Other streets, running parallel and perpendicular to this, created *insulae* approximately 100 × 45 m. In the Roman period a second major thoroughfare united the agora of the new town with the temple of the existing native city. The road was colonnaded in Roman times. One would like to think that this arrangement of temple and agora, not only signifying the physical unification of the two elements of the city but also symbolically indicating the cultural fusion of Greek and Asiatic, was part of the original Hellenistic design. Unfortunately, this cannot be proved and in reality such an arrangement is more suited to Roman planning concepts.[14]

Throughout Syria the Seleucids continued a policy of colonisation and urbanisation which was first begun by Alexander. The cities were to be centres of Greek military, economic and cultural domination. The simple method of planning reflects the need to

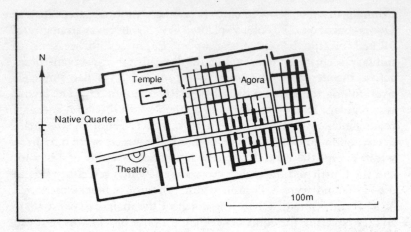

Figure 27 Damascus

establish such urban centres as quickly and as easily as possible. Many of the original Seleucid cities subsequently became prosperous and important provincial centres of the Roman Empire. It is to the credit of the original planners that when they laid out the cities they allowed for future expansion and the subsequent extensions strictly conformed to the original plan. Other foundations never lived up to original expectations. At Doura-Europus, which is admittedly on the eastern frontier of the Seleucid empire, the agora was never fully developed and by AD 250 an eastern-style bazaar quarter had developed on part of the site. Many of the original Greek buildings were never fully completed.[15] In Syria the Seleucids had laid the foundations of Greek urban life but it was left to the Romans to instil fresh impetus into the cities.

The primary aim of Seleucid colonial planning was the establishment of Greek cities in an area where the traditional Greek way of urban life was alien. To the west, along the coast of Asia Minor, Greek cities and the Greek way of life had a long history. The planting of new cities and the remodelling of existing ones continued throughout the Hellenistic period. Strabo's description of Smyrna, removed from its original location at the mouth of the River Hermos and rebuilt on the slopes of Mount Pagos by Antigonus and Lysimachos, is illustrative of the interest which the powerful Hellenistic kings had in promoting cities. He describes Smyrna as 'the best city of all' and his account suggests a well-ordered town, which embraced the harbour, the lower town and the fortified upper city in a unified scheme.[16] Several of the public buildings were conveniently situated close to one another and the streets, wherever possible, were straight and paved. His only criticism was the failure of the builders to provide an adequate drainage system, an omission which had disastrous consequences whenever it rained.

The Carian city of Herakleia-under-Latmos, in the tradition of Knidos and Priene, was situated on the steeply sloping lower slopes of Mount Latmos. Also, like Knidos and Priene, the original city was abandoned and refounded close by, hence its name. There is much discussion concerning the date at which the city was refounded.[17] The impressive city walls are thought to have been constructed by Mausolus who captured the city, but the sophistication of the defences suggests that they are post-Alexandrian. Nor can any of the excavated buildings be firmly dated to the fourth century BC. What is certain is that Hellenistic Herakleia was a new, physical refoundation, occupying a site slightly removed from the Classical city. Despite the difficulties of the terrain, it was, nevertheless, regularly planned with its street system orientated to the cardinal points of the compass. The public buildings conform to the grid pattern with the exception of the temple to Athena which stood on a commanding hill overlooking the harbour. The often steeply sloping ground, however, encouraged scenic landscaping. The large Hellenistic agora had a lower level on its southern side where the ground fell away to the harbour. Close by stood the bouleuterion, whilst the theatre and a nymphaeum were situated higher up the slope. Other temples occupied commanding positions throughout the city.

The progressive silting of the Maeander River ensured that Herakleia was not successful, and the construction of the cross wall to reduce the defensible circuit of the fortifications confirms that the city never attained its expected size. Nevertheless, its public buildings exploited the natural advantages of the site. It was the combination of spectacular locations, large-scale landscaping, monumental buildings and complexes of buildings, together with the political will and the financial resources of the Hellenistic dynasts which transformed the cities of the Hellenistic world.

Despite its successful application to such sites as Knidos, Priene and Herakleia, the inherent danger of grid planning was the artificial creation of an ordered urban environment. All buildings ultimately had to conform to the street plan. More impressive were those cities in which the terrain was utilised in a free-ranging and natural way. In Asia Minor in particular, large-scale landscaping and experiments in composition fundamentally affected Hellenistic planning as powerful, and often only semi-Hellenised, rulers employed the city as permanent and lasting monuments to their achievements. Scenographic landscaping was not new but the monumentalisation of traditional Greek urban buildings and their combination into large landscaped complexes resulted in some of the most visually spectacular cities of the Greek world.

The Carian city of Alinda is indicative of these developments. Here the sloping ground allowed extensive terracing and the main public buildings climbed the slopes in a monumental but free-ranging way.[18] The theatre stood immediately below the principal hill of the town which acted as Alinda's acropolis. Further down the slope still was the most spectacular building of the city – a large agora with an associated market building. The latter was over 90 m in length and stood three storeys high. The upper storey opened northwards on to the agora whilst the lower two floors were terraced into the slope and faced southwards. Monumental market buildings became a common feature of cities in the Hellenistic period and indicate the importance of the economic basis on which the success of these cities was founded.

The agora of Assos illustrates how monumentality, visual composition and the terrain were combined to enhance the heart of the traditional Greek city.[19] The agora stands on the southern slopes of the city's acropolis and was approached from the main west gate by means of a paved road. The agora itself measures 150 m in length and 60 m in width although it narrows to the east. Its northern and southern sides were flanked by stoas, with the double-storeyed northern stoa terraced into the slope (Figure 28). The southern stoa was only a single storey overlooking the agora itself, but on its southern side there was a second lower storey to compensate for the declivity of the ground. The eastern and western ends of the agora were enclosed respectively by the bouleuterion and a temple. The design of the agora at Assos was not regular. It responds to the topography of the site. Nevertheless, it is both visually pleasing and combines architecturally the chief

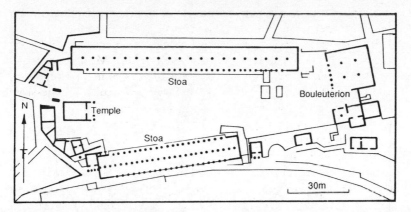

Figure 28 The agora of Assos

commercial, administrative and religious functions of a Greek city centre.

By far the most impressive example of monumental planning is Pergamon. The city on the western coast of Asia Minor was transformed by the efforts of Attalus II. The city itself occupies the summit and southern slopes of an otherwise precipitous hill overlooking the Caicus valley.[20] The difficult terrain necessitated extensive and complex terracing which was the key to the success of the town. The main road, only 5 m in width, climbed in a series of bends from the southern gate to the acropolis. This road formed the essential link between the majority of the public buildings, which are terraced along it (Figure 29). On the lowest terrace there is a large market building, open to the south and surrounded by a two-storey colonnade which gave access to rows of shops on its other sides.[21] From the rear of the market building the road climbed to the next level where there was a complex of terraced buildings including three interconnecting gymnasia, several temples and a fountain house.[22] From the terrace of the gymnasia the road finally reached the acropolis, the most spectacular part of the city. The focal point of the complex of buildings on the acropolis was the theatre which was situated on the steeply sloping western side and was supported by a massive retaining wall. Other skilfully terraced buildings were arranged fan-like around the top of the theatre. The buildings included a second agora, several temples, the great altar, a library, barracks and the royal palace.[23]

87

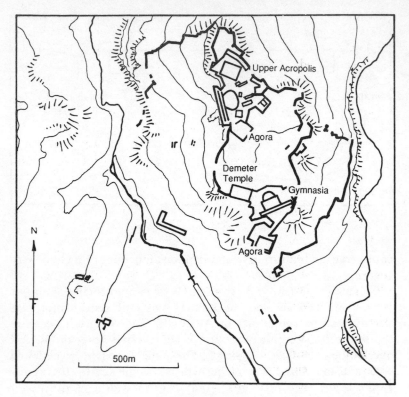

Figure 29 Pergamon

The water supply to the Hellenistic city was no less impressive. Water was piped from the surrounding hills in a high-pressure system to Hagios Georgios, the summit of the mountain above the city.[24] From settling tanks here it was distributed to the city itself. Sewers were provided to control rain-water which must have been a particularly bad problem on such a steep site.[25]

Pergamon represents the pinnacle of Hellenistic urban design. It combined monumental architecture within a monumentally conceived layout, and at the same time fully exploited the difficulties of the terrain to produce one of the most impressive and visually spectacular cities of the ancient world. The origins of this form of planning remain obscure and consequently disputed. Certainly, it seems unlikely that the 'Pergamene' style of planning was developed at Pergamon. The city in its final form was the product of one hundred and fifty years of development and its overall design is highly refined and complex. The idea of exploiting the terrain for scenographic effect is found in the Classical period. However, often the buildings remain essentially individual structures and visual unity is achieved by the sloping terrain.

Some scholars believe that a possible forerunner to Pergamon is to be found in Halicarnassus, Mausolus' capital.[26] There the terrain was skilfully utilised and the buildings were extensively terraced for visual effect. But the underlying design of Halicarnassus differs from that of Pergamon.[27] Although the plan has a certain visual unity, the focal point of the city is Mausolus' tomb, the Mausoleum. The tomb is not located on high ground overlooking the city but it is positioned along the central avenue of Halicarnassus, and can be seen from any point within the city. It thus interrupts views upwards from the harbour, and dominates the views from the theatre and other vantage points throughout the city. The layout of Halicarnassus utilises the terrain to direct the vision towards the centre-piece of the town, the tomb of Mausolus.

The design of Pergamon is different. As already stated, the acropolis of Pergamon was the product of one hundred and fifty years of development. There is no dominant building at Pergamon. Instead, on both the lower slopes and on the acropolis the individual buildings are grouped as integrated series of complexes, which are so composed to provide a united and spectacular urban landscape. It seems likely, therefore, that the origins of Pergamene planning lie elsewhere. Strabo's description of Alexandria, planned by Deinocrates, with its complex of interconnecting buildings and courtyards, suggests an architectural as well as a visual unity. At Alexandria, however, order was imposed by the rectangular street grid. Actual experiments in visual and architectural landscaping which elicited order from the site itself in a natural way must have taken place on a more modest scale.

The sanctuary to Zeus Stratios at Labraunda, close to the Carian city of Mylasa, offers an interesting parallel to the arrangements at Pergamon.[28] The original sanctuary was embellished by Mausolus and his brother, Idreius, although by no means on a monumental scale. The site is steep and the reconstruction necessitated terracing and the construction of ramps and stairways for access

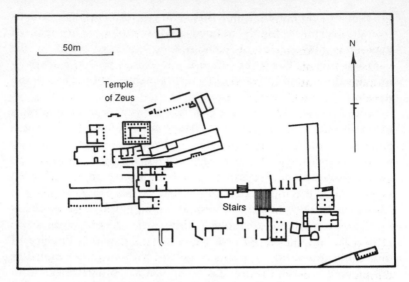

Figure 30 The sanctuary of Zeus Stratios (Labraundos) at Labraunda

(Figure 30). The precinct was approached from the east, and two imposing entrance-ways gave access to a group of buildings and a monumental staircase. The main building complex was situated at a higher level at the western end of the site and included the temple itself, dining-rooms, houses and a stoa, which were all arranged on different levels but nevertheless display a united and cohesive arrangement.

The sanctuary at Labraunda has neither the same complexity nor the same monumentality in construction and design as Pergamon. Nevertheless, its simple landscaping and effective terracing brings a sense of unity to the buildings and a cohesion to the site which ultimately looks forward to the achievements of Pergamon. It is surely at Labraunda and other more modest sites that the direct antecedents of Pergamene planning were to be found.

The effects of Hellenistic monumental planning were felt beyond Asia Minor. The Hellenistic kings became great benefactors to cities throughout the Greek world and many Greek cities benefited from the gifts which the Hellenistic kings endowed. It was not by public buildings alone that cities were improved. The cities provided education and even doctors' services for their citizens. Better water supply and drainage facilities improved the quality of life in cities throughout the Hellenistic world.[29] Even so the provision of such facilities was not uniform, as Hellenistic Smyrna and Amastris in Bithynia make clear.[30]

Developments in Hellenistic planning were not confined to the monumentalisation of the traditional Greek city. Parallel with the developments which were taking place in the co-ordinated design of building complexes was the growing tendency towards symmetry and axiality. Grid planning, in which public buildings had to fit the rectangular street network, was obviously influential in this development. The tendency towards a dominating central axis has already been noticed in the laying out of the Seleucid cities. It is seen within towns in the construction of the agora as a symmetrical horseshoe shape, enclosed on three sides by stoas and on the fourth side by an independent portico. Axial planning was also employed independently of grid planning in the design of such building complexes as the temple to Asclepius at Cos and the temple to Athena on the acropolis of Lindos, Rhodes.

The temple complex to Asclepius on Cos was constructed on three regular terraces.[31] The lowest terrace of the precinct was approached by means of a wide stairway which led through a monumental entrance (Figure 31). The entrance-way was set in the rear wall of the three-sided portico which flanked the piazza of the lower terrace. The latter was connected to the middle terrace by a second flight of steps, which was misaligned in relation to the other flights of stairs. On this terrace there was a cluster of altars and shrines, including a large altar, probably of later date, and an Ionic temple. Another flight of stairs led from the rear of the middle terrace up to a roadway which separated the latter from the highest terrace, which in turn was approached from the road by a stairway. On the highest terrace there was the Doric temple to Asclepius surrounded on three sides by a portico with projecting wings.

The fourth-century/Hellenistic building complex which occupies the acropolis of Lindos on Rhodes was also axially arranged.[32] A monumental stairway led up to a large piazza on which stood an imposing stoa with short projecting wings. Another flight of monumental stairs ran through the centre of the stoa into the so-called propylaea. The propylaea, in fact, consisted of a complex of interconnected colonnaded stoas and porticoes, which surrounded two sides of the courtyard of the temple to Athena on the summit of the hill.

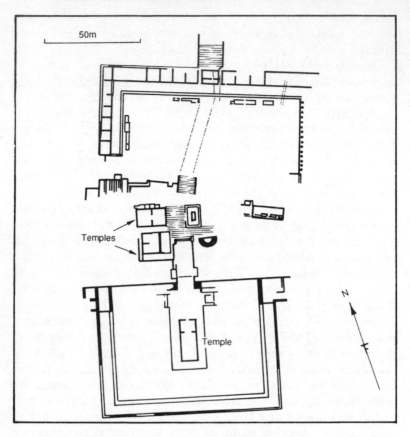

Figure 31 The precinct of Asclepius on Cos

The axial arrangement of both complexes is clear and unmistakable. Yet in neither place was the symmetry consistently maintained. In the case of Cos the lower terrace was not strictly orientated with the central axis, and the irregularity of the monuments on the middle terrace helps to reduce the symmetry of the complex. The abandonment of the axial arrangement is just as striking at Lindos. Because of the lack of space the eastern projecting wing of the propylaea, corresponding to the western wing, could not be constructed. More incongruous is the location of the temple itself. This abandoned the central axis of the complex and was positioned on the edge of the cliff overlooking the sea below (Figure 32).

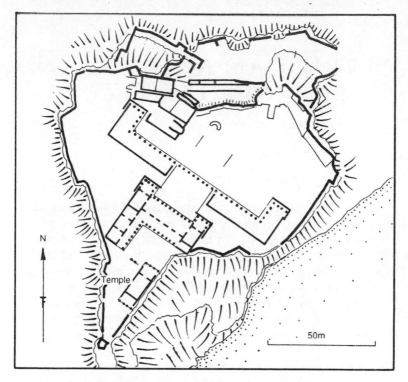

Figure 32 The acropolis of Lindos, Rhodes

The achievements of Hellenistic planning are diverse. The real success of Hellenistic town planners lay not in the continued application of the grid pattern, but in the monumentalisation of the typical Greek city. Ultimately, however, Greek planning was hostage to the physical environment of the site and the building materials which were available. It was left to the Romans to introduce new ideas, and different constructional methods and building materials, to the cities of the Greek east. These innovations not only transformed regular planning but also completely altered the character of the cities of the Greek world.

6

ETRUSCAN AND ROMAN PLANNING IN ITALY

The proposal for the migration was defeated and they began to build the city without plan of any kind. . . . Such was their haste that they did not take care to lay out the streets, since all the boundary distinctions had been lost and they were building *in vacuo*. This is the reason why the old drains, once running through public property, now in many cases pass under private houses, and why the appearance of the city resembles one that has been occupied rather than being properly planned.

Thus Livy ends his account of the sack of Rome by the Gauls and the defeat of the proposal that the Romans should abandon their city and move to Veii.[1] Until the great fire of AD 64 Rome remained essentially unplanned. Livy blames the irregularity of the republican city of Rome on its destruction by the Gauls and the subsequent haste with which the city was rebuilt after the departure of the enemy. Unlike at Athens during the Persian war, this explanation is not totally correct. Livy himself admits that Rome had not been totally destroyed during the Gallic attack.[2] He concedes that they had been restrained in their destruction of the city and consequently the resulting damage was limited. Therefore, in many cases, the Romans would have returned merely to renew and renovate. Existing property boundaries, which Livy says were destroyed, would have remained and would have formed the basis of the restoration of the city. In fact, in another passage Livy admits that it was in part official policy and in part the wishes of the individuals that were major contributory factors in the rebuilding of the city and the subsequent irregularity of Rome.[3] After the departure of the Gauls the Romans would have found

94

it difficult to undertake a radical redistribution of land, which regular planning would have entailed, for the same reasons that they had found it impossible to move to Veii when the proposal had been put forward.[4] The opponents of the move had argued that many of Rome's most sacred places were inside the city and a transfer of the population to Veii would have necessitated the abandonment of these traditional places. There were also forceful social and political reasons why the transfer of Rome to Veii was impossible. Rome had already been inhabited for centuries. Landholding and landownership within the city were firmly established. The proposed occupation of Veii would have meant the abandonment of existing property and necessitated a new distribution of land at the new site, with potentially far-reaching social, economic and possibly even political consequences for the people of Rome. Any planning scheme involving a radical redistribution of land within Rome itself would have had the same effect and so could not be contemplated. Thus, for historical reasons and because of the reluctance of both the government and individuals with vested interests extensive replanning was impossible. Consequently, after the departure of the Gauls the city of Rome continued to expand in the same haphazard way as before.[5] The consequences of this were a vital factor in the disastrous fire of AD 64. Conditions in Rome were typical of conditions in native towns and cities throughout central and northern Italy and contrasted markedly with many of the Greek colonies of southern Italy.[6]

The history and development of town planning in Italy are both complex and controversial, involving not only the Greeks but also the Etruscans and the Romans. In the past, scholars have argued for an independent tradition of regular planning in Italy which was based on the Etruscans and their predecessors, the Villanovans. Other authorities, however, have maintained that there is no evidence for an independent planning tradition, and Etruscan and Roman planning came about through direct contact with the Greeks of southern Italy.[7] The ambiguities in part arise from the fact that in many cities, especially in central Italy, Greeks, Etruscans and Romans came into direct and close contact. Native cities were influenced or occupied consecutively and sometimes even concurrently by the Greeks and the Etruscans. Therefore it is often difficult to unravel the exact contribution which each made to the development of a particular town.

The whole question of the origins of planning in Italy and the specific question of the Etruscan contribution to its development is further obscured by the fact that excavation of early Etruscan sites has not been extensive and where evidence is found, it often remains inconclusive. The problem is further confused by Roman literary tradition, which emphasised the importance of the Etruscans in the development of Roman city-foundation ritual. Thankfully, archaeology has now begun to clarify the problem. The increasing evidence for early Greek planning in Italy, together with the scarcity of evidence for regular planning at early Etruscan towns and their Villanovan forerunners, is an indication of the importance of the Greeks in the transmission of town planning ideas to the indigenous peoples of Italy. The suggestion that town planning in Italy had developed independently of any Greek influence can now almost certainly be discounted.[8]

Proof comes from the earliest Etruscan cities, which in all cases were unplanned. Like their counterparts in the Aegean, defence was a primary consideration in the choice of site, and the rugged, sometimes virtually inaccessible locations of the early Villanovan and Etruscan settlements made systematic planning difficult. However, not every site was unsuitable.[9] The volcanic tufa out of which the southern part of Etruria is formed weathers particularly easily into relatively flat plateaus. Even where the terrain allowed, planning did not take place. Regular planning involves central co-ordination. But such central co-ordination was not necessary with a small population. Occupation at a site took place wherever conditions allowed. Towns grew from small villages as the population increased. The early settlements of Italy differ in detail from their Aegean counterparts. Geographical and topographical conditions varied; there are differences in constructional methods and building types; but the underlying processes which determined the development of the towns were broadly similar.

The Etruscans were the first true city-builders of central and northern Italy. Before them there existed only the hut villages of the early Iron Age peoples of Italy, known as the Villanovans. In the course of the seventh century BC changes began to take place.[10] New, more substantially built cities began to appear as the Etruscans, building in stone and mudbrick, replaced the less substantial wattle and wooden huts of the Villanovans. In some cases new sites were occupied and Villanovan settlements were completely abandoned. Sometimes occupation continued at an

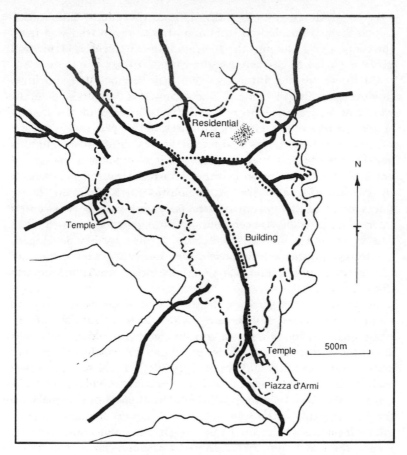

Figure 33 Veii

established site, although even then the new building techniques were introduced. Despite these changes and innovations regular planning did not take place, and both the new towns and the existing centres continued in the same irregular manner.

Veii offers a typical example of the development of an early Italic settlement (Figure 33). Because of its rivalry with and its eventual destruction by Rome, Veii is probably the most famous town in southern Etruria.[11] The town occupied a virtually inaccessible hill protected on all sides, except the north-west, by rivers. Earliest occupation comprised a number of independent Villanovan hut villages, each with its own cemetery, which were

97

situated at different points throughout the site.[12] The tracks, which formed the basis of the later street system, radiated from the centre of the site into the surrounding countryside. Habitation initially tended to concentrate along these routes.[13]

Of the succeeding Etruscan town little remains. It is possible, however, to discern some of the changes at Veii, when, in the course of the seventh century BC, the huts began to be replaced by substantial stone and mudbrick houses.[14] But progress was only gradual; new houses appear alongside the existing Villanovan huts and no attempt was made to bring order to the new residential areas. The only exception to the total irregularity of Veii was on the citadel of *Piazza d'Armi* at the southern end of the site. Here, traces of a regular system of streets, possibly with two central intersecting axes, have been found, although why this area alone was so laid out is unclear. Elsewhere, as the new city developed, no attempt was made to impose order. Even the temples, the only identifiable public buildings at Veii, remained scattered throughout the site.[15]

A significant geographical feature of southern Etruria is the innumerable rivers and ravines which criss-cross the region. Consequently, flooding was a constant problem at Veii, as it was at many Etruscan sites. This problem was alleviated by the construction of drains and water channels.[16] Rock-cut and stone-built drains are a feature of both the houses and streets of Veii. Street drains have been found close to the *Pontanaccio* sanctuary on the western side of the site. Part of a larger drainage system, which led water out of the Capenan gate, has also come to light. It included converging street drains, a settling tank and gutters.

More substantial hydraulic engineering projects were also undertaken. The *Ponto Soto* relieved the possibility of flooding of the River Valchetta on the north-western side of the town and an underground channel carried water from the *Fosso di Formallo* to the *Fosso Piordo*. In addition to the drainage works adequate supplies of water were maintained by the construction of cisterns, some of which tapped natural underground sources by means of rock-cut channels. The water installations of Veii are impressive, since they not only emphasise the skill of the Etruscans in the field of hydraulic engineering, but also indicate an area of urban planning in which the Etruscans were to make a significant contribution.

The remains of other Villanovan and early Etruscan settlements confirm the picture of Veii. Unplanned Etruscan towns succeeded Villanovan villages at Tarquinii and Luni sul Mignone.[17] Swedish excavations at San Giovenale and Acquarossa and research at the northern Etruscan city of Vetulonia reveal the same development and add detail to the general picture.

San Giovenale lies on a tributary of the River Mignone 15 miles to the east of Tarquinii,[18] and stands on a rocky tufa plateau which is protected on two sides by rivers. The original Villanovan hut settlement was replaced in the course of the seventh century BC by a substantially built city, with the walls of the buildings constructed of tufa socles supporting a mudbrick superstructure. However, like Veii, free-standing huts also continued in use and the new town was not regularly laid out. The streets were narrow, irregular and sinuous, hugging the contours of the hills as they wound between houses and other buildings. Only the central area of the town, which was probably a later addition, appears different. Here the buildings were more orderly arranged. A system of narrow streets and alleys created narrow but regular blocks of adjacent houses.

Acquarossa and Vetulonia grew in the same way. The former, close to the later Roman town of Ferentium, was built around the middle of the seventh century BC and occupied a naturally defensive site.[19] The earliest evidence of habitation, in well-constructed tufa and mudbrick houses, was totally irregular, and only later in the course of the sixth century BC was a regularly planned extension added. Vetulonia, on the other hand, continued to develop in an irregular manner with well-made cobbled streets winding through the irregular blocks of houses.[20] The evidence of early Etruscan towns remains meagre. It is, nevertheless, certain that they were not initially regularly laid out, and the regular extensions, which several of the towns had, were later additions.

Etruscan expansion northwards into the Po Valley and southwards into Campania brought the Etruscans into contact with the Greeks. Undoubtedly this expansion not only introduced them to Greek ideas of regular urban design but also provided the opportunity to put the ideas into practice.[21] In northern Italy the Etruscans came into direct contact with the Greeks at Spina, which lies between Venice and Ravenna, and it is possible that it was here in this international trading port that the Etruscans were first introduced to Greek concepts of town planning.[22] A much more likely source of inspiration for Etruscan planning was the

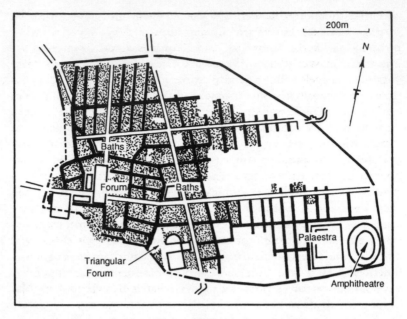

Figure 34 Pompeii

Greek cities of southern Italy. In Campania in particular, the Etruscans came into direct contact and eventual conflict with the southern Italian Greek cities. Trade and commercial intercourse flourished, and both the Greeks and the Etruscans vied with each other for control of and influence over the native towns. Undoubtedly, ideas as well as goods were exchanged; and the cross-fertilisation of ideas in the Campanian towns not only helped to formulate Etruscan planning but was also the inspiration of Roman planning methods.

Of the Campanian towns, Pompeii, preserved as it is by the eruption of Vesuvius in AD 79, exemplifies the interaction of Greek, Etruscan and later Roman ideas and methods (Figure 34). The original Oscan centre, which occupies only the south-western corner of the later city, was small and, although it assumed a general regularity, based on the intersection of two roads, it was unplanned.[23] The roads do not meet at right angles, the lesser streets are narrow and sinuous, and the buildings do not conform to the arrangement of the streets. In the course of the fifth century BC the original town was greatly increased in size by the addition of a series of approximately orthogonal extensions.[24] Two parallel east-west streets, the *Via dell'Abondanza* and the *Via di Nola*, and a north-south arterial street, the *Via di Stabia*, not exactly perpendicular to the above streets, formed the basis of the new layout. The new town developed in relation to these arteries but at the same time also had to take into account the existing native district. The resulting residential *insulae* differ in size and shape, but overall the plan maintains a high degree of unity and cohesion.

As Pompeii developed so public buildings were added, although the majority of the preserved buildings today are either Roman in date or at least are Roman renovations of earlier buildings. The public buildings concentrate in three areas of the city in particular. The forum, situated in the original Oscan city, acted as the political, religious, legal and economic centre of the town; and the buildings, including the forum itself with basilica, temples and a food market, emphasise the multiplicity of functions of a forum. The theatre, a roofed odeion and temples were located in the vicinity of the so-called triangular forum on the southern side of the city, whilst in the south-eastern corner of Pompeii a Greek-style palaestra with a swimming pool of Augustan date and the oldest known amphitheatre in the Roman world provided leisure and entertainment facilities. There were also three public bath houses. A notable feature of Pompeii was the paved streets with raised pedestrian walkways and a comprehensive system of underground drains. For water the city relied on underground sources and cisterns, until the construction of the aqueduct.

The urban development of Pompeii is complex, the result of the combined efforts of the Greeks, Etruscans and Romans over several centuries. It is consequently difficult to disentangle the exact contributions of the Greeks and the Etruscans to the original development of the plan. The overall street system is definitely Greek-inspired. The fortifications are Greek as are some of the original buildings. But there are also features at Pompeii which are not Greek. They include the subtle combination of the different elements of the town into a coherent unit, which takes into account the existing native centre, the suburban roads and the general topography of the area. The well-made roads with raised pavements and the complexity of the hydraulic installations are also not typically Greek. Pompeii offers a unique glimpse of a small but flourishing Italian town and at the same time emphasises the complex interaction of the Greeks, Etruscans and Romans in its development.

From Pompeii we turn to Capua, by far the most important Etruscan centre in Campania. Like Pompeii, the small, original native settlement was greatly expanded by the addition of a new, rectangular extension.[25] Again there are difficulties in interpreting its development. Its importance as an Etruscan trading post suggests that the expansion of the city can almost certainly be credited to the Etruscans. The town plan, however, is typically Greek. The regular layout, reconstructed from aerial photographs, consisted of five, or possibly six, wide, east-west avenues, and running perpendicular to these were a series of regularly spaced cross streets. The resulting elongated *insulae* were characteristic of the Greek cities of southern Italy. Also like Pompeii, the original town, occupying the south-western corner of the site, was skilfully amalgamated with the new extension.

Several other of the Campanian cities illustrate the interaction between Greek, Etruscan and Roman planning methods and the consequent cross-fertilisation of ideas. At the same time they also exemplify the difficulties in trying to identify the specific contributions of each. The Etruscan colonies of northern Italy are more helpful.

Commercial interests and the exploitation of the natural resources were two of the key factors which drew the Etruscans to the Po Valley where they planted the first true cities in the region, and places like Bologna, Spina and Marzabotto became important Etruscan centres. Unfortunately, little remains of Etruscan Bologna, although extensive evidence of the preceding Villanovan settlement has come to light.[26] More is known about Spina. Lying in the lagoons and sandbars at the mouth of the River Po, the city was an impressive feat of engineering. Even though it was built on water, its layout was, nevertheless, regular.[27] A main canal, along which flowed the River Po, ran through the centre of the town. Other narrower canals lay parallel and perpendicular to this waterway, creating rectangular *insulae* on which the buildings were constructed.

Legend accorded the foundation of Spina to the Greeks and, in consequence, it is possible that the Greeks were responsible for the development of the city. However, its greatest period of expansion and prosperity came in the fifth century BC under Etruscan influence; and the expertise of the Etruscans in hydraulic engineering, proof of which is seen in the construction of a canal linking Spina to Atria, suggests that the Etruscans were probably instrumental in the design and the construction of the town. Despite the uncertainties, the Greeks and the Etruscans lived in close contact at Spina and the result was a remarkable, flourishing and lively international port.

Evidence of the Etruscan colonisation in northern Italy continues to increase. A regular grid plan has been found at Casalecchio.[28] Yet Marzabotto remains the most interesting and instructive Etruscan colony in the Po Valley region.[29] The town, called after the local modern village since the ancient name is unknown, was established on the flood plain of the River Reno to the south-west of Bologna towards the end of the sixth century BC, in order to exploit the commercial potential and the natural resources of the surrounding region. Its plan is regular (Figure 35). It was laid out with three broad east-west avenues and at right angles an axial, north-south avenue and numerous, narrower streets. The resulting *insulae* formed elongated rectangles of characteristically Greek type. However, the street network was not arbitrarily imposed on the site. The *insulae* vary in width according to the nature of the terrain and take into account the differing topographical features of the land. An important feature of the town plan is the emphasis placed on the intersection of the two central axes in the residential zone. The importance of these two streets in the layout is further confirmed by the discovery of a stone *cippus* under the street surface, which was inscribed with two intersecting lines, corresponding to the direction of the two roads.[30] It was possibly at this point that the surveying instrument, used to lay out the town, was placed. Uninscribed *cippi* also marked the junctions of the other road intersections.

The hill on the north-west side of the city acted as the citadel. Here a series of temples and altars was built. All were aligned in the same direction as the lower town and the area was united with the lower town by the central east-west avenue. There is also slight evidence of a road running around the inside of the town in the manner of the 'pomerial' road common in Roman cities.[31]

Planning at Marzabotto went beyond merely laying out the streets and the organisation of districts. Civic organisation was no less impressive. Some of the streets were paved and the major roads had raised pedestrian pavements reminiscent of Pompeii. There was a comprehensive drainage system which not only

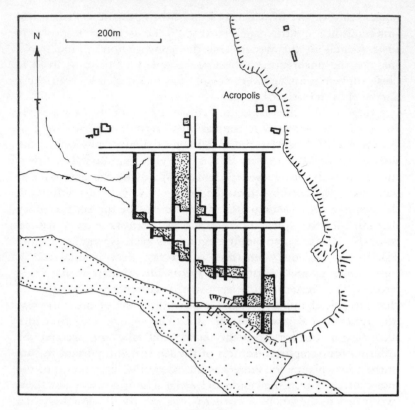

Figure 35 Marzabotto

controlled water, but also helped to define and segregate private building land from the public streets.

Wells provided drinking water for the houses but the remains of an aqueduct, which distributed additional supplies of water to the industrial establishments, has also been found. Industrial and commercial activity was also fully integrated into the town. Workshops and industrial establishments occupied prominent positions throughout the city and along the main streets, as well as in specific industrial areas on the outskirts.[32]

In total, the evidence for Etruscan planning is not extensive and so conclusions can only be tentative. Nevertheless, it is certain that the Etruscans played a major role both in the urbanisation of central and northern Italy and in spreading the idea of town planning throughout the area. Etruscan planning methods without a doubt were Greek-inspired. The influence of the Greeks can be seen not only in the overall street plans but also in specific details. The Etruscans, however, were not mere imitators. Their cities have an originality which indicates that they made a valuable and independent contribution to the development of town planning in Italy. The town plans display greater flexibility than their southern Greek counterparts. At Marzabotto the stone markers found under the streets suggest a theoretical approach to the laying out of the street grid.[33] Etruscan planning skilfully tried to integrate the different elements of the town. The incorporation of the existing towns of Pompeii and Capua into the new schemes contrasts with Greek practice at Naples, Naxos and Himera. At Naples the new town which was built on the other side of the harbour to the existing town became a distinct and separate suburb. At Naxos and Himera the original settlements were swept aside when the new layouts were drawn up. Again the integration of commercial and industrial activity at Marzabotto, and probably also at Capua, can be contrasted with Greek practice at several colonies where industrial activity was purposefully separated from the residential districts. Etruscan planning excelled especially in the provision of basic services and amenities. Roads were paved, drains were constructed, and adequate supplies of water were maintained. Certainly Etruscan cities benefited from contact with the Greek world. But the transfer of ideas was not necessarily one way. It could even be suggested that the improvements to the Greek cities of southern Italy and Sicily, especially in the field of hydraulic engineering, were due to direct contact with the Etruscans.[34]

It remains to consider the long-held views concerning Etruscan towns, namely that Etruscan planning was based on concepts of axiality and celestial orientation.[35] The idea that Etruscan cities were axially arranged is based on the axiality of Etruscan temples and on ritual foundation lore, as recorded by the Romans. Its importance in urban planning is more difficult to substantiate. Only Marzabotto, and possibly the regularly planned district of Veii, have produced evidence of an axial arrangement, but in both cases it is not the dominating feature of the plan. The same is true of the idea of celestial orientation. Both the street systems of Marzabotto and Capua were orientated to the points of the compass. But it might seem obvious to employ such an orientation if other geographical and topographical factors were not relevant. Indeed, at Marzabotto, the celestial orientation coincided with the slope of the terrain, which was exploited to improve the efficiency of the drainage of the site. Rather than seek evidence of celestial orientation in Etruscan towns it is better to emphasise again the flexibility of Etruscan planning, noting its use where appropriate, but also realising that it could be abandoned when circumstances dictated.

The actual importance of the Etruscans in the history of planning in Italy will remain a source of controversy and debate until the early history of Etruscan cities is more clearly understood. There is, however, no reason for thinking that the Etruscans were only the passive recipients of Greek practice. They made a positive and independent contribution to the development of planning in Italy. It was this combination of Greek and Etruscan achievement which laid the foundations of Roman planning.

Roman planning began with the conquest of Italy. As a result of expansion, the Romans not only came into direct contact with existing regularly planned towns, but also, in planting their own colonies, were faced with the practical difficulties of how to establish new cities. The Romans colonised primarily for military and strategic reasons. They established colonies first of all in Latium and central Italy to protect their own territory. Subsequently colonies were established throughout the peninsula in order to secure conquered lands and as bases for further expansion. Where towns already existed, the new colonists were added to the native population, although often the native city was extensively refurbished on Roman lines. At the Greek city of Poseidonia for instance, where a Roman colony was founded in 273 BC, the Romans strengthened the walls, added Roman public buildings, and remodelled the street plan by widening into an axial road the so-called *Via Sacra* which passed through the southern gate.[36] At Thourioi, renamed Copia by the Romans, the remodelling was more comprehensive and involved the slight displacement of the new colony from the original Greek location.[37] Such renovation was not merely an attempt to Romanise Greek or native cities. It is indicative of the specific needs of the Romans in colonisation and the contribution which they made to urbanisation in Italy.

In areas of Italy without a tradition of urbanised life, new towns had to be created and in order to achieve this the Romans

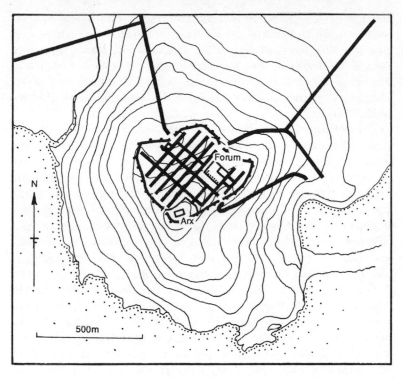

Figure 36 Cosa

naturally turned to regular planning. Rome benefited greatly from the wealth of planning experience which was already available in Italy. In the early Roman colonies of Norba, Alba Fucens and Cosa, Rome's undoubted debt to the Greeks and the Etruscans is most obvious.

Cosa, the last of the three colonies, is probably one of the finest examples of early Roman planning, and is an indication of the skill of the Romans in learning, yet adapting, the ideas of other peoples (Figure 36). The colony was established in 273 BC on an easily defensible hill on the Etruscan coast, 85 miles north-west of Rome.[38] Despite the difficulties of the site, the town plan reveals a high degree of unity and expertly combines the military and civil requirements of the colony. The fortifications exploited the defensive qualities of the site, resulting in a totally irregular perimeter. Nevertheless, the street plan was both rectangular and fully co-ordinated with the walls. In accordance with tradition, the number of gates was reduced to three, in the north-western, north-eastern and south-eastern walls.[39] There was also a postern gate allowing access to the citadel. The two roads from the north-eastern and the south-eastern gates met in the centre of the town. The road from the north-western gate led to the forum. In addition a 'pomerial' road followed the irregular course of the walls.

The forum of a Roman colony was usually positioned at the centre of the town where the major roads met. However, because of the unevenness of the terrain the forum of Cosa was located on relatively flat ground close to the south-eastern gate and the road which led down to the harbour, a position recommended by Vitruvius as most appropriate for coastal cities.[40] Besides the temples situated in the vicinity of the forum, two other temples stood on the two hills which dominate the south-western and the south-eastern corners of the town respectively. The rest of the city was divided into rectangular, residential *insulae*.

Together with Paestum, Cosa was founded shortly after the departure of Pyrrhus of Epirus to guard the coastline of the Tyrrhenian Sea. The town is a monument to the skill and the success of Roman planning. The town plan fully exploits the location and at the same time fulfils the strategic and civilian role which the Romans required of a colony. The success of Cosa is an indication of the experience which the Romans had already gained in planting colonies.

The essential features of the layout of Cosa were already apparent when Alba Fucens was colonised thirty years previously, and even earlier at Norba. Like Cosa both were founded on steep, easily defensible hills. At Norba the rectangular grid pattern was preserved not only in some rectangular *insulae* on the southern side of the acropolis, but also in the series of regular terraces which climb the site.[41] Alba Fucens was established on a prominent hill overlooking the Fucine Lake after the surrender of the Aequi in 303 BC in order to control two strategic routes: the one coming from Campania and the south, and the other, the *Via Valeria*, climbing over the Apenines to the north-east.[42] The street system was rectangular although the streets were not strictly regular (Figure 37). The main road through the town was the *Via Valeria*, which followed a slightly irregular course. At right angles to the *Via Valeria* there was another important road which led from the eastern gate, although it was not directly aligned with it.

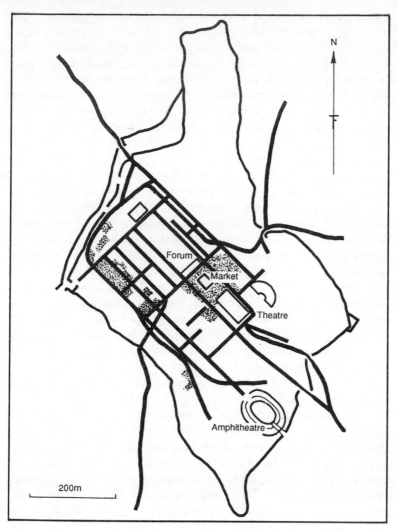

Figure 37 Alba Fucens

Another major road paralleled the *Via Valeria* to the east of the public buildings and led out of the northern gate. With the exception of the amphitheatre and two temples, which overlooked the colony on the southern and the eastern sides, the public buildings concentrated in the centre of the town along the *Via Valeria*. Like Cosa, the urban walls took full advantage of the

109

terrain and followed an irregular course around the colony.

The colonies of Alba, Cosa and Norba are proof of the influence of the Greeks on the formation of Roman planning. The overall grid pattern is Greek-influenced as are specific details, such as the portcullis on the gates of Cosa and Alba Fucens.[43] But these towns were not mere copies of Greek originals. They display clear Roman traits which formed the basis of a specifically Roman system of planning, conceived on Italic lines and adapted to Roman planning needs. In fact by the time that Cosa was established the Romans had already planted no fewer than nineteen colonies. In doing so the Romans developed a type of urban colonial design which became a veritable 'blue print' for Roman cities, not only throughout Italy but also ultimately throughout the empire. Certain of the traits can be seen in the arrangement of Cosa and were most probably inspired by Etruscan planning methods.[44] The street system itself placed considerable emphasis on the intersection of two major roads. These two major axes, erroneously termed the *decumanus maximus* and the *kardo maximus*, led from the city gates and met in the centre of the town, where the forum was situated. Unlike Cosa, Alba Fucens and Norba the perimeter was often square or oblong in shape and the residential *insulae* were similarly square or oblong rather than rectangular.

The pattern had already been formulated when the small citizen colony of Ostia was planted towards the end of the fourth century BC. Established to protect the mouth of the River Tiber, the original colony is now buried below the bustling harbour town which subsequently grew up on the site. The plan of the original colony, however, has been recovered (Figure 38). The earliest colony was a small rectangular-shaped settlement measuring 193.94 × 125.70 m. Two main roads led from corresponding pairs of gates to meet in the centre of the town.[45] The *decumanus maximus* took its alignment from the direction of the River Tiber and was incorporated into the main east-west road of the later harbour town. The town plan of Ostia was repeated in other early colonies including Pyrgi, Minturnae, and Terracina. All were small, accommodating usually only 300 Roman citizens, were either square or slightly rectangular in shape, were well defended, and with the exception of Minturnae, where only the course of the *Via Appia*, which acts as the colony's *decumanus*, has been located with certainty, contained two axial roads.

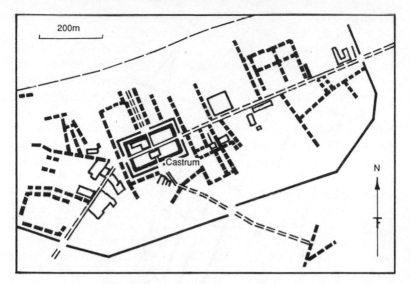

Figure 38 Ostia – the Roman *castrum* underlies the later port

This scheme became standard in Roman colonies throughout Italy down to the end of the Republic and laid the basis for the towns which Rome established throughout the empire. Unfortunately, because of later colonisation and in many towns continuous occupation from antiquity, it is often difficult to obtain detailed information concerning the earliest phases of many of the towns. Often, however, the street systems and the perimeters of the colonies have been preserved in the later street plans. Thus Placentia (Piacenza), originally established as a colony in 218 BC in the territory of the Celtic Anamares, had a square perimeter measuring 480 m and the *insulae* were approximately 80 m square.[46] The plan of Placentia was repeated elsewhere. At Bononia (Bologna), for instance, the perimeter of the original colony was probably square, although as the colony increased it was redrawn and the residential *insulae* were oblong.[47] Cremona, planted in 218 BC as the first of Rome's colonies beyond the River Po, was also square in plan and revealed traces of paved roads including the remains of the 'pomerial' road, 6 m in width.[48]

Roman planning was based on a theoretical 'blue print' which could be applied repeatedly at any new location. The Romans, however, did not impose the design arbitrarily without regard for

111

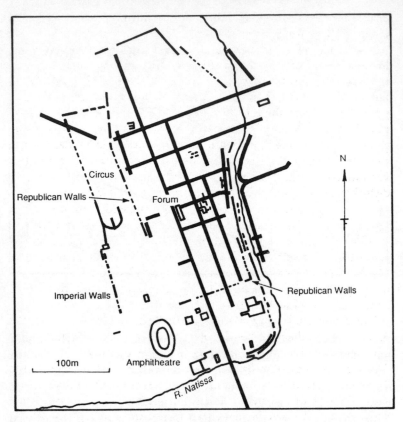

Figure 39 Aquileia

other factors. At Aquileia (Veneto) (Figure 39), planted in 181 BC and successively expanded later, the rectangularity of the perimeter and the uniformity of the street grid was abandoned in places.[49] The colonies of Lucca, which was planted in 177 BC, and Luni were planned as squares but in both cases the rectangularity of one side was abandoned for topographical reasons.[50] Similarly at Ariminum (Rimini), which was situated at the junction of the *Via Aemilia*, the *Via Flaminia* and the *Via Popilia*, the perimeter was irregular in order to utilise to the full the defensive qualities of the site.[51] Yet the street system was rectangular. Roman colonial planning developed in response to a set of circumstances which were broadly the same whenever a new town was planted, but one of the achievements of Roman planners was their ability to adapt and at times even abandon established practice should circumstances necessitate.

The army reforms of Marius together with the large-scale and lucrative wars of the first century BC had far-reaching effects on the Republic and ultimately were one of the major causes of the failure of the Senatorial government.[52] Successful generals were obliged to reward their armies not only in terms of booty and pay but also by obtaining land for their veterans after campaigning. Often the troops were settled in the provinces. But Sulla, Caesar, the Triumvirs and Augustus settled a large proportion of their veteran troops in Italy. This policy caused hardship and civil disturbance, but political expediency and military security outweighed the grievances of the dispossessed peasants. The Caesarian and Augustan colonies of the late Republican period in particular form an homogeneous group of towns of extremely standard design. Augusta Praetoria (Aosta), Augusta Taurinorum (Turin) and Verona offer the clearest examples of the scheme, but it is repeated at Allifae, Comum (Como), Ticinum (Pavia), Fanum (Fano), and Venafrum (Venafro).

The Augustan colony at Verona, situated on a bend in the River Adige, replaced an earlier Latin colony at the same site.[53] The perimeter was rectangular although like the perimeter of Augusta Taurinorum the south-eastern corner was truncated (Figure 40). The street system was based on the intersection of the two major axes which ran from the gates and met in the centre of the town. The rest of the streets delimited approximately square *insulae* 75–80 m per side, the area of which corresponds to 2 Roman *iugera*. The amphitheatre and the stadium lay outside the city but they were aligned to the streets and were connected to the city by the drainage system. Augusta Praetoria[54] and Augusta Taurinorum[55] follow a similar pattern, although in both cases the *kardo maximus* was displaced from its central location to one side, in the manner of army encampments. The military influences on the planning of these colonies are further seen at Aosta where the wall towers correspond to the ends of the streets.

There can be little doubt that although the origins of Roman town planning are rooted in established Greek and Etruscan practice, in Italy the Romans developed a specific and identifiable system of planning adapted to the problems which they themselves faced in colonising Italy. Of the factors which influenced the development of Roman grid planning the army and

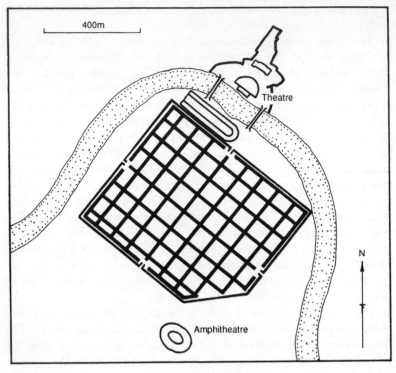

Figure 40 Verona

land surveying were probably the most influential.[56]

Unfortunately, evidence of direct influence between Roman military camps and town planning is deficient. The nature of legionary camps of the Republican period remains unclear, and references in both Frontinus and Polybius argue that Roman colonial planning antedated the appearance of regularly planned army camps. Frontinus, at one time the governor of Britain and later the curator of aqueducts at Rome, maintained that it was not until the Romans had overrun the camp of Pyrrhus of Epirus that they developed an orderly arrangement for their own army camps.[57] This happened in 275 BC, three decades or more after the foundation of Ostia, Norba and several other colonies, and only two years before the foundation of Cosa and Poseidonia. Similarly Polybius' comparison of the regular arrangement of Roman army camps with regularly planned towns also supports the priority of Roman colonial planning.[58]

Despite this evidence, Rome's early colonies were overtly military. They were established as strongholds to protect Roman territory, for securing and consolidating new territories acquired in the wake of Rome's victorious armies, or as offensive bases for future military operations. The military importance of Roman colonies is clearly stated both by Cicero and Appian. Cicero, writing of Narbo Martius in Gaul, describes the town as a watch-tower and a bulwark of the Roman people, and a defensive barrier against the hostile tribes which threatened the province.[59] Appian, commenting upon the conquest of Italy, states that the Romans built new cities or occupied existing towns in the newly conquered territories as strategic outposts.[60] Furthermore, the colonies were often positioned to exploit and control the system of military roads which the Romans developed in Italy. Indeed in many cases they were built across a road, which acted as one of the main arteries of the colony. The military nature of the colonies is also evidenced by the fact that the new colonists arrived at the site in military formation,[61] and military terms were often used to describe the colonists.[62]

This evidence is inferential. However, the evidence from the town plans themselves is direct and undoubtedly confirms the importance of the army in the formation of Roman colonial planning. There is a clear relationship between the military and civil requirements of the settlements. The defences are fully co-ordinated with the street system, which includes a 'pomerial' road around the inside of the walls. The city gates, always the weak point in a defensive wall, were reduced to one per side to reduce the number of points of entry. Certainly in later colonies the military considerations underlying the plan become increasingly apparent. The perimeters of both the Sullan veteran colony of Allifae and the Augustan colony at Fanum were rectangular with rounded corners, reminiscent of the army forts of the imperial period (Figure 41). At Aosta the towers which protect the walls are directly related to the system of streets within the city.

Although military, Roman colonies, almost without exception, were also agricultural and commercial. Aquileia, mentioned above, emphasises the combined strategic and agricultural/commercial importance of Roman colonisation. Established after the conquest of Italy as a base for operations against the Carnici, and also utilised later for operations against other hostile tribes in the region, the centuriation of its territory from the initial

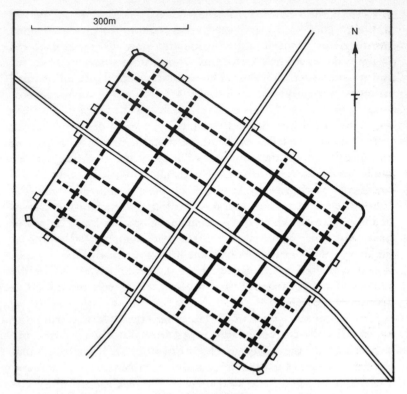

Figure 41 Allifae

foundation of the colony also indicates that it was intended to foster peaceful agricultural and commercial conditions in the area. Thus, the second important factor which influenced the development of Roman colonial planning and to which the historian Appian draws attention, is land surveying.[63] In the ancient world there was an intimate and reciprocal relationship between town and country. A city controlled and exploited the territory surrounding it. For the individual, land was a means of wealth and an indicator of social position. Thus an essential feature of the reorganisation of a district after conquest, at times to the annoyance of the local population, was the assessment of the erstwhile enemy's land and the confiscation of part of it.[64] Of this confiscated territory a portion was retained by the Roman state for public use. The rest was allotted to the new colonists who had been sent to live in the area. In both cases land surveying was an

116

integral aspect of the reorganisation of a district. The Latin word *colonia* emphasises the agricultural notion implicit in the foundation of a new Roman city, and the apportionment of land to the colonists was a significant aspect of the foundation of a new colony. It would seem natural, therefore, that the techniques of the land surveyors, who accompanied the foundation of a new colony, would be used not only in the apportionment of the surrounding land but also in the laying out of the town; and their techniques are again reflected in the axial arrangement of the towns with their two main arterial roads. In fact the use of the terms *decumanus* and *kardo* implies the importance of the land surveyors, although their actual usage with reference to urban centres lacks ancient authority.[65]

Evidence of direct links between towns and centuriated land is also available. The use of a common base line for the town plan and the surrounding agricultural land is found in Africa,[66] but up to now it has been rarely found in Italy. However, recent work at Faventia indicates that the orthogonal plan of the town and the surrounding centuriated land shared a common base line in the *Via Aemilia*.[67] Similarly it has been suggested that there is a relationship between *Regio* 6 of Pompeii and the centuriated land to the north of the city.[68] There also seems to be correspondence between land division and the dimensions of the *insulae* of certain colonies. The use of a 75–80 m square in the planning of several of the Caesarian and Augustan colonies in Italy corresponds in area to 2 *iugera* of land, which was the normal allocation of land to a colonist, and is further confirmation of the relationship between colonial planning and centuriation.[69]

The area of a colony was often small, the inhabitants living and working in farms and dependent villages throughout the territory.[70] Thus the town also acted as the administrative, social and religious centre for the surrounding territory. In order to fulfil these functions basilicas, fora, bath houses, temples, amphitheatres and circuses became a regular feature of the Roman urban environment. Such buildings not only themselves became standardised but were also usually incorporated into the town layout and conformed to the dimensions of the *insulae*. The larger public buildings, or those which were added later, were constructed on the outskirts of the city. Such buildings should not be considered mere appendages to the town proper. At Verona, the axis of the amphitheatre, situated on the south-eastern side of the town, lies parallel to the street system of the town and was probably incorporated into the colony's drainage system.[71] On the northern side of the town the axis of the circus was also aligned to the streets. Similarly at Lucca the amphitheatre was aligned to the street system and linked to the town by the *kardo maximus*. In addition the roads themselves were often well constructed with paved surfaces and raised pedestrian walkways.[72]

Another field of urban planning which the Romans developed from the Etruscans, and in which they were to excel, was the provision of water and drainage.[73] A comprehensive system of street drains accompanied the planning of Roman colonies and in several cases the drainage system covered an area wider than that which eventually became inhabited, suggesting that from the beginning drainage was an integral aspect of the original town plan and was not only developed as the towns expanded.[74] Together with drainage, water was also provided. Public cisterns supplemented private wells as a source of water. Subsequently, aqueducts were constructed which delivered water to the city, whence it was distributed to fountains and roadside basins for public use.[75]

Axial grid planning became the characteristic feature of Roman colonies and towns throughout Italy. Roman planners, however, did not confine their experiments to grid planning alone. From the first half of the second century BC onwards, Rome became directly involved in the affairs of the Hellenistic kingdoms and became increasingly influenced by the Hellenised Greek world. Despite the opposition of certain members of the Roman nobility,[76] contact with the kingdoms of the Greek east transformed every aspect of Roman life. Architecture was no exception. Public buildings as well as private houses were directly influenced by Hellenistic concepts of monumentality and grandeur. Nor was monumentalisation confined to individual buildings. There were experiments in the composition and the construction of ensembles of buildings, recalling the monumental designs of the Hellenistic cities of Asia Minor. Thus for instance at Morgantina the lower and upper agoras were linked by a set of monumental stairs.[77]

The systematic development of several important sanctuaries involving the construction of ramps, stairs, terraces, porticoes and other buildings is also indicative of the Hellenised influences to which Roman architecture and planning were subjected. Examples

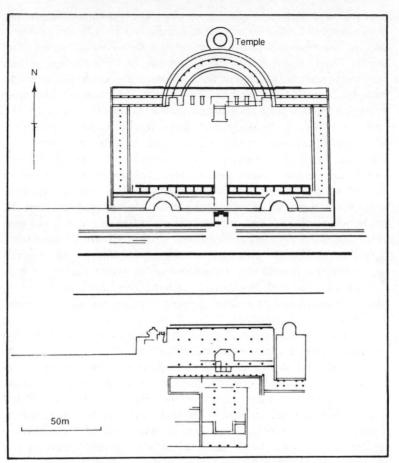

Figure 42 The acropolis at Praeneste

include the sanctuary of Jupiter Anxur close to Terracina and the sanctuary of Heracles Curinus, in the vicinity of Sulmona. At both, intrusive Hellenised traditions were combined with Roman methods and techniques. The sanctuary of Fortuna Primigenia, overlooking the lower city at Praeneste (Palestrina), is particularly impressive (Figure 42). The original Etruscan town was situated on a hill 36 km to the east of Rome, commanding the road from Poseidonia to Etruria. As the town grew, a second city, independent of the upper town but united with it by extending the fortifications, developed on the lower slopes of the hill. Sulla

119

captured and destroyed the town after the younger Marius had fled there in 82 BC. He then established a colony of veterans there and undertook a vast programme of renovation and building. The whole of the slope above the forum of the lower town, which curiously was unconnected with the upper sanctuary, was cut back in a series of regular terraces. On the terraces rows of shops, a second forum with associated public buildings including the curia, a large building resembling a basilica, nymphaea, a treasury, and a temple were constructed.[78] Above this again, climbing the slope in a series of seven regular terraces which were connected by stairs and ramps, was the sanctuary to Fortuna Primigenia itself. The complex, planned in the shape of a triangle with the temple at its apex, comprises a series of colonnaded porticoes, shops, niches, a large piazza culminating in a stepped colonnaded hemicycle and the small circular Corinthian temple.

Hellenistic Greek influence is apparent both in the overall concept of the sanctuary, in specific architectural details such as the use of Ionic and Corinthian columns, and even to a certain extent in its symmetrical arrangement. Yet its overall design and construction are typically Roman. Its building materials are concrete, covered in stuccoed *opus incertum*, and tufa columns with travertine capitals. Although axial symmetrical arrangements were employed in the design of such Hellenistic building complexes as the sanctuary of Asclepius at Cos and the acropolis of Lindos on Rhodes,[79] the extreme axial arrangement of Praeneste, which unites the two independent complexes, reflects the tradition in axial planning which had long been a central part of Etrusco–Italic design and construction.[80] It is in such experimentation in the design and construction of whole building complexes that the basis of Roman monumental planning in the imperial period was laid.

Roman town planning was undoubtedly built upon the achievements of the Greeks and the Etruscans. At the same time the Romans introduced new ideas which were adapted to their own particular planning requirements. The result was a highly standardised, but nevertheless flexible, approach to town planning. This combination of adaptability within a standardised arrangement laid the foundations for the urbanisation of the Roman Empire in the succeeding centuries.

7

PLANNING IN THE ROMAN EMPIRE

At its height the Roman Empire embraced the whole of the Mediterranean basin, a large part of northern and central Europe including Britain, and the Middle East as far as the Euphrates River. This vast territory contained a variety of peoples of different cultures, beliefs and traditions; and Rome was faced with major problems both in governing this vast area and maintaining peace and security within it. In order to achieve these aims the central government relied heavily upon the city. Cities were the primary level of the administration of the empire, upon which the central government devolved a heavy burden of responsibility for the administration of both local affairs and certain imperial duties. At the same time the Romans believed the city to be the institution most capable of maintaining peace and promoting civilisation in the Roman sense. Thus Rome encouraged the growth of towns and cities throughout the provinces of the empire.[1]

In the first two centuries of the Christian era in particular, the Roman Empire enjoyed an unparalleled period of peace, security and material prosperity, all of which had important consequences for the development of cities and urban life within the empire. With the Roman army protecting the frontiers, defence was no longer an important consideration either in the initial siting of a new city or its subsequent development. Consequently, except in frontier areas, urban walls were not required. They became a mark of privilege and ostentation not a military necessity. Indeed walls could not be constructed without the express permission of the emperor.[2]

Cities also took advantage of the new and vast economic opportunities which the *pax Romana* offered. Some cities were

121

moved to better, more accessible locations,[3] and others, like Lugdunum (Lyon) and Colonia Agrippinensis (Cologne), developed rapidly to exploit the complex network of rivers of Europe which the Roman peace opened up.

Furthermore, a spirit of competition was fostered both within cities and between cities. There was a deep and genuine feeling of civic pride and civic patriotism, especially amongst the leading citizens of the towns, and this patriotism had a profound effect on the development of towns throughout the empire. In Apuleius' *Golden Ass*, Byrrhaena, one of the eminent female citizens of Hypata, boasts to the hero of the story, Lucius, of the facilities and amenities that even this small Thessalian town had to offer.[4] Evidence of competition and the resulting benefactions abounds.[5] Eminent citizens vied with each other for public recognition and the senior civic posts. Cities competed with each other for honorific titles.[6] This spirit of rivalry engendered by the Roman Empire had several important consequences. Lavish shows and games were put on, a range of civic amenities was provided, and there was a massive increase in building activity.[7] This, in turn, fostered architectural and decorative developments as cities strove to emulate and surpass rivals in the splendour of their public monuments and the variety of their urban facilities.

The effects of such rivalry were not always beneficial. The desire to beautify and aggrandise also put an increasingly unbearable strain on the resources of the cities and their citizens. Moreover, benefactors tended to bestow such gifts as would increase their own standing and prestige, but often ignored less prestigious but nevertheless essential urban facilities. The case of Amastris, mentioned by Pliny, typifies this ambivalent attitude. An otherwise beautiful and well-laid-out city was, according to Pliny, spoilt by the fact that an open, foul-smelling sewer ran down the central road.[8] Presumably, none of the citizens thought that such an essential task as the covering of the main sewer would gain appropriate recognition and sufficient return, and so it was left to the provincial governor to ensure the task was completed.

The spirit of rivalry also brought other potential dangers. Pliny's letters catalogue numerous ill-conceived, unfinished and completely dangerous public building projects which were undertaken by the cities of Bithynia.[9] The reasons for this situation are various. Sometimes the project was too ambitious, or failed through lack of funds. It is also clear, however, that personal profit might also be involved.[10]

New Roman ideas, techniques, buildings and building materials were employed in an effort to built even grander and more imposing buildings. Architectural decoration increased. Buildings became more ornate and decoration more complex. But it is a short step from splendour to gaudiness and empty grandiosity. Despite these dangers, the success of Rome in both fostering the growth of cities in the unurbanised provinces and transforming existing cities is astounding, and the measure of this success is the continued occupation of many originally Roman cities down to the present day.

The task of urbanising the empire was, however, complicated. In some areas, notably parts of the Greek east and the coastal regions of the Mediterranean, there was already a long tradition of urban life through the colonising efforts of the Greeks and the Phoenicians, and sometimes urban traditions had already been passed on to the indigenous population.[11] Although even in the Greek east the Romans still found many opportunities to create new cities, the real success of Roman planning in these regions was to encourage Roman ideas and amalgamate Roman and native traditions. In other parts of the empire, towns in the Graeco-Roman sense were rare or totally lacking. In these areas the concept of the city had to be introduced and towns physically created. Consequently, the Roman response to these differing conditions had to be flexible. Roman cities were built and an urban administrative machinery of local government, typical of that at Rome,[12] was encouraged, but rarely were they forcibly imposed upon an unwilling population.[13]

In the western provinces of Europe in particular the first task of the Romans was to create cities, and here the experience which they had gained in planting and laying out towns throughout central and northern Italy proved invaluable. The process of urbanisation was facilitated by the fact that there was no tradition of urbanised life and so the Roman concept of the city could be introduced wholesale. The result was that Romanised towns, usually laid out in typical Roman grid fashion, and including typical Roman urban buildings, sprang up throughout the west. The military surveyor and the engineer continued to play a major role in the construction of these new cities.

The Roman towns of Britain provide a suitable starting-point.

Before the arrival of the Romans there were effectively no towns,[14] and so urban centres had to be created by the implantation of colonies and the encouragement of local towns. The military must have played an important part in this process. Not only did the army have the technical expertise in planning and constructional methods, which would not have been available initially to the local population, but the implantation of veteran colonies provided specific examples of Roman urbanised life. The close relationship between the army and planning is evidenced in the British colonies of Camulodunum (Colchester), Glevum (Gloucester), Lindum (Lincoln) and the native towns of Isca Dumnoniorum (Exeter) and Viroconium (Wroxeter). Not only were the civilian towns established on the sites of the original legionary forts but they also incorporated the ground plans of the forts in their street systems, and in the case of Exeter the military bath house was re-used.[15]

Colonies were established both for military security and, in areas without traditions of urban life, to introduce and familiarise the provincials with law-abiding government.[16] Four colonies were eventually established in Britain. Towns were also encouraged as administrative centres for the native *civitates*, or they grew up spontaneously at river crossings, road junctions and around Roman forts.

The level of urbanisation achieved by the towns in Roman Britain varied according to local conditions. Those settlements which had developed spontaneously were often unplanned and remained concentrations of houses and other buildings stretched ribbon-like along roads or around forts and other official installations. The more important towns and those chosen as *civitas*-capitals were usually regularly laid out.

Verulamium (St Albans) is typical of a Romanised native town of Britain, and its success was such that it achieved the status of a *municipium*.[17] The new town, which replaced an existing native centre a short distance away, occupied a strategic position where Watling Street crossed the River Ver (Figure 43). Verulamium was first inhabited in the Julio-Claudian period and the town plan was developed as a series of approximately square *insulae* which were framed by a network of rectilinear streets. The traditional Roman plan was, however, adapted to suit the geographical and topographical conditions found on the site. The strictly axial arrangement with two centrally intersecting roads, typical of

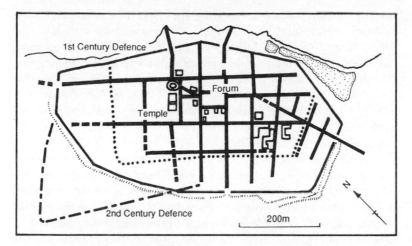

Figure 43 Verulamium (St Albans) in the fourth century

many of Rome's new towns, was abandoned at Verulamium, and the two roads which led out of the city to the north and to the west met at a point much closer to the bridge across the River Ver. In addition, the town also incorporated an oblique stretch of Watling Street, which entered the city from the south-western gate.

Unlike many new cities of the empire the original Julio-Claudian city was surrounded by a ditch and bank rampart, which unfortunately proved totally ineffective during the Boudiccan revolt. A more ambitious series of fortifications was initiated towards the end of the second century BC encompassing a far larger area than the original town. Well-constructed stone gates were erected as the first stage of the project but the fortifications were built in earth. Subsequently, they were replaced in stone. The total projected area of the town, surrounded by the second-century defences, proved too ambitious and the city was again reduced in size when new defences were built in the course of the third century AD.

As the town developed so public buildings were added. These concentrated at the junction of the two main roads and included the elaborate forum, the basilica of which was dedicated by the governor Agricola and destroyed by fire in the second century AD. A stone-built market hall was added towards the end of the first century AD. The forum was later rebuilt in the reign of

125

Antoninus Pius after a devastating fire, one of several which the city suffered during its history, and at the same time a theatre was added. There were also several Romano-Celtic temples throughout the town, and two triumphal arches commemorated the original Claudian extent of the town when it was increased in size towards the end of the second century AD. In addition, evidence of a drainage system and piped water also reveals the level of sophistication in the planning of Verulamium which was absent from many other native British towns.

Verulamium reveals Roman influence not only in design but also in constructional methods. The stone socle with timber-framed buildings of the early phases of the town are typically Roman. The forum, more elaborate than the fora of many British towns, suggests possible continental influences. Like the fora of several Gallic towns, it is oblong in plan with entrances on the shorter sides. The precinct itself is surrounded on three sides by shops or offices and porticoes, and on the fourth side there stood the basilica. It lacks only the temple which was a common feature of Gallic fora.[18]

The Romans found the Silures of South Wales particularly intractable during the early years of the invasion. It was not until the Flavian period that the Silures were finally pacified. Once the pacification of South Wales had been completed, the small town of Venta Silurum (Caerwent) near Newport in Gwent, eventually developed as the *civitas*-capital of the Silures.[19] Its plan is typical and emphasises the influences of the military on the towns of Britain (Figure 44). Its perimeter, defined towards the end of the second century AD by the construction of ramparts, is oblong, although the walls are not perfectly rectilinear. A road uniting the eastern and western gates effectively bisects the town into two. The gates in the northern and southern walls were offset and the roads from them pass either side of the forum. The forum itself occupies the usual position in the centre of the town and in area covers a complete *insula*-unit. Space within the town was restricted and the majority of the *insulae*, into which the town was divided, were fully developed with houses, shops and other buildings. Public buildings included a bath house and an intramural temple of Romano-Celtic type. In addition, outside the walls to the east of the city there was another circular temple.

Caerwent was small, and some of its public buildings appear impoverished even by British standards. Nevertheless, several of

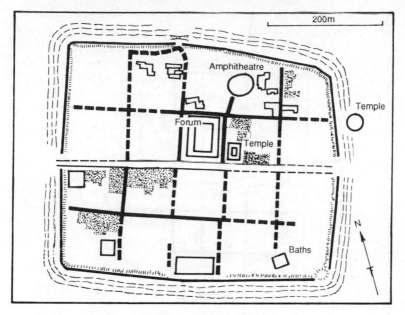

Figure 44 Venta Silurum (Caerwent)

the houses were of a high standard, and some, with peristyle courtyards, imply a continental influence, perhaps due to veteran soldiers who settled in the town from the nearby legionary base at Caerleon.[20]

Calleva Atrebatum (Silchester), the tribal capital of the Atrebates, not only offers an interesting comparison with Caerwent but its arrangement and development are an indication of the level and speed of acceptance of urban life in Britain. Although it has an irregular perimeter, its plan, with two major intersecting roads, looks typically Roman (Figure 45). The site was already an important Belgic centre before the arrival of the Romans and it was developed as the tribal capital of the Atrebates. The overall plan is Roman and contains two intersecting major roads and a rectangular grid of streets enclosing almost square *insulae*.[21] Detailed analysis of the plan, however, reveals several inconsistencies and anomalies. The forum-basilica complex was misaligned in relation to the *decumanus maximus* and did not cover the total area allocated for it. One of the earliest Roman buildings on the site, the bath house, was radically altered when the streets were laid down, indicating that the preserved grid was not

127

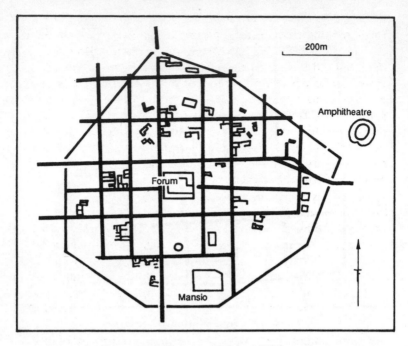

Figure 45 Calleva Atrebatum (Silchester)

original, and indeed there is some evidence from the earliest buildings which suggests an earlier, different alignment. Furthermore, the fact that parts of the grid seem to date to the late first/early second century AD also suggests that all the streets were not laid out at the same time. In all, four defensive circuits have come to light, of which two date to the pre-invasion and immediate invasion period before the town became a *civitas*-capital. Like Verulamium, the enlargement of the urban defences was found to be too great, and soon after, the north–western corner of the town was truncated by a secondary bank and ditch.

The *insulae* themselves differ in size and internal arrangements. Occupation was heaviest along the main streets, but even here buildings were rarely contiguous. In other *insulae* occupation was more sporadic. The buildings were interspersed with free space and market gardens and were not necessarily aligned to the direction of the streets.

Yet, despite the discrepancies, the layout of Calleva achieved a remarkable degree of unity and cohesion. The temple precinct, in

128

the vicinity of the eastern gate, is linked to the forum by a major road, running to the south of the *decumanus maximus*, although its alignment is not strictly parallel to the latter. Both the early defences and their later successors were integrated into the street system. The whole arrangement of the town gives the impression of a spacious market town, built to a Roman design by local planners to suit local needs, and increased and adapted as necessary. Its internal arrangements, with gardens and farm outbuildings, emphasise the agricultural nature of the town and are a salutary warning against drawing too great a distinction between town and country in the Roman world.[22]

The towns of Britain are indicative of the ways in which Rome fostered urban life in a totally unurbanised province by direct example and by indirect encouragement. The picture in Gaul was more complex. Some areas were, like Britain, totally unurbanised. In contrast, along the southern coast some Greek cities had long been established and indeed in other districts even native Gallic settlements had reached a level of settled, urban existence which fell only just short of full urban life in the Classical Graeco–Roman sense.[23]

The suitability of the native site played a large part in deciding whether an existing native town was developed or abandoned and replaced. Thus, the Aeduan capital of Bibactre was replaced in 5 BC by Augustodunum. Other native centres, like Nemausus, Arelate and Augusta Treverorum, were developed as fully Romanised native towns.

Augusta Treverorum, the modern Trier, lies on the banks of the River Moselle and was the tribal capital of the Treveri.[24] Its importance as an urban centre was recognised as early as the reign of the emperor Claudius, when it was granted colonial status, and later not only did it become the capital of the breakaway 'empire of the Gauls' in the third century AD but also, under Diocletian's reorganisation of the empire, it became the capital of the western provinces. Like many of the Romanised native towns of Gaul, Augusta Treverorum was orthogonally laid out with two major axes which met at the forum (Figure 46). The forum itself occupied the equivalent of four *insulae* and was fully co-ordinated with the street grid. As the town grew the original *decumanus* was replaced by a second major east–west road more to the south. The later additions to the city, nevertheless, respected the original grid pattern.

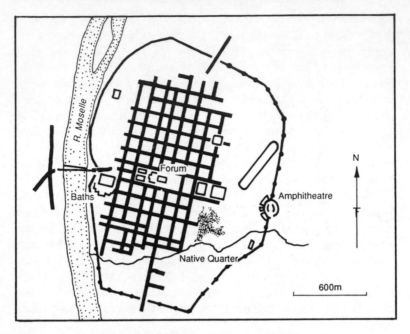

Figure 46 Augusta Treverorum (Triers)

The architectural development continued with the construction of typical Roman public buildings. An amphitheatre was located on the eastern side of the town along the same axis as the forum and was utilised as one of the gates when the town was later fortified. The sumptuous baths of St Barbara were constructed close to the River Moselle in the second century AD. Another large bathing establishment was added during the reign of Constantine and, when Augusta Treverorum became an important capital city, a palace was constructed.

Despite its Romanised appearance Augusta Treverorum remained an important native religious centre for the Treveri. As such, when the town plan was laid out, it had to take into account the existing religious district. This area, which lay to the south of the baths of Constantine and contained several major temples to various Celtic deities, was incorporated into the town and was fully co-ordinated with the rest of the city.

The Romans faced a similar situation at Nemausus (Nîmes) to that at Trier. The site, according to Pliny the capital of the Volges Arecomices, was already an important strategic and religious

130

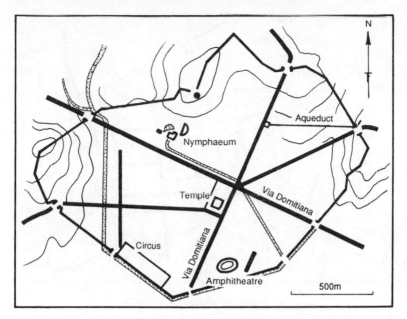

Figure 47 Nemausus (Nîmes)

centre.[25] Consequently, when the town was regularly planned, the planners had to incorporate the existing Gallic district (Figure 47). Nemausus nonetheless assumes the typical Roman layout with two centrally intersecting axes.[26] The *Via Domitiana*, acting as the eastern part of the *decumanus Maximus* and the southern part of the *kardo maximus*, entered the city through the eastern gate and left through the southern gate. In addition to the two major axes, two other important roads led respectively from the north-eastern and south-western gates diagonally across the town to the forum. The layout of most of the town corresponds to the direction of the *decumanus* and *kardo*. There are, however, anomalies. The perimeter of Nemausus abandoned the strictly rectangular arrangement of Roman towns in favour of one which made full use of the natural advantages of the terrain. Both the circus and the amphitheatre did not conform to the street grid. Most noticeable of all the south-western residential area, where the original native settlement was located, did not respect the main street grid. Despite these anomalies, the town plan of Nemausus presents a unified and fully co-ordinated scheme, which offered variety and

131

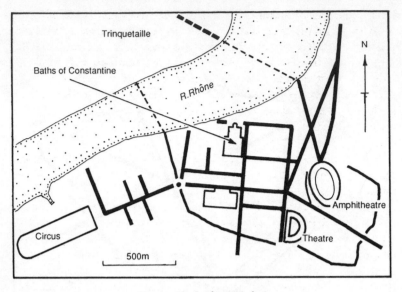

Figure 48 Arelate (Arles)

flexibility within the traditional Roman arrangement.

At Arelate (Arles) an existing native settlement on the banks of the River Rhône was combined with a veteran colony which was established by Julius Caesar.[27] The plan of the colony was typically Roman with two intersecting orthogonal axes which dictated the orientation of the street grid. The main east-west axis, however, was not straight but followed the line of the river to unite the existing Gallic settlement with the new town.

As Arelate grew so new districts were added (Figure 48). One to the north-east lay outside the original ramparts. Like the original Gallic settlement its orientation was different from that of the colony, yet it was closely linked to the overall plan of the town and the direction of the river. Across the river a veritable second city developed (Trinquetaille) as the commercial centre of Arelate. The district was incorporated into the existing town both by a ferry and by a pontoon bridge over which one of the main roads, leading from the northern gate of the town's amphitheatre, was carried. The street grid of Trinquetaille was again conditioned by the bank of the Rhône.

Despite the differences in orientation, the main east-west road of the town united the old Gallic centre, the new colony and the later extension by joining the circus at the western end of the city with the amphitheatre and theatre on the eastern side. The main northern road from the amphitheatre was also instrumental in uniting the district across the river with the existing town. The town plan of Arelate was not the product of abstract rules and theory but developed in response to conditions on the site. That such a degree of unity and cohesion was achieved between the different areas is an indication of the skill of the planners who originally designed the town.

Within the regular framework of these Romanised native towns of Gaul, other features, typical of the Roman process of urbanisation, developed. The public buildings were larger and often more elaborate than their British counterparts, indicating not only that parts of Gaul had been under Roman influence for a longer period but also that the process of urbanisation had penetrated deeper into the native population. In addition to baths, fora and basilicas, and amphitheatres some towns even had theatres and circuses like their Italian counterparts. Some of the towns of Gaul in particular display Roman skills in hydraulic engineering. Water was often brought great distances by means of aqueducts and then was distributed to fountains and other buildings throughout the town. Complementary to this was the provision of adequate drainage and sewerage facilities to carry off waste. On the other hand, urban defences, which the central government was always loathe to sanction, virtually disappeared until they were hastily erected, often reducing drastically the defended area, during the years of crisis in the third century AD.

In founding new towns and developing existing native centres in the western provinces, the Romans used techniques which had been tried and found to work in the colonisation of Italy. Although the methods were familiar the resulting towns were not the same. Each was the product of its own immediate geographical and historical factors and it was adapted to its own local circumstances. Roman grid planning formed the basis of these towns and controlled future growth but the development of the town progressed at a rate which was acceptable to the local population and the availability of resources.

In the western provinces Rome created cities of Mediterranean type, where before none had existed, and in doing so laid the foundations for the full urbanisation of Europe. The success of Rome in fostering cities in the west can be judged from the number of modern towns which not only occupy the sites of their Roman forerunners, but in many cases retain the original Roman street system in their modern town plan.

In those parts of Africa and the Greek east where cities already existed and had a long history of development, Rome's problems were different. The Romans continued to plant colonies and cities in these parts of the empire as the opportunity arose or necessity demanded. However, in the urbanised parts of the empire the success of Rome in the field of urban planning and design was built upon the radical transformation of the existing native cities. New ideas and techniques, different materials, Roman concepts of monumentality, architectural composition and symmetry, as well as specifically Roman building types, transformed the native cities of the Greek and African provinces. Even the long-established cities of the Aegean such as Athens did not remain untouched by these developments. The effect was the creation of fully Romanised provincial towns of spectacular visual appearance and diverse character. Moreover, the provincial cities of the eastern half of the empire benefited greatly from the spirit of rivalry that had long been a characteristic of their existence and the vast resources which were to be found in the east.

In the Republican period north Africa was important to Rome, both as a source of grain to feed the large urban population of the capital and as a source of luxury commodities, slaves and exotic beasts for the increasingly popular animal shows with which the capital entertained the urban masses. In the imperial period Roman colonies were planted and Romanised native towns flourished.

We begin by studying the two almost contemporary colonies of Thamugadi (Timgad) and Cuicul (Djemela). These two towns not only illustrate the continuing importance of founding new cities as strategic and civil centres, but comparison of them also indicates the range and adaptability of Roman planning techniques. Thamugadi, established early in the reign of the emperor Trajan for veterans from the legionary fort at Lambaesis, represents Roman planning at its simplest.[28] The plan is rigid and stark, and emphasises the continued importance of military thinking in colonial planning (Figure 49). Not only was the perimeter with its square shape and rounded corners reminiscent of the shape of a fort, but the two main streets of the colony even reflect the main road system of a fort. A colonnaded street bisects the town and

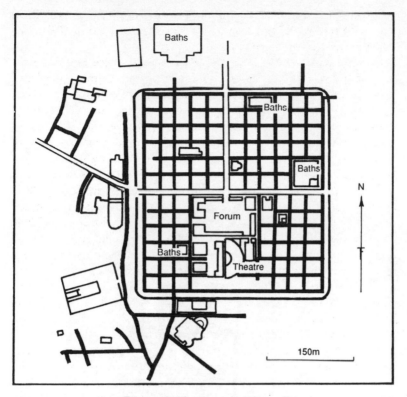

Figure 49 Thamugadi (Timgad)

unites the eastern and western gates. Another street, also colonnaded, runs from the northern gate to meet the *decumanus maximus* at the centre of the town. This arrangement originates from and corresponds to the characteristic 'T' junction arrangement of the *via principalis* and the *via praetoria* of a military fort. With the exception of a large area stretching from the *decumanus maximus* to the southern ramparts, which was occupied by the forum, its associated buildings and the theatre, the rest of the area within the walls was divided into small, almost square *insulae*. The rigid arrangement inside the city can be contrasted with arrangements outside the walls. Here, all sense of order was abandoned and the buildings, including several major public structures, developed without any order at all.

The rigid, military layout of the colony is relieved by the fine, impressively decorated public buildings. The two main thorough-

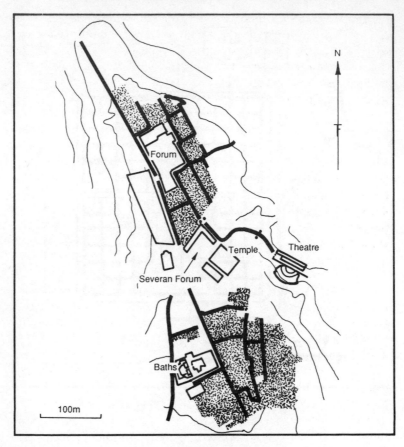

Figure 50 Cuicul (Djemila)

fares were colonnaded. In the main civic area, in addition to the forum and the theatre with a seating capacity for approximately four thousand spectators, there was even an ornately decorated public latrine. There were several impressive temples, a public library, no less than eleven bath houses, which is clear testimony to the importance of these buildings as a social institution in Roman towns, and several notable churches.

The contrast between Thamugadi and the almost contemporary colony of Cuicul (Djemila) is both obvious and striking (Figure 50). The latter was established on a high, precipitous spur of rock commanding two strategic routes in the mountainous inland region of modern Algeria.[29] The original colony, dating to the reign of Nerva, occupied the northern end of the hill. One major road, though not exactly straight, ran through the city alongside the forum and conditioned the alignment of the other streets and buildings. Thus, a certain regularity was achieved without the strictly formal rectangularity of Thamugadi.

As the colony grew it became necessary to expand on to the higher ground to the south. Here a new residential district was laid out, linked to the original area of occupation by a greatly enlarged civic centre. Although the plan of Cuicul lacks the rigid layout of Thamugadi and many other of Rome's colonies throughout the Mediterranean, nevertheless, through the siting of its public buildings and the employment of a major road across the town, it achieves a remarkable degree of unity. It was the ability of the Roman planners to adapt to local conditions and circumstances which helped to transform the cities of Africa and the Greek east.

Both Thamugadi and Cuicul were conceived and planned as Roman cities, housing veterans from Rome's legions in Africa. Native cities were Romanised by the addition of new Roman buildings and new quarters and sometimes by complete remodelling. The scale of the Romanisation of these native African cities varied according to local conditions. Thugga (Dougga) is a typical native town which was progressively Romanised in the imperial period. Situated on a steep, naturally defensible location, the native city was aggrandised by the construction of fine and imposing public buildings.[30] In particular, a new Roman civic centre was created with the construction of a forum, several temples, including the impressive capitolium, a market building and a bathing establishment. Further away, overlooking the surrounding plain, there was a theatre. The Romanised centre, built progressively over the second and the third centuries AD, was installed within the existing native town, which in other respects maintained its characteristically narrow, winding streets and cramped, bazaar-like domestic quarters.

Sabratha was more extensively Romanised than Thugga, yet still maintained its native character. The original town had been established by Phoenicians in the sixth century BC on the coast of Tunisia, and over the succeeding centuries it had developed into a flourishing, densely populated port.[31] Under Roman control the city was greatly enlarged. In the mid-first century AD a large

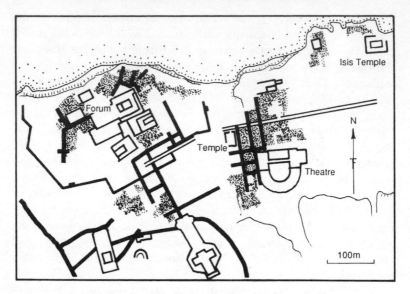

Figure 51 Sabratha

Roman-style forum replaced the small irregular market place of the original town, and beyond this to the south and east two new residential areas were constructed. Both followed the typical grid pattern; the southern district taking its orientation from two axial roads which ran through it, whilst the eastern residential zone was aligned to the main east-west road which was extended eastwards following the line of the coast (Figure 51).

In spite of the fact that the alignments of the new extensions to Sabratha differed, the overall town plan still forms a coherent unit. The forum is the essential link which unified the new districts with the old town. The native character of the old quarters was maintained in the new extensions. The shops, offices and streets of the new districts subtly imitated the character of the native quarter. Although they were regularly planned, the new buildings followed the same traditional constructional techniques, and the streets were lined with colonnades in the same way as the old town.

Lepcis Magna is arguably one of the finest Roman towns of Africa. The site, one of the few good natural harbours along the coast of Tripolitania, was first inhabited by Phoenicians in the sixth century BC. From the time of Augustus onwards it

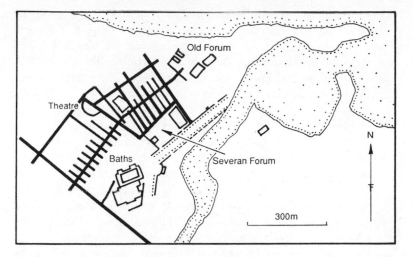

Figure 52 Lepcis Magna

prospered and flourished.[32] Its expansion, culminating in the extensive improvements of the emperor Septimius Severus, was progressive. The old road, curving south-westwards out of the city, led to the rich agricultural land to the south and was the focal point of the expansion. Along it a series of gridded extensions was built. As at Sabratha the forum, with its basilica and three ornate temples, acted as the essential link between the old town and the new extensions (Figure 52).

The prosperity of the town is reflected in its public buildings which were successively added throughout the first two centuries of the Christian era. A market building and the theatre were added in the reign of Augustus. Hadrian dedicated an imposing bath house close to the Wadi Lebda on the southern side of the town, and some time in the third century AD the so-called 'hunting baths' were constructed on the western perimeter.

Lepcis' greatest period of growth and prosperity came during the reign of Septimius Severus, who was born there. Under his patronage there was an extensive programme of remodelling and rebuilding, which not only sumptuously transformed the city, but also skilfully united its various parts. A large, finely embellished colonnaded street, which ran from the newly built harbour to pass behind the bathing establishment of Hadrian, together with a new forum, was the basis of the new town. The architectural

139

decoration of the street was lavish. The raised porticoes on either side were constructed with marble, imported from the Aegean island of Karystos, and the supporting columns carried arches and not the usual architraves. A new, ornate nymphaeum was built at the point close to Hadrian's baths, where the street turned southwards. A new, richly adorned forum and basilica, skilfully constructed on a difficult site at the side of the colonnaded street, also helped to unify the different public elements of the city.

Under the Romans Lepcis Magna greatly exceeded in grandeur and scale its Punic forerunner. Its buildings are magnificent and fully Romanised, yet they still retain original Punic details such as decorative motifs.[33] The combination of intrusive and native forms was one of the key factors in the successful transformation of the cities of the eastern provinces. The conquest of the east by Alexander and the creation of Hellenised kingdoms by his successors had united Greek and Oriental traditions. Rome, in conquering the Greek east, inherited and built upon this established tradition.[34] Public buildings, even the most utilitarian types, were imposingly constructed and elaborately decorated. Symmetry, by which groups of buildings were arranged along a central axis, a technique only occasionally found in the Hellenistic period,[35] was encouraged, and height and size were utilised to impress and overawe.[36]

If Roman architectural and planning concepts helped to transform the cities of the east, so did the vast resources which were available. The public-spiritedness of their leading citizens, admittedly for motives of personal advancement, coupled with the benefactions of leading Roman officials and even the emperors themselves, contributed greatly to the development of the cities of the Greek east. In Greece itself, Corinth was rebuilt and became the capital and one of the foremost cities of the Roman province of Achaea.[37] Because of its illustrious past and its reputation Athens was particularly favoured by wealthy Roman patrons. When Pompey visited the city whilst in the east, he gave 50 talents to assist renovation.[38] The centre of Athens was transformed by the Romans. Julius Caesar began a new forum, completed by Augustus. Marcus Agrippa built an odeion as the focal point of the old agora. Amongst the many benefactions of Herodes Atticus were a new theatre and a stadium in pure white marble, which he built to thank the Athenians for the honour they bestowed upon him in putting him in charge of the Panathenaic festival.[39] The emperor Hadrian showed the city special favour. Under his patronage a new extension was constructed on the south-western side of the city, the temple of Olympian Zeus was finally completed, and the water supply was vastly improved by the construction of a new aqueduct and holding tank on the lower slopes of Lykabettos. The efforts of these and other patrons not only embellished the city, but altered the character of the original Classical and Hellenistic city centre.[40]

Similar changes took place throughout Asia Minor as the Romans founded new colonies and remodelled existing Greek and native cities. On the west coast great cities such as Miletos, Pergamon, Ephesos, Smyrna and many others were further aggrandised. New buildings were added, existing buildings were renovated, and generally urban facilities were improved. At Miletos, Trajan completed the monumentalisation of the area in front of the Hellenistic bouleuterion with the construction of an imposing, three-storeyed nymphaeum, decorated with niches for statuary and columns in the manner of a theatre façade.[41] Under Marcus Aurelius, Miletos especially prospered. The large theatre was completed and his wife, Faustina, contributed vast resources for the construction of the large bathing establishment overlooking the Bay of Lions, which bore her name. The latter, one of the best-preserved buildings at Miletos, is further proof of the willingness of the Romans to abandon theory in the face of prevailing conditions, because it is neither symmetrical in arrangement nor does it conform to the alignment of the street grid.

Changes were no less spectacular in other cities of Asia Minor as remodelling and renovation took place. Monumental arches, propylaea and colonnaded streets became particularly widespread throughout the cities of the eastern provinces. Not only were such structures used to embellish and beautify the cities, but they also had the practical application of directing and controlling the spectator's vision, and so hiding any unsightly or mundane structures behind. The two main intersecting streets at Perge, on the Pamphylian coast, were colonnaded probably in the reign of Hadrian.[42] The main north-south street was particularly grand and was part of a much larger scheme of renovation. Like its east-west counterpart, it had a double carriageway which was separated by a stone-built water channel. It began at an ornamental nymphaeum, decorated with Corinthian columns, and ran southwards in two sections past the large, square agora to pass through the old gate of the Hellenistic fortifications. The inner courtyard of the gate was decorated with statuary and a new large courtyard was created on the outer side. This included a monumental gateway, a stoa and a two-storeyed nymphaeum approached through a propylon. Other facilities were also improved. New bath houses were constructed, and a stadium and a large Graeco-Roman theatre were added.

The area of direct Roman control extended as far as Mesopotamia. Throughout this region, much of it desert, the Romans came into contact with the Greek cities which the Hellenistic kings had established to maintain their political and military supremacy. As elsewhere, often the basis of these cities was already well established and the town plans themselves could not easily be changed without major disruption. Nevertheless, the addition of new areas, like the Roman extension to Antioch-on-the-Orontes, and the architectural embellishment and aggrandisement of existing areas, meant that many of the cities enjoyed their greatest period of prosperity. The axial roads of the Hellenistic quarters were often widened, porticoes proliferated, Roman architectural ideas were combined with native traditions, and new buildings and new designs were added, which helped to break up the monotony which had become the inherent danger of regular planning in the Hellenistic east.

Gerasa (Jerash), set in the Jordanian desert, is one example of an original Greek town which underwent extensive renovation and improvement in the Roman period.[43] The shape of the town and its internal topography was conditioned by the River Chrysorrhoas, which cuts the city into two unequal portions (Figure 53). On the western side of the river the main public buildings were concentrated; the eastern side was given over largely to private development and spacious gardens. An arterial road ran down the western side of the town and this was intersected by two other major roads which were carried across the Chrysorrhoas ravine on bridges and united the two parts of the town. All three roads were porticoed as were many of the secondary streets, and the intersection of the north-south road with the southernmost cross street was marked by a triumphal arch, which was built in a large circular space surrounded by shops. At the southern end of the town the rectangularity of the grid was abandoned. The road from the south gate led obliquely on to an oval, colonnaded

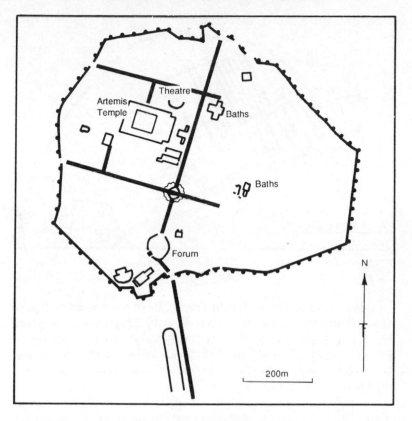

Figure 53 Gerasa (Jerash)

plazza. Associated with the plazza there was a theatre, one of two which the city had, and a temple to Zeus, which was constructed in Romano-Syrian style and set upon a high podium.

The large temple to Artemis stood in the centre of the town on the western side of the river. The temple, one of the major religious monuments in the Roman east, was approached through an ornately decorated propylaea which led on to the precinct itself via a monumental staircase. The temple itself, richly decorated and with a deep porch, was placed on a high podium in order to increase its grandeur. Close to the propylaea there was an impressive scenic nymphaeum, whilst the city's second theatre stood to the north of the temple precinct. East of the arterial road two bath buildings have also been found.

143

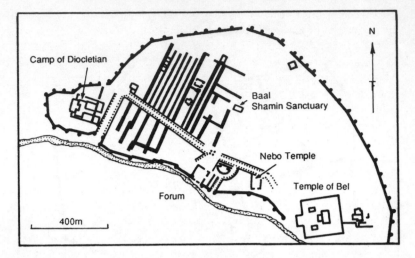

Figure 54 Palmyra

Further east, in the Jordanian desert, Palmyra was another city which flourished as a result of the Roman Empire and the peace which it brought.[44] Its prosperity was based on the revenue which it received from the taxation of all goods and services, both within its territory and from those goods which passed through its territory.

Its wealth is reflected in its urban architecture. The original town plan was not homogeneous, but the wide axial road which passed through the city, linking the different monuments, brought a sense of order and unity (Figure 54). This road itself ran in three differently aligned sections from the great temple of Bel to the south-west to the funerary temple on the north-western side of the city. The lavish porticoes of the street were adorned with statuary, the fixing brackets for which, as at Gerasa, are still visible. The two changes of direction in the route were marked by an elaborate arch and a tetrapylon respectively.

The majority of Palmyra's public buildings lay along the route of the colonnaded street. They include the temple to Nebo, a theatre, a forum, the baths built in the time of Diocletian, and a large ornamental nymphaeum. The temple to Bel is the largest of the three major temples at Palmyra and it dominates the eastern side of the town. The large square court, in which the temple itself is situated, was artificially raised and was approached by means of a monumental stairway. The temple to Nebo was similarly lavish and set upon a high podium.

The grandiosity and lavish decoration which typified the public monuments of Palmyra were also applied to domestic architecture. Many of the private houses at Palmyra were sumptuously decorated, combining both Hellenistic and native Syrian architectural traditions.

Gerasa and Palmyra are typical of the changes which the Romans introduced in the cities of the east. They contain many characteristically Roman public buildings; the use of axial roads brings unity even when the towns are not strictly rectangular in plan; their public architecture is sumptuous and lavishly decorated, fusing new Roman ideas with established traditions; buildings are tall and their height, which is often further increased by the construction of artificial podia, is intended to impress and overawe; and round and oval areas were introduced to break up the monotony of the rectangular designs and rectilinear street system.

Roman planning in the east in particular relied heavily upon the visual impact it could create. Buildings and groups of buildings were arranged axially and vistas were created by the careful location of buildings; the use of height and the introduction of new building materials freed urban buildings from their physical environment and allowed the creation of artificial townscapes; colonnades, arches and propylaea not only embellished the cities but also were vital aspects of planning, used to control and direct vision. Buildings were so employed, designed and constructed to hide the unsightly or to obscure the awkward.

There are dangers in such planning and construction. Sometimes, buildings, like the nymphaea of many cities, were mere façades. They impart a false sense of solidity which is not in fact there. Increasingly grander buildings and increasingly ornate decoration not only helped to beautify the cities but they are also an indication of the intense rivalry which existed between the cities of the empire as they competed for honorific titles and recognition of their success. Even the smallest towns were fired with the same sense of competition.[45] But even the intense rivalry is not without danger if the tasteful decoration for the constructive enhancement of the buildings should degenerate into vanity and sterility.

As already stated above, the letters of Pliny to Trajan from Bithynia abound with evidence of ill-conceived building projects.

New buildings were started but not completed. Others, too ambitious, ran out of funds, and others suffered simply from bad planning and jerry-building. Trajan's advice to Pliny regarding the request of the people of Claudiopolis to rebuild their gymnasium on a much grander scale is illuminating. The emperor granted their request, but tells Pliny that they will have to be content to build a gymnasium to suit their needs not their aspirations.[46] Ostentatious display was less important than practical economics.

Pausanias' description of Panopeus also warns that not all the cities of the empire enjoyed equally a successful programme of public building activity,[47] and his description of the Megalopolis basin in the Peloponnese, if it can be believed, is one of decay and abandonment.[48] The ability of the city to attract resources from the emperor, wealthy patrons and ultimately their own rich citizens was a crucial factor in the development of a city. Some cities prospered better than others and attracted the interest of wealthy patrons. Sometimes the official policy of encouraging urban life brought official assistance from the central government. But more often it was left to the individual cities and citizens to contribute to the public building programme. Nor was the financial commitment over after the construction was completed. The maintenance of the public buildings was a continuing drain on the financial resources of the cities. Evidence of lack of repair and the decay of public buildings abounds.[49] The problem of maintenance and renewal of public buildings became more acute as the public-spiritedness of the urban aristocracy was eroded by other factors, including the increasing demands from the central government which were made upon their resources.

Other changes are also apparent. Towns usually contained certain public and monumental buildings which typified the Roman concept of urban life. Within the broad uniformity which the Romans encouraged, regional styles and local variations and adaptations continued. However, the growing cosmopolitanism of the later imperial period led to the emergence of a broadly uniform style of architecture which gradually diminished the regional differences.[50] This increasing tradition of uniformity is witnessed especially in the widespread transport of marble as a building material throughout the Mediterranean basin. As early as the reign of Hadrian imported marble and indeed even ready-cut imported columns were being used both in new buildings and in the remodelling of existing buildings at Lepcis Magna.[51] The changes at Lepcis Magna merely reflect the growing uniformity in architecture and architectural design throughout the Mediterranean which was stifling regional styles and provincial variations.

The emergence and eventual triumph of Christianity also effected the cities of the empire. Although Christianity flourished in the cities of the empire, ironically it also brought changes. In the first place, ancient urban life was essentially public and communal. The citizens came together in large groups to exercise political rights, and for entertainment and religious festivals. The upper classes, on whose generosity the vitality of the cities was maintained, built public buildings, provided games and distributed largess to the whole community in return for public recognition and position. Christianity, however, brought about a fundamental change in attitudes. Present, secular life became less important than future salvation. Smaller, more intimate, gatherings of Christians in their churches replaced the mass meetings of the population, which was a feature of pagan communal life. Indeed, much of the communal life of the towns was centred on pagan religion and this would naturally disappear as conversion to Christianity continued. Tertullian specifically rejected those public buildings which typified the entertainments associated with pagan public life.[52] Moreover, the upper classes, on whose generosity urban life depended, found in the Church another means of escape from the overwhelming financial burdens which they had to endure to maintain urban life and public services.[53] Thus, at one level Christianity brought about a reorientation of loyalties and values away from the communal life of the pagan city.[54]

Secondly, as the population of the cities became increasingly Christian, so many of the buildings associated with pagan life became useless. Some were re-used as churches. But curiously and surprisingly in many cases the old public buildings were either abandoned completely and left to fall into ruin, or used as virtual quarries for the new churches which were springing up throughout the cities.[55] The churches themselves, which were the new focal points of communal life, were built in closer association to the people, whom they served, and so they are found scattered throughout the residential areas of a city.

The military crisis of the third century AD also affected cities throughout the empire. Many of the provinces had to endure destructive incursions from beyond the frontiers, and the cities, after the long period of peace, found that they were ill-equipped to cope. Cities were attacked and plundered by the enemy or by Roman forces trying to drive out an occupying force. As already noted above, in Gaul urban defences were hastily erected, often encompassing the minimal area possible and abandoning much of the town to the enemy.[56] Some towns were sacked and never recovered.

The question of whether these points indicate the ultimate decline of the cities of the empire or merely reflect changing conditions is difficult to answer. They are generalisations, and the true picture is much more complex. In reality, individual cities reacted in different ways and at differing rates to the conditions. Developments were consequently neither uniform nor consistent. The restoration of order by Diocletian after the period of anarchy included the rebuilding and refurbishment of many cities, and cities continued to prosper even after the withdrawal of the Romans from a province.[57] In Britain, for instance, there is evidence of continued prosperity in the fourth century AD.[58] Public building activity in several towns continued even beyond the withdrawal of the Romans.[59] In the eastern provinces cities continued to be a fundamental institution of life. Even though Christianity altered aspects of pagan urban life, it also helped existing cities and fostered new ones. Constantinople was founded as a Christian city, and in many parts of the east the city remained the basis of life in the Byzantine empire.

The achievements of Roman planning in the western half of the empire differ from those in the east. However, overall Rome was highly successful in encouraging Romanised urban life throughout the provinces. The extent of her success is best measured by the number of cities which were not only founded but also continued even after the collapse of the empire itself.

8

THE ANCIENT CITY AND THE URBAN INFRASTRUCTURE

Planning formed the framework within which the ancient city developed. But town planning involves more than the laying out of the streets and the distribution of space. True urban planning should seek to improve the quality of life for the inhabitants by providing services and facilities, and by regulating the component parts of the city in order to gain the best possible situation for the buildings and the most advantageous conditions for the citizens.[1] The extent to which the Greeks and the Romans dealt with the practical problems of maintaining and ameliorating urban life varied. Indeed the response varied from city to city. Nevertheless, in general both the Greeks and the Romans offered a high standard of services and amenities to the inhabitants of the cities. The object of this chapter is to analyse those facilities and their location in the urban environment.

Until the reality of the *pax Romana* the largest and most expensive urban monuments were city walls. They were a sign both of the community's independence and the unstable military and political situation in ancient Greece and Italy before the domination of Rome. Early settlements in Greece and Italy usually occupied naturally defensible locations,[2] offering protection from raids rather than long-term security from a determined enemy.[3] Not all early towns were so located. Old Smyrna was situated on a low-lying peninsula and was in consequence surrounded by a full town wall from the middle of the ninth century BC onwards.[4] The small settlement of Zagora on Andros was similarly defended by a wall on the landward side in the eighth century BC.[5] Such early town walls were, however, exceptional and it was only in the course of the sixth century BC that urban fortifications became a regular feature of Greek cities.[6]

In Italy early Etruscan towns were similarly positioned to take advantage of the natural defensive qualities of the terrain, and, although the natural defences of early Etruscan settlements were sometimes supplemented by terracing, it was not until the fifth century BC, as a result of warfare against the Romans and the incursions of the Gauls, that the Etruscans began to build full urban defences.[7]

The Greeks and the Romans, probably following Etruscan practice, differed fundamentally on the relationship between the city plan and its walls. Greek fortifications neither follow the shortest perimeter nor are they co-ordinated with the street system. They often weave and deviate, encompassing outlying hills and other features.[8] Even with the introduction of regular planning the walls remained independent of the town plan.[9] Thus, at Miletos the original town walls not only encompassed the old acropolis of Kalabaktepe to the south of the town proper, but also there was no positive correlation between the gates and the regularly planned street system. The main street through the southern residential district of the city had to deviate to pass through the original 'sacred gate' of the Classical city. It was only when the new cross wall was built in the Hellenistic period that the co-ordination of the street and the gate was achieved.[10] The walls of Knidos, Priene, Doura Europos and many other original Greek foundations were similarly unrelated to the town plan. They loosely follow the contours of the hills and the topography of the ground, and at Priene even include the almost inaccessible acropolis above the city.[11]

There were both civil and military advantages in including within the circuit of the walls, areas greater than were at first required. The extra space allowed for subsequent expansion, whilst the inclusion of adjoining hills within the defensive circuit prevented the enemy from dominating the heights. Yet the military disadvantages were also recognised and this often led to the construction of cross walls to reduce the perimeter which had to be defended.[12]

Because of the military influences on Roman colonisation, Roman planning fully integrated urban defences with the city plan and the street system. The walls and the streets were laid out concurrently as part of the co-ordinated planning of the city. The main streets led directly from the centre of the town to the gates, and a 'pomerial' road ran around the city immediately inside the walls. Even at Cosa, where the walls take full advantage of the terrain and follow an irregular course, the co-ordination of the gates and the walls with the internal city plan is still apparent.[13] The same is probably true at other early Roman colonies.

Town walls did not only have a military function. As previously stated, they were also a sign of independence and, in the imperial period, a mark of status and privilege. City walls and their gates were important public monuments. Consequently expense was lavished on them and their maintenance was part of a public figure's duty.[14] The comparison of the towns of Britain and Gaul in the unsettled conditions of the late second and third centuries AD illustrates the distinction between the purely defensive role of city walls and the construction of fortifications as prestigious, civil monuments as well as for security.[15]

The walls of the Gallic towns show all the signs of haste in their construction. Re-used building materials were extensively employed. The areas of the towns, encompassed by the walls, were often drastically reduced in size, effectively providing strong points for defence but at the same time abandoning much of the city to the enemy. The situation in Britain was different. There is no sign of haste and there is little evidence for reduction in the size of the intramural space. Although the fortifications were originally built of earth, they were subsequently replaced by well-made stone walls. Moreover, imposing stone gateways were constructed as the initial phase of the fortification of Corinium (Cirencester) and Verulamium (St Albans).[16] Whatever the reason for the initial change in construction from stone to earthwork ramparts, the stone gateways at both towns suggest that the original intention was to build stone walls. Furthermore, whatever the nature of the military threat to Britain might have been, the walls of British towns were conceived and built not only for defence but were also impressive civic monuments and reaffirm the importance of walls as an integral part of the urban landscape.

As places through which people passed, the gates of a town in particular might also have an economic significance. Sometimes the agora or forum might be situated close to a gate.[17] Shops lined the roads which led from the gates, and if space was available, temporary stalls could be erected. At Rome both the vegetable market (the *forum holitorium*) and the cattle market (the *forum boarium*) were situated immediately on the edge of the old city. The former stood immediately outside the so-called 'Servian' wall on the roads which led from two of the crossings of the Tiber.[18] Similarly the *forum boarium* was situated on the north-western side of the city, immediately inside the old walls.[19] Such locations obviated the necessity of country dwellers, who brought their produce and livestock into the town centre, with its attendant problems of congestion and escaping animals.[20]

City walls were a means of defining the limits of the city.[21] Occupation, however, did not end at the city walls and consequently distinctions between intramural and extramural land should not be overemphasised. Most cities had suburbs. Yet the question of what constituted suburban occupation in the ancient world is complicated. Although space within a walled city was finite, it is misleading to consider the suburbs of ancient towns as overspill areas, which were developed once urban land was used up.

It is equally wrong, by drawing analogies with medieval cities, to view the suburbs of Greek and Roman cities as areas where the less favourable elements of the town and its population were to be found.[22] The suburbs of Graeco–Roman cities were an integral aspect of the city itself. Certain elements of the town were usually located in the suburbs. Cemeteries and graves, either through religious scruple or through lack of space, were often located outside the city.[23] Industrial activity or large, industrial establishments might also be located in the suburbs.[24] Similarly, the larger public buildings were often, although not invariably, located in the suburbs. Stadia, amphitheatres and circuses, all of which made demands on urban space, were to be found outside the city proper, but the rules regarding their position were not rigidly fixed. The suitability of the location and of the natural geography of the site, rather than the actual availability of land, determined the position of these buildings.

Although waste was dumped outside the city[25] and urban drains usually merely emptied through the city wall, suburbs were often places of peace and serenity, characterised by shrines, monuments, gardens and trees. Plato gives an idyllic description of the district around the Ilissos stream at Athens, as being suitable for girls to play in.[26] The peaceful conditions of the suburbs attracted temples, cultural and intellectual buildings such as schools, gymnasia and libraries,[27] and bath buildings.[28] They also attracted residential occupation, and suburban farms are a common feature of the Graeco–Roman city.[29] The convenience of having a suburban house with land gave to the owner the advantages of the countryside whilst at the same time living in close proximity to the town.[30] The distinction between urban and suburban was even less meaningful as city walls were abandoned in the peaceful conditions of the imperial period. Suburbs then were not merely adjuncts to the cities which they served. They were an integral and important part of the town, having a parallel and a complementary role to the city itself.

The ancient city was a community and the community expressed itself in its public activities and its public buildings. By far the most important area of a Greek city was the agora, which served as the political, religious, social and economic focal point of the community. Essentially the agora was an open space, conveniently situated at the centre of the city's street system. Its architectural development was often slow and piecemeal. Administrative buildings, stoas, temples, altars, statues and other public buildings accumulated around it as the city developed, but they remained independent of each other.[31] Initially even regular planning had little effect on the development of the agora, which in several early colonies continued to grow in the same piecemeal fashion.

Pausanias contrasted the agora of Elis, which, he says, was constructed in the old manner with independent stoas, with the agoras of Ionian cities.[32] Certainly, the agora was adapted to the gridded street pattern of regular planning. Its dimensions were determined by the size of the *insulae* and it was adapted to the street grid. Architecturally its development was also standardised. The Ionian agora of Pausanias is probably to be identified with the agoras of the regularly planned cities, in which the open area was enclosed on three sides by a continuous portico, whilst another free-standing stoa enclosed the fourth side.[33]

The vast economic opportunities brought about by the conquests of Alexander led to the development of independent commercial buildings.[34] These, often large enclosures surrounded by porticoes, developed as independent structures, although often in close association with the agora itself, or in the case of harbour towns with the port facilities and wharves. Despite the progressive enclosing of the agora and the development of other specialised public buildings, to the Greek mind the agora remained an open space linked to the network of roads and accessible to all except criminals and the accused.

The equivalent area of a Roman town was the forum and it developed in much the same way as the Greek agora as the centre of public life. Indeed, under Greek influence porticoes were added, whilst rectangular planning tended to regularise its shape. However, the forum is not merely a Roman copy of the Greek agora. Its evolution was conditioned by other factors as well. In the first place, whereas the Greek agora attracted commercial and economic activity to its environs, the economic importance of the forum was early on emphasised by the specific inclusion of rows of shops as an integral part of it.[35] Secondly, there was the tendency to monumental axiality typical of Etrusco-Roman traditions, which far exceeded the simple axial arrangements of the Greek agora.

The forum differs most markedly from the Greek agora in its concept as an open space. The agora remained essentially an open public square which attracted public buildings. The forum, on the other hand, surrounded by shops, offices and porticoes, evolved as an enclosed area, linked to but independent of the street system and other public buildings. Vitruvius emphasises the importance of the forum as an enclosed area suitable for the production of gladiatorial shows.[36] In many provincial cities, especially in the western half of the empire, the forum developed as a fairly standard, self-contained administrative and commercial centre, surrounded by porticoes and shops, a basilica, which acted as the town hall, and often with an associated temple.

Religion was an inextricable part of ancient life and its importance in the architectural development of the city is emphasised by the number of temples, shrines and precincts, and the sanctity of several ancient places within the city. Theatres grew out of religious practice, public buildings were dedicated to specific deities, and shrines were associated with public buildings. The protective nature of religion is witnessed in the location of temples in commanding positions, and in the case of Roman cities, the concept of the sacred *pomerium* encircling the city.

The complexity and antiquity of many religious practices and observances meant that, although temples and shrines concentrated around the acropolis and agora or their Roman equivalents, they were often to be found throughout the city. Nevertheless, regular planning was influential. Wherever possible, temples conformed to the orientation of the street system, although religious scruple took precedent over conformity to the orientation of the town

154

plan.[37] Areas were specifically set aside for sacred use as part of the initial laying out of the city, although the close relationship between the temples and other public areas, emphasising the overall unity of the city, was maintained by the road system.[38]

An integral aspect of ancient Graeco-Roman religion was entertainment. The increasingly important role that entertainment and leisure played in the life of the ancient city is reflected in the number and types of specialised buildings which were developed. The agora or forum offered space for entertainment. Most cities boasted a theatre and many also provided stadia and, under Roman influence, amphitheatres. In the cities of the Greek world the gymnasium assumed an increasingly important social and relaxational role.[39]

More so than the Greeks, the Romans realised the importance of providing leisure and entertainment for the general happiness and well-being of the urban population.[40] Games, shows and recreational facilities became an essential aspect of Romanised urban life. Leading citizens of the cities of the empire vigorously competed with each other to provide games and shows, and to dedicate buildings or parts of buildings for such purposes. Amphitheatres became increasingly popular and the bath house became one of the most important social centres of the cities of the empire, combining with or sometimes even supplanting the gymnasium in the cities of the east.

The location of such buildings in the urban landscape was dependent upon the size of the structure and the availability of space. Wherever possible, theatres were situated in natural hollows, although the introduction, by the Romans, of concrete and the widespread use of brick, freed the theatre and other large buildings from the physical constraints of the terrain. Similarly the size of a stadium, circus or amphitheatre, and the need for a relatively flat piece of ground on which to build, often forced such buildings to the outskirts of the city.

The location of buildings for leisure and entertainment was not always opportunistic. Some cities show a tendency to group such buildings in close proximity. For instance, at Rhodes a gymnasium and a small theatre as well as a temple and a fountain house were located near the stadium on the lower western slopes of the acropolis. Similarly one of the gymnasia at Priene adjoins the stadium, and at Miletos the area between the southern and western agoras included the stadium, gymnasium and the baths of

Faustina. As the position of the amphitheatres of Verona, Lucca, Arelate and Augusta Treverorum show, even when such buildings were positioned on the outskirts of the town they were directly linked to the city by the road system and drainage system.

A large proportion of urban land was given over to residential exploitation. Regular planning permitted the orderly development of such areas and could offer solutions to the problems of the cramped conditions which were characteristic of many unplanned towns. Residential areas developed as multiples of the basic *insula*-unit.

Greek planning preferred rectangular housing blocks with houses arranged in two parallel rows, which allowed each property direct access to the street. It was employed at Olynthos, and was also found at Naxos, Himera, Abdera, Paestum, and Akragas. Similar rectangular *insulae* were used in the Roman towns of Cosa, Alba Fucens, Norba and Carthage. However, the Roman method of planning, based on two centrally intersecting axes, tended to produce square or slightly oblong *insulae*.

The organisation of *insulae* into uniform, regular-sized houses promoted the idea of equality and allowed the construction of the *insula* as a single unit. However, such arrangements were not universal. Indeed, often house plots varied in size and continuous occupation resulted in changes to the internal arrangements of house blocks. The surviving remains of *insulae* from towns such as Priene, Rhodes, Pompeii and Herculaneum display little internal uniformity. Within the *insulae* the houses differ in size, shape and overall configuration depending on existing availability of land and the wealth of a property owner to enable him to expand into adjoining property.

Access to properties which did not front directly on to the street was an obvious problem in residential development. There were no general rules. Sometimes access was by private arrangement between neighbours; sometimes alleys and lanes which subdivided the *insulae* were incorporated into the original layout.[41]

Streets were areas of public space but there was always conflict between the demands of the individual and the need to maintain passage. Consequently, in many cities the streets were often maintained only at the minimum viable width, and it only required a street to go out of use for it to be built upon. Regular planning assisted the viability of the streets. By clearly defining public buildings and residential *insulae*, passage could be maintained.

Indeed in some cities main streets were often monumentally wide, indicating the importance that the planners attached to the roads. In addition, laws laid down the minimum widths of urban and rural streets, and forbade encroachment and damage to street surfaces.[42]

In spite of the importance of the streets as arteries of communication, the surfaces of many roads of Greek towns in particular often remained only of beaten earth, gravel or shells and potsherds.[43] Even the streets of Rome were not extensively paved until the time of Caesar.[44] By the reign of the emperor Vespasian, Rome's streets were in need of extensive repair and renovation, which the emperor undertook,[45] although, if Juvenal is to be believed, the efforts of Caesar and Vespasian were either ineffective or not comprehensive.[46] In times of war, unpaved streets could be advantageous if an enemy succeeded in entering the city,[47] but they also caused problems. Regular repair was necessary and indiscriminate dumping of waste, which was rapidly absorbed into the street surface, raised levels and restricted passage.[48]

Some cities improved the quality of the streets. The roads of Old Smyrna were cobbled in the sixth century BC[49] and in the fifth century BC some parts of the streets of Olynthos were also cobbled.[50] Cobbled or paved surfaces were also a feature of the streets of Mantinea,[51] Colophon[52] and even Seuthopolis in Thrace.[53] At Delos, on the other hand, only a few of the main thoroughfares were fully paved.[54]

As far as it is possible to generalise and such generalisations are valid, the Etruscans, and through them the Romans, accepted that the streets were an important part of urban planning and the urban infrastructure, and consequently were well built and maintained. Cobbled streets were discovered at the Etruscan town of Vetulonia,[55] and the well-constructed roads of Marzabotto, some with raised pedestrian pavements, look forward to the well-made streets of Pompeii.

Under Roman influence paved streets became a widespread feature of urban design and were another of the amenities to which leading citizens and patrons willingly contributed.[56] It was also under Roman influence that the full monumentalisation of urban streets took place. Imposingly wide roads linked the public buildings of different areas of the city. In the eastern cities in particular, sumptuously decorated colonnades were added to embellish major roads. Such colonnaded streets became, in effect, public monuments in their own right and, as with other public buildings, they were an important status symbol for the city.

Besides providing a network of communications the roads were also the means by which public services were provided. Drains and water supply pipes ran underneath and even along the surfaces of the streets.

Street lighting was rarely provided, and the lighting for which Antioch was famed was exceptional.[57] For the most part, streets remained unlit except for any lighting which came from public buildings such as bath houses[58] or which an individual might provide outside his own property.[59]

Water was an essential requirement for urban life.[60] An adequate supply of water was one of the major factors in deciding the location of a new city, and many cities were so situated as to take advantage of naturally occurring supplies of water from springs, wells and even rivers.[61] Natural supplies could be supplemented by the digging of both private and public cisterns.[62] The replanning of Old Smyrna in the course of the seventh century BC involved the construction of a public spring house;[63] and many of the Greek tyrants constructed fountain houses and spring houses, both as a public amenity and an embellishment.

Contrary to the general opinion regarding the inadequacy of Greek hydraulic engineering,[64] the Greeks, whenever necessary, were both prepared to and had the technology to channel water by means of aqueducts. The aqueduct of Eupalinos on Samos needs little comment.[65] The Peisistratids brought water by means of an underground terracotta pipeline from the Ilissos stream to a newly constructed fountain house in the south-eastern corner of the agora; and later the system was improved and extended.[66] By the middle of the fifth century BC Akragas was supplied with an impressive underground aqueduct system,[67] and one of several aqueducts supplying Syracuse measured approximately 17 km in length.[68] Similarly at Olynthos, water was brought to the city from springs 7 miles away by means of a terracotta pipeline laid in an underground tunnel.[69]

The steeply sloping terrain on which many Greek cities were built could at times assist the distribution of water throughout the city. At Priene an aqueduct brought water to the city from 2 miles away and fed it into settling tanks above the city proper. From here the water was distributed to small street fountains which were located at key points in various parts of the city.[70]

Probably the most impressive water system of the pre-Roman Greek east was that at Pergamon.[71] Until the reign of Eumenes II, the citizens of Pergamon relied on wells and cisterns for water. But the expansion of the city under Eumenes included the introduction of a public supply of water. Water was brought under pressure from the surrounding territory to settling tanks above the city. Thence it was distributed by means of three aqueducts. One was a Roman improvement but the other two date from the Hellenistic period and distributed water to the gymnasia, the public fountain house and other points in the city.

In general, the political instability of the Greek world before the arrival of the Romans made many cities reluctant to rely on sources of water which were too remote from the city.[72] External sources could be cut.[73] Even at Pergamon, where water was introduced by aqueducts, the fact that municipal legislation still ensured that private house cisterns were well maintained and kept clean is an indication of the continued military threat which Greek cities felt if they relied on external sources of water alone.[74]

The achievements of the Romans in the field of hydraulic technology are well known.[75] Supplies to existing towns were improved[76] and the supply of water became an important aspect of the development of new towns. Aqueducts became a common and widespread feature of urban planning. Furthermore, their construction was often instrumental in the revitalisation of cities.[77] The skills of the Roman hydraulic engineers, based upon the practice and achievements of the Greeks and the Etruscans, together with the security which came about through the *pax Romana*, enabled water to be brought to towns from far greater distances. By the end of the first century AD Rome itself was supplied by nine aqueducts drawing on sources between 19 km and 80 km away. In Gaul the aqueduct supplying Forum Iulii (Fréjus) ran for a distance of 40 km, and that supplying Nemausus (Nîmes) tapped sources 50 km away.[78] The aqueduct supplying Carthage, however, ran for 132 km.[79] Once the water reached the city it was carried to water distribution tanks and towers, whence it was distributed to public fountains, public tanks, public buildings, and even to private individuals on payment of a fee.[80]

Water was not merely needed for drinking purposes. It was an essential civic amenity, providing for the general health and happiness of the city population.[81] In Classical Athens the provision of water, together with the planting of trees and the laying out of paths in the Academy, were part of the civic improvements undertaken by the Athenian general and politician, Cimon.[82] In the Roman Empire, the evidence from Britain, parts of Asia Minor and even Ostia suggests that the primary reason for the construction of aqueducts was to supply the urban bath houses, which were increasingly becoming the essential urban amenity of the cities of the empire.[83] Even the fountain houses and public latrines themselves were not simply utilitarian. In the African and eastern provinces in particular, highly ornamental nymphaea, together with large, sometimes lavishly decorated public latrines, were constructed to enhance and embellish the cities.[84]

Despite the undoubted skills of Roman hydraulic engineers and the popular image of majestic arched structures crossing the countryside, the supply of water presented problems. Juvenal wrote of the dripping arches of the aqueduct which entered Rome at the Capenan Gate.[85] Damage and the resultant need to effect repairs interrupted supply.[86] The Romans faced constant problems with the Aqua Claudia, necessitating extensive repairs and loss of supply. Bad design, inferior construction and over-ambition were other problems: thus Pliny notes the two abortive attempts by the citizens of Nicomedia to construct an aqueduct.[87] Moreover, despite the importance of water for the continuation of urban life and as an essential civic amenity, several cities did not have aqueducts.[88] Sometimes the availability of a source or technical difficulties of bringing the water to the city were influential. Often, however, it was the expense of construction and the consequent ability to attract the necessary resources that was the crucial factor in deciding whether a city had an aqueduct.[89] Sinope did not have an aqueduct until the governorship of Pliny. But Trajan's reply to Pliny's request that an aqueduct should be built, emphasises that the project had to be affordable for the citizens.[90] Similarly, Hadrian was annoyed when the actual cost of constructing the aqueduct for Alexandria Troas turned out to be seven million drachmae, not the three million that Herodes Atticus had estimated. Whereupon Herodes promised to pay the excess himself.[91]

Even with the widespread introduction of aqueducts other means of supplying, collecting and storing water were not abandoned. The Pergamene law requiring householders to maintain cisterns has already been cited. This law reflects the general pluralistic approach which many cities had to the question of the supply of water, whereby public and private efforts were harmonised in order to reduce the dependency on one source alone.[92]

As cities increased in size so the problems of drainage and sewerage became more acute. The physical growth of a city itself created difficulties. Gulleys, natural runnels and channels, along which rain- and storm-water ran, were increasingly blocked by houses and other buildings. Paved and cobbled streets prevented the absorption of water through the street surface. Thus, without adequate drainage facilities, roads became veritable open drains after rain.[93] The raised pedestrian pavements of Pompeii, Marzabotto and other cities are an indication of the problem when streets were constructed with an impervious stone surface. Alternatively, as already observed, the surfaces of unpaved streets, which allowed a certain amount of seepage, could easily be turned into a rutted quagmire of mud when it rained.

To a certain extent the use of cisterns to supply water for everyday purposes alleviated the problem by collecting at least some of the run-off from roofs of buildings. Many cities realised that drainage was a problem and tried to deal with it through legislation and the provision of adequate public sewerage systems. Beforehand, drainage often remained a matter of private concern. In those towns without adequate drainage facilities, the general rule was to keep property dry. The house drains of Olynthos emptied directly onto the street.[94] In Athens individuals were allowed to drain water on to the street and to build sewers as long as they were properly covered.[95]

Changes did take place either through force of circumstance as the cities themselves increased in size, or through the example of improved drainage facilities from other parts of the Greek world. The construction, renovation and later extension of the large drain along the western side of the Athenian agora, initially to control the storm-water which must have flooded down from the saddle between the Areopagus and the Hill of Nymphs, came in response to the architectural developments in the vicinity of the agora.[96] The limited evidence from Thasos and other Greek towns suggests a similar slow and piecemeal development.[97]

City builders and planners, however, increasingly realised that adequate drainage facilities were a necessary part of urban planning. The stone-built drain at Miletos and the system of cobbled surface channels at Old Smyrna have already been noted.[98] Similarly, surface channels have been found along the cobbled sections of the streets at Olynthos.[99]

More complete underground systems were also introduced. At Akragas prisoners captured in the battle of Himera were used to build a comprehensive underground drainage system.[100] An underground drainage system seems to have been part of the original town plan of Rhodes.[101] Stone-built drains of uniform sizes drained water from the houses and buildings into street sewers, which in turn emptied into main collectors, large enough to allow passage for maintenance. The example of Rhodes was followed by several of the new towns constructed in the fourth century BC and Hellenistic periods. The system at Priene is one example;[102] Seuthopolis, built in the second half of the fourth century BC, was provided with an underground drainage system.[103] Nevertheless, as Smyrna reveals, the inclusion of a drainage system as part of the planning and construction of new cities was not always the rule.[104]

The supremacy of the Etruscans, and through them the Romans, in the construction of drainage systems has to be accepted. It is feasible that the sewers of Greek cities such as Akragas were directly influenced by the established models already to be found in the cities and towns of central and northern Italy. Underground and surface, stone-built and rock-cut channels were a feature of the streets of Veii and other Etruscan towns. The development of Rome's system of sewers began as early as the sixth century BC with the construction of the *Cloaca Maxima*, which drained water from the forum and surrounding valleys.[105] Already by the time of the sack of Rome by the Gauls the city had an elaborate drainage system.[106]

Under Roman influence drainage and sewerage facilities became a necessary public amenity, not only to control rain-water and storm-water, but also to take away the overspill and waste from bath houses, public latrines and fountain houses. As with other aspects of Roman urbanisation in the provinces, the actual evidence varies. Few towns in Britain seem to have been provided with drainage systems and none approaches the sophisticated system of the colony of Lincoln.[107] Provision in the towns of Gaul was far superior.[108] In other cities existing drainage was improved and extended to cope with the demands of Romanised urban life.

The efficiency of these drainage systems must sometimes be doubted. Despite the drains at Rhodes, the city suffered from three particularly disastrous floods, of which the last one caused great loss of life;[109] and Lysimachos blocked up the drains of Ephesos as a way of forcing the unwilling inhabitants to move to the new city which he had built.[110] Ultimately the aim of the drains and sewers was to keep the houses, other buildings and streets of the city relatively clean and free from water, and to remove the waste from public and domestic latrines. Usually, however, the drains and sewers merely emptied their contents through the city walls or into convenient streams and rivers.[111]

The provision of drainage systems able to cope with the increasing complexity of urban life does not stand in isolation. Together with assured supplies of water, bath houses and public and private latrines, they formed an important part of urban planning, which, as well as improving living conditions in towns and cities, also helped the public health of the inhabitants in general.

The comments of Thucydides and Strabo illustrate the differences which existed between the cities of the Graeco-Roman world. The construction of public buildings and the provision of urban facilities and amenities varied in response to the growing complexity of urban life and the availability of funds. Not every city provided every facility. Nevertheless, a wide degree of comfort and prosperity was enjoyed by the majority of the inhabitants of the cities.

9

EPILOGUE

The development of city life in the Graeco-Roman world was a long and complex process of which town planning forms an early and integral part. The priority of the Greeks in the introduction and initial dissemination of regular grid planning is certain. But the achievement of the Greeks has to be put into perspective. The Romans and indeed the Etruscans made valuable and independent contributions to the development of urban planning.

Current thinking emphasises the essential continuity in the practice of town planning through Greek and Roman times. The individual contributions of the Greeks, Etruscans and Romans are placed within the 'wider framework of a single organically developing tradition'.[1] Whilst such an evolutionary development is undoubtedly true in general terms, the development is not smoothly progressive and the basic distinctions and differences between the contributions of the Greeks and the Romans should not be lost. Such distinctions are illustrated by Greek and Roman attitudes to what might be termed 'visual planning'. Whereas the Romans at times created artificially ordered townscapes, the Greeks retained a sense of plasticity and spontaneity in design, which was seen to be characteristic of their whole way of life.

Analysis of the evidence for town planning and indeed urbanisation in general suggests that many of the changes and developments came about not through a continual process of evolution, but through the interaction and reciprocity of ideas and practices. Such interaction is seen in the cities of central and southern Italy, where Greeks, Etruscans and Romans came into close contact, and in Asia Minor and the Near East where the combined traditions of Greek and Hellenised barbarian were later amalgamated with Rome.[2]

Whilst the Greeks invented grid planning, the Romans made equally important and fundamental contributions to the development of urban planning. Not only did they give the Graeco-Roman world the political stability and military security in which towns could flourish, but their ability to learn and to adapt what they had learned, combined with the introduction of new ideas, methods and materials, ensured the spread of comfortable, well-planned and visually spectacular cities throughout many parts of Europe, the Mediterranean and the Near East.

APPENDIX

TOWN PLANNING AND THE LAW

A juridical concept is central to the theme of town planning. It is seen in the clear differentiation of areas for particular use and the demarcation of those areas by means of *horoi* (boundary markers), roads, drains and stone curbs. However, even the most auspiciously planned city could not solve all the problems of urban life. In those cities which had grown without any rational planning the problems were particularly severe. Legislation was needed.

Legislation dealt with many aspects of communal living, and the actual laws which were introduced varied greatly from city to city, reflecting the problems and difficulties of the individual town. In general, laws operated in three main areas. First, laws defined the relationship between the state and the individual, together with the responsibility which the individual had to the community. Secondly, relations between the individual and his neighbour had to be regulated. Thirdly, the general health and well-being of the citizens and the overall maintenance of the city and its services had to be ensured.

Urban land was finite. The enactment of laws to organise and control space and to define the individual's responsibility to public land, civic buildings and the community in general was an important aspect of town planning. Encroachment by individuals was an ever-present threat. It has already been observed how the construction of the western extension of the 'great drain' at Athens allowed neighbouring property owners to expand their properties.[1] Even the agora of Athens was not immune: squatters and artisans crowded onto its northern and western bounds after the destruction of the city by Mardonius and the Persians.[2] Similar problems existed in other cities, as Caesar's legislation

166

forbidding the occupation of and construction on public buildings and property illustrates.[3]

Encroachment on to public streets became an increasingly serious problem and the maintenance of the viability of streets was a recurring source of legislation. Laws established the widths of streets,[4] but often streets were maintained only at their minimum viable width. Overhanging balconies, illegal dumping, and the digging of drains and cesspits created problems for the pedestrian, as roads became constricted and blocked.

Legislation was introduced but often proved to be ineffective or inadequate. At Athens, Hippias taxed overhanging balconies, and doors and shutters which opened outwards on to the road.[5] Although this might seem good planning its main purpose was economic. It was a single tax on the property owners and its real importance as a source of revenue for the state is seen when it was re-enacted in the fourth century BC.[6] In Rome laws established a minimum width of 2.90 m for urban streets precisely to allow for overhanging balconies.[7] Yet the streets of Rome still became congested. The emperor Domitian forbade shopkeepers from displaying their goods on the street and so restricting passage.[8]

Damage to the street surface was the object of legislation in many cities. Damage could be caused through private building activity such as the mixing of mortar, the dumping of building waste, or the digging of drains, cesspits and other constructions. In Athens, street surfaces in the vicinity of the triangular sanctuary in the south-western corner of the agora rose to such an extent through the accumulated chippings of marble workers, who had occupied the site, that the boundary markers of the shrine were partially obliterated.[9] Demosthenes details a similar transgression.[10] At Pergamon such activity was expressly forbidden and the offender had to remove waste.[11] Similar legislation was operative in Piraeus[12] and in Rome.[13] In Athens, the digging of private drains was allowed, so long as the property owner covered the channel and adequately repaired the street.[14]

The above evidence is indicative of the concern to prevent private encroachment on public land and damage to public property. Encroachment by the state was another matter. There is evidence from several cities that the community could encroach upon and even expropriate private land for building purposes. At Megara Hyblaea the public buildings of the agora spread into the adjacent residential *insulae*.[15] At Tanagra in Boeotia a law, passed to transfer the ruined sanctuary of Demeter and Kore into the city, allowed officials to obtain any land and even private houses for the site if necessary.[16] The charter of Urso permitted the state to construct aqueducts through private property and generally allowed city officials to build, repair and dig channels, so long as the private buildings remained undamaged.[17] The main avenue on the northern hill of Olynthos was widened at the expense of the private houses along which it passed.[18] Even the street plan itself could be altered. At Priene and Augusta Raurica, the construction of the agora and baths respectively led to alterations in the adjoining street systems to accommodate the buildings.[19]

Legislation not only dealt with the relationship between the individual and the community but also regulated an individual's responsibility to his neighbour. Ancient sources abound with evidence of private litigation over property and boundary disputes between neighbours. Legislation at Gortyn on Crete forbade the construction of either dung heaps or ovens within 10 feet of house walls, presumably to avoid damage to neighbouring property.[20]

The astynomic inscription from Pergamon devoted a whole section to the difficulties associated with party walls and the problems of adjoining properties.[21] The text details responsibilities for repair dependent upon the extent to which a party wall was shared: if both neighbours used a shared wall equally, the cost of repair was shared equally; if, on the other hand, the party wall divided a house from a vacant plot the house owner was responsible for two-thirds of the cost of repair whilst the owner of the empty plot paid only one-third. It was, furthermore, forbidden to damage a common wall by digging a ditch, or planting or resting wine jars against it.

The problems were compounded on steeply sloping ground. In a city such as Pergamon, the problems of damage to neighbouring properties from water were particularly acute. The astynomic law specifically allowed property owners at a lower level to build a second wall on his neighbour's property if vacant, in order to create a gap for drainage purposes. The gap, however, had to be roofed and the space above it remained the property of the owner of the land.

Rubbish from building activity, although potentially hazardous to the individual, was not a serious health risk to the community in general. But organic waste and sewage were potentially dangerous to all citizens. In our modern consumer-orientated, throw-away society it is often forgotten that in more rural economies there is relatively little organic waste. Much organic waste is recycleable either as fodder for animals or as fertilizer and manure for crops. Dung heaps had an economic worth to their owners and at times were included in property sales.[22] This said, there was still an increasing potential threat from human and animal detritus.

Aristophanes gives a picture of evil-smelling alleys and fouled streets in Athens.[23] Juvenal draws attention to the problems of walking under open windows at night.[24] Inadequate or non-existent sanitary facilities meant that the streets, public places and empty building plots were used for dumping, even when statutory dumps were provided, as occurred at Pergamon.[25] The legislation passed in an attempt to control this problem suggests that the evidence of Aristophanes and Juvenal, even if exaggerated, probably conveys general conditions in many cities, especially in the residential districts. Even the hekatompedon on the Acropolis at Athens was not immune from the indiscriminate dumping of animal manure.[26]

The overall supervision for the maintenance of the streets was entrusted to a city officer. At Athens the responsibility fell to the *astynomoi*.[27] At Pergamon minor officials, known as *amphidarchoi*, exercised control of the streets under the overall supervision of the *astynomoi*.[28] At Thebes the task of ensuring that the streets were free from waste and dung was undertaken by a minor public official entitled a *telearchos*, a position once held by Epaminondas.[29] In Republican Rome the aediles exercised general supervision over the maintenance of the roads, whilst the actual responsibility for the cleaning of the streets was commuted to two boards of minor officials: one for the streets within the city and another for cleaning the streets within one mile of the city.[30]

According to Aristotle the Athenian government employed a gang of public slaves in the maintenance of the streets.[31] However, it appears from legislation in several cities that the state relied upon private responsibility and private enterprise. Property owners, either as individuals or in associations, were responsible for the maintenance of streets and the removal of waste.[32] The involvement of city officials in the upkeep of the streets and the removal of waste was supervisory. They ordered the citizens to carry out their responsibilities, imposed fines for refusal, contracted out the work, and then recouped the expense. In this respect the state was also considered a property owner and where public property bordered a street it paid a share of the maintenance.[33] It is difficult, however, to see how such a system of private arrangement worked in practice and the fine well-made roads of the cities of the empire could hardly have been maintained through private efforts alone. It seems likely that there must have been some method of commuting an individual's responsibility.

NOTES

1 INTRODUCTION

1 See Lampl, 1968: *passim*.
2 Homer, *Od.* ix 105–15.
3 Thucydides, i 2.
4 Tacitus, *Agr.* 21.
5 Alcaeus, *Frag.* 28; see also Aelius Aristides, xliii 64.
6 Herodotus, viii 61.
7 Thucydides, vii 77.
8 Herodotus, viii 41.
9 Herodotus, viii 62.
10 Pausanias, x 4. 1.
11 Apuleius, *Metamorphoses* ii 19; see below, p. 122.
12 Aelius Aristides, xiv 93–94.
13 See Martin, 1974: pp. 130–47 for full discussion of these points.
14 Plato, *Leges* 778 a–d.
15 Plato, *Leges* 778 e–779 b. The arrangement of houses so as to present a common barrier for defence was not uncommon in the Aegean. The houses of the late eighth-century settlement at Vroulia on Rhodes were arranged in two parallel rows facing the sea, and their rear walls, facing inland, acted as a defensive barrier on the landward side, Kinch, 1914: pp. 112–14. The houses at Lato on Crete were also arranged to assist the defence of the town, see below, p. 24; and a similar need for defence conditioned the arrangement of Mesta on Chios, see Plommer, 1977: p. 79.
16 Plato, *Leges* 779 c–d.
17 Aristotle, *Pol.* 1330b–1331b.
18 Hippocrates, *Aer* 3–4.
19 Vitruvius, i 4. 1–7, 6. 1–3; see Salway in Grew and Hobley, 1985: p. 68.
20 See note 17 above. Both Athens and Corinth had adequate water supplies. Thourioi and Cyrene were chosen for their nearby springs.
21 See note 18 above; see also Xenophon, *Oeconomica* ix 4–5 on the orientation of houses, and Vitruvius, v 1. 4 on the siting of basilicas.
22 Vitruvius, i 7. 1–2.

171

23 Vitruvius, i 4. 9; see note 19 above.
24 See below, p. 30.
25 Strabo, viii 8. 1 (388).
26 Boardman, 1980: pp. 189–90.
27 Salmon, 1969: pp. 25–26.
28 See below, pp. 64–65.
29 Strabo, xiv 1. 22 (640).
30 e.g. Sabora in Spain, *CIL*, II 1423.
31 Ward-Perkins, 1974: p. 38; Drews, 1981: p. 135; compare Lampl, 1968: pp. 7–9.
32 Thucydides, i 10.
33 Boardman, 1980: p. 161.

2   URBAN DEVELOPMENT AND THE 'OLD' CITIES OF GREECE

1 Ps-Dicaearchus, i 1 = Müller, 1841: p. 254, no. 59.
2 Tacitus, *Ann*. xv 38.
3 Juvenal, iii 190–99; see MacDonald, 1965: pp. 25–31.
4 Cicero, *De leg. agr.* ii 96.
5 Tacitus, *Ann*. xv 43.
6 Aristotle, *Pol.* 1330b.
7 Plutarch, *Pyrrhus* 32–34.
8 Thucydides, ii 4.
9 Vermeule, 1964: pp. 181–83; Taylour, 1964: pp. 99–104.
10 Snodgrass, 1980: p. 31.
11 Thucydides, i 5.
12 Thucydides, i 10.
13 Mitchell, 1964: pp. 103–4; Forrest, 1980: pp. 28–29.
14 Roebuck, 1972: pp. 99–103; Salmon, 1984: pp. 75–80; Williams, 1984: p. 12.
15 Travlos, 1960: p. 23; Travlos, 1971: p. 158; Martin, 1974: pp. 292–94.
16 Thucydides, ii 15.
17 Popham and Sackett, 1972: pp. 8–19; 1980: pp. 11–25.
18 Details of excavations can be found in, *AD* esp. 1966: pp. 218–27; 1967: pp. 278–83; 1968: pp. 227–44; 1969: pp. 189–209.
19 Tomlinson, 1972: pp. 24, 67; Martin, 1974: p. 80.
20 Kleiner, 1966: pp. 14–17; Martin, 1974: pp. 291–92.
21 See below, pp. 38–39.
22 The evidence from Rome suggests that the villages out of which Rome grew were originally independent, Scullard, 1967: pp. 244–47; see also Drews, 1981: p. 145.
23 Cook, 1958/9: pp. 1–3.
24 ibid., pp. 10–17; Nicholls, 1958/9: pp. 120–37.
25 See below, pp. 32–33.
26 Cambitoglou, 1971: pp. 1–5; Snodgrass, 1971: p. 426.
27 Cambitoglou, 1971: pp. 33–36.
28 Coldstream, 1977: p. 306.

29 Cambitoglou, 1971: pp. 7-9. The inhabitants of Karphi on Crete faced similar problems. Natural springs close to the site were few and the discovery of potsherds above the levels of the roofs suggested to the excavators that rain-water was collected and stored in jars, see Pendlebury, 1937/8: p. 63.

30 Boardman, 1967: pp. 34–40; Martin, 1974: p. 291; Coldstream, 1977: pp. 306–9.

31 Boardman, 1967: pp. 38–39.

32 ibid., p. 249.

33 Political meetings in the agora are one of the features of urban life mentioned in Hesiod, *Opera* ii. 27–41.

34 See below, p. 25.

35 Willetts, 1965: p. 58.

36 Hommel, 1960: p. 40.

37 See Thompson, 1940: pp. 106–11; Young, 1951: pp. 149–68; Thompson, 1957: pp. 99–100; Thompson, 1968: pp. 58–64. For early roads at Argos, see Courbin, 1956: pp. 182–218.

38 Cobbled streets with covered drains were a feature of the rebuilding of Old Smyrna in the sixth century BC; see Cook, 1950: p. 10.

39 Young, 1951: pp. 135–288; Thompson and Wycherley, 1972: pp. 119–20.

40 e.g. Thompson, 1954: pp. 51–53; Shear, 1969: pp. 383–94.

41 Thompson, 1937: pp. 14–21.

42 See Lauter and Laute-Bufe, 1971: pp. 109–24; Shear, 1973: pp. 146–56.

43 e.g. on the northern slopes of the Areopagus, Thompson, 1959: pp. 99–105.

44 Thompson and Wycherley, 1972: pp. 197–203; Wycherley, 1978: pp. 89, 250.

45 Mussche, 1970: p. 131.

46 For full reports of the excavations of the Classical town see Mussche, 1965: pp. 5–46; 1967: pp. 48–70; 1968: pp. 57–71; 1969: pp. 121–34; 1970: pp. 125–35; 1971: pp. 103–33; 1975: pp. 45–54.

47 Mussche, 1968: pp. 61–64.

48 See in general Bruneau, 1968: pp. 633–709; Papageorgiou-Venetas, 1981: *passim*.

49 Papageorgiou-Venetas, 1981: p. 81, fig. 63, pp. 113–14.

50 Chamonard, 1924: pp. 76–96.

51 Bruneau, 1968: pp. 667–68.

52 See Hiller von Gaertringen, III 1904: esp. pp. 75–77.

53 Evans, 1895/6: pp. 169–94; Demargne, 1901: pp. 282–307.

54 Hadjimichali, 1971: pp. 167–222.

55 See above, note 35.

56 See above, note 6.

57 Thucydides, i 15; Popham and Sackett, 1972: p. 19.

58 Kriesis, 1958: p. 41.

59 Thucydides, ii 17.

60 Xenophon, *Poroi* ii 6.

61 Tod, ii 1948: no. 202, pp. 294–301. Corinth similarly appears to have

been spacious; see Williams, 1984: pp. 18–19.
62 See below, pp. 32–33.
63 Demosthenes, xxiv 149.
64 Boersma, 1970: pp. 44–45.
65 Willetts, 1965: p. 57.
66 Van Effenterre, 1963: p. 235.
67 Boardman, 1980: pp. 54–84.
68 Snodgrass, 1980: pp. 31–32; see below, p. 50.
69 Thucydides, ii 16; Aristophanes, *Acharnae* 26–42.
70 See below, p. 48.

3 THE ORIGINS AND DEVELOPMENT OF GREEK PLANNING IN THE MEDITERRANEAN

1 Blake, 1959: p. 72.
2 Aristophanes, *Aves* 995–1009; see Wycherley, 1937/8: pp. 22–31.
3 Lampl, 1968: pp. 26, 31.
4 ibid., p. 40.
5 ibid., pp. 113, 120.
6 ibid., pp. 19–20.
7 *CAH*² III. 3, pp. 5–7 for evidence of Phoenician contacts with the Greeks.
8 Boardman, 1980: pp. 38–54.
9 Compare the maps in Desborough, 1972: pp. 356–57 and Coldstream, 1977: pp. 386–87.
10 See above, p. 15.
11 Cook, 1962: pp. 71–72.
12 As, for example, at Akragas, probably Megara Hyblaea and other colonies.
13 Cook, 1947: p. 42.
14 Nicholls, 1958/9: pp. 58–63.
15 Cook, 1958/9: pp. 23–24; Nicholls, 1958/9: pp. 126–28.
16 Compare Giuliano, 1966: pp. 38–40 and Martin, 1974: pp. 289–90.
17 Cook, 1950: p. 10.
18 Kleiner, 1966: pp. 18–20; Martin, 1974: pp. 291–92.
19 See below, p. 54.
20 von Graeve, 1973/4: pp. 69, 78–80.
21 Hommel, 1960: p. 40.
22 See below, note 58, for the foundation inscription from Black Kekyra.
23 See Boardman, 1980: pp. 169, 172, 185, 189–90. Where the native population already occupied a site they were usually forcibly ejected, e.g. at Naxos, Leontini and Syracuse. At Syracuse a destruction layer, which is possibly associated with the ejection of the native population, has been found, see *AR*, 1982: p. 87.
24 Ward-Perkins, 1974: p. 11.
25 Martin, 1974: pp. 326–27.
26 *AR*, 1977: p. 67.
27 *AR*, 1982: p. 88.

28 Martin, 1974: p. 326.
29 Waşowicz, 1975: pp. 41–45.
30 See Castagnoli, 1971: p. 10; Berlin de Ballu, 1972: pp. 17–20, 27, and compare Waşowicz, 1975: pp. 77–78; Finley, 1977: p. 196.
31 Martin in Finley, 1973: pp. 97–101. Massilia followed the same arrangement.
32 For Syracuse in general see Stillwell, 1976: pp. 871–73. For a summary of recent excavations, see *AR*, 1982: pp. 86–87.
33 Pelagatti, 1964: pp. 149–65; 1972: pp. 211–19; Martin, 1974: pp. 314–16.
34 *AR*, 1981/2: pp. 92–93.
35 For Megara Hyblaea in general see Dunbabin, 1948: pp. 18–21; Schmiedt, 1968/9: pp. 412–13; Vallet in Finley, 1973: pp. 84–110; Martin, 1974: pp. 309–11; Ward-Perkins, 1974: pp. 23–24; Vallet, 1976: *passim*. The colony was founded in the second half of the eighth century BC although there is a discrepancy between the traditional date as recorded by Thucydides (vi 4) and the archaeological evidence; see Holloway, 1978: p. 560.
36 Holloway, 1978: pp. 561–62; compare Ward-Perkins, 1974: pp. 23–24.
37 *AR*, 1982: p. 89.
38 Ward-Perkins, 1974: p. 24.
39 Vallet in Finley, 1973: p. 88.
40 For discussion of the town plan, see Bradford, 1957: pp. 218–27; see also Voza, 1963: pp. 223–32.
41 Ward-Perkins, 1974: p. 119.
42 Bradford, 1957: pp. 220–21; Castagnoli, 1971: p. 44.
43 Castagnoli, 1971: pp. 35–39; Ward-Perkins, 1974: p. 118.
44 See *AR*, 1976/7: pp. 60–61.
45 Castagnoli, 1971: p. 134.
46 Giuliano, 1966: pp. 44–49; Adamestaneau in Finley, 1973: pp. 49–62; Martin, 1974: pp. 323–25.
47 Ward-Perkins, 1974: p. 118.
48 Evidence for the possible relationship between town planning and rural land division is slowly appearing, see Boyd and Jameson, 1981: pp. 327–42; see below, pp. 67–68.
49 Martin, 1974: p. 316; *AR*, 1976/7: p. 73; 1982: p. 99.
50 Graham, 1972: pp. 300–1; Martin, 1974: pp. 314–16.
51 For Cyrene, see Castagnoli, 1971: pp. 133–34; for Eusperides, see Goodchild, 1952: pp. 208–12; Castagnoli, 1971: pp. 17–18.
52 Wycherley, 1951: p. 234; Giuliano, 1966: p. 50; Schmiedt, 1968/9: pp. 398–400; Castagnoli, 1971: pp. 10–11; Ward-Perkins, 1974: p. 23.
53 Genière and Theodorescu, 1979: pp. 385–95; Genière, 1981: pp. 211–17; *AR*, 1976/7: pp. 60–61.
54 Miro, 1957: pp. 135–40; Giuliano, 1966: pp. 49–50; Schmiedt, 1968/9: pp. 401–2; Castagnoli, 1971: pp. 19–24; Martin, 1974: pp. 91–92, 321.
55 Metraux, 1972: p. 175.
56 Diodorus Siculus, xiii 81–84; Tertullian ascribes the quotation to Diogenes concerning Megara, see *Apologeticus* 39.
57 Diodorus Siculus, xi 25.

58 *SIG*³, 141; Jeffrey, 1976: p. 55.
59 Waşowicz, 1972: pp. 199–229.
60 As at Naxos and, according to Athenaeus, at Sybaris; see below, p. 152.
61 Vallet, 1976: p. 302; see also above, note 58, for Black Kekyra.
62 See below p. 156.
63 Ward-Perkins, 1974: Introduction.
64 For the general characteristics of Near Eastern planning, see Lampl, 1968: pp. 19–22, 29–32.
65 See the arrangements at Zernaki Tepe and Megiddo II, above, p. 31.
66 Snodgrass, 1980: p. 32.
67 For a brief description of Phoenician cities, see Harden, 1971: pp. 122–26.
68 Lampl, 1968: p. 40.

4 PLANNING IN THE CLASSICAL PERIOD

1 See von Gerkan, 1924: pp. 42–61; Wycherley, 1964: pp. 135–39; Giuliano, 1966: pp. 94–107; Castagnoli, 1971: pp. 80–84; McCredie, 1971: pp. 95–100. Martin, 1974: pp. 95–100; Burns, 1976: pp. 419–48.
2 Ward-Perkins, 1974: p. 14.
3 The Athenian colony at Amphipolis was only established after earlier, unsuccessful attempts by both the Milesians and the Athenians to establish a city at the site; see Thucydides, iv 102.
4 See above p. 27.
5 Boersma, 1970: pp. 45–46.
6 von Gerkan, 1924: pp. 38–41; Giuliano, 1966: pp. 80–84; Kleiner, 1968: pp. 25–27; Castagnoli, 1971: pp. 12–14.
7 Ward-Perkins, 1974: p. 116.
8 Martin, 1974: pp. 122–23.
9 Aristotle, *Pol.* ii 1267b, 22ff; vii 1330b, 21ff.
10 Photios, s.v. *Nemesis Hippodamou.*
11 Thucydides, i 93; on the question of the date of the plan and the age of Hippodamos, see Wycherley, 1964: pp. 137–39; Boersma, 1970: pp. 46–50; Burns, 1976: pp. 421–28.
12 *IG*, i² 887–96; Hill, 1932: pp. 254–59; McCredie, 1971: pp. 96–98; Garland, 1987: pp. 140–41, 225–26.
13 Pausanias, i 1. 3 states that Piraeus had two agoras, one near the sea and the other inland; Garland, 1987: pp. 141–42.
14 Judeich, 1931: pp. 430, 451; Rider, 1964: pp. 222–24; McCredie, 1971: pp. 96–98; Jones, 1975: pp. 98–100.
15 See above, note 12.
16 Diodorus Siculus, xii 10. 6–7. On the possible identity of Hippodamos see Castagnoli, 1971: p. 135, note 33.
17 On the efforts to locate Thourioi, see Colburn, 1967: pp. 30–38; Rainey, 1969: pp. 261–74. The Roman colony of Copia partly overlay Thourioi and had two intersecting central axes; see Stillwell, 1976: p. 870.

18 Strabo, xiv 2. 9 (654).
19 Strabo, xiv 2. 5 (652).
20 Diodorus Siculus, xx 83. 2.
21 For discussion of the town plan, see Kondis, 1954: pp. 1–31; Bradford, 1956: pp. 57–69; Bradford, 1957: pp. 277–86; Kondis, 1958: pp. 148–51; Castagnoli, 1971: pp. 14–15; McCredie, 1971: pp. 99–100; Ward-Perkins, 1974: pp. 14–15; Martin, 1974: pp. 148–49.
22 For examples of arterial roads see *AD 1967*; 1969: p. 440; *AD 1968*, 1969: p. 535; *AD 1970*, 1973: p. 509.
23 Castagnoli, 1971: p. 131.
24 Bradford, 1956: p. 67.
25 Stillwell, 1976: p. 756.
26 Diodorus Siculus, xx 83. 1–2.
27 Diodorus Siculus, xix 45. 1–8.
28 Bradford, 1956: p. 68; Kondis, 1958: pp. 152–53.
29 Burns, 1976: pp. 425–27.
30 Aelius Aristides, xliii 6.
31 McCredie, 1971: pp. 99–100.
32 Boyd and Jameson, 1981: pp. 335–42; see below, pp. 67–68, for Halieis and Mantinea.
33 Akragas had been supplied with drains after the defeat of the Carthaginians; see above, p. 47.
34 Martin, 1974: pp. 122–23.
35 Pausanias, vi 24. 2; Wycherley, 1962: pp. 70–78.
36 On the synoecism of Olynthos, see Thucydides, i 58. For the layout of the town see Robinson and Graham, 1938: pp. 1–44; Robinson, 1946: pp. 167–78.
37 Robinson and Graham, 1938: pp. 21–22.
38 ibid., pp. 29–37; Plato advised that houses should be so arranged that they presented a unified appearance; see above, p. 4. For objections to enforced unification with Olynthos from neighbouring communities, see Xenophon, *Hellenica* v 2. 11–19.
39 Robinson, 1928: pp. 11–14; Robinson, 1946: pp. 95–114.
40 A common amenity; see, for example, the fountain at the Dipylon Gate at Athens, Travlos, 1971: pp. 302–3; Glaser, 1985: p. 64. A spring house was similarly located outside the southern gate of the Pisidian city of Kremna.
41 For examples of cobbling see Robinson, 1928: pp. 10–11, 14, 100; Robinson and Graham, 1938: pp. 172–73, 183; Robinson, 1946: p. 237; for drains, Robinson, 1928: pp. 11, 38; Robinson and Graham, 1938: p. 23; Robinson, 1946: pp. 237, 240–41, plates 83, 91.2, 92.1, 202, 207.1. It could be that cobbled streets and drains were more extensive than the excavators thought.
42 For recent excavations see Mellink, 1968: pp. 137–39; 1969: pp. 216–19; Love, 1970: pp. 149–55; 1972: pp. 61–76; 1973: pp. 413–24.
43 van Berchem, 1970: pp. 198–205.
44 Wiegand and Schrader, 1904: *site plan*; Martin, 1974: pp 207–8.
45 Wiegand and Schrader, 1904: pp. 74–77.

46 Stillwell, 1976: pp. 849–50.
47 Ward-Perkins, 1974: p. 15.
48 Petsas, 1958: pp. 246–54; 1964: pp. 74–84; Makaronas, 1966: pp. 98–105.
49 Coleman, 1970: pp. 155–61.
50 Martin, 1974: p. 297.
51 Graham, 1972: pp. 295–300.
52 Quilici, 1967: pp. 159–86; Martin, 1974: p. 325; Ward-Perkins, 1974: pp. 117–18.
53 For results of recent excavations, see Jameson, 1969: pp. 311–42; Boyd and Rudolph, 1978: pp. 332–55.
54 Fougères, 1898: pp. 162–63; Martin, 1974: pp. 118–20.
55 Diodorus Siculus, xvii 52.
56 See von Gerkan, 1924: pp. 67–71; Martin, 1974: pp. 116–17.
57 Strabo, xvii 1. 6–10 (791–95).
58 Martin, 1974: p. 118.
59 For the Hekatomid building programme, see Hornblower, 1982: pp. 294–331.
60 Vitruvius, ii 8. 10–11; Hornblower, 1982: pp. 297–305.
61 See below, p. 89.
62 Plutarch, *Moralia* 818 D; *Cimon* 13. 7.
63 See above, note 38.
64 See below, Appendix.

5 TOWN PLANNING IN THE HELLENISTIC WORLD

1 Ward-Perkins, 1974: p. 18; Martin, 1974: pp. 154–55.
2 Hammond, 1967, p. 666; Martin, 1974: pp. 299–300. The foundation date is disputed. Although a few fifth-century roof tiles have been found in the *katagogion* the majority of the buildings on the site date to the third century BC.
3 Hammond, 1953: pp. 135–40; Hammond, 1967: pp. 154–56; Martin, 1974: p. 301.
4 Dimitrov, 1961: pp. 91–102; Martin, 1974: p. 307; Hoddinott, 1975: pp. 93–97.
5 Martin, 1974: p. 301; for a brief resumé of current work see *BCH*, 1971: pp. 914–46; 1972: pp. 719–25; 1974: pp. 660–62; 1975: pp. 658–60.
6 *BCH*, 1972: pp. 721–25; Martin, 1974: p. 301; Stillwell, 1976: pp. 267–68; *BCH*, 1980: pp. 636–40; 1981: p. 819.
7 Lauffray, 1958: pp. 8–11; Downey, 1961: pp. 26–28; Martin, 1974: pp. 166–67.
8 Saugavet, 1941: pp. 38–48; Lauffray, 1958: pp. 13–14; Martin, 1974: pp. 167–68.
9 Lauffray, 1958: pp. 11–12; Martin, 1974: pp. 169–71.
10 Lauffray, 1958: pp. 12–13; Martin, 1974: p. 169.
11 Cumont, 1926: pp. 25–27; Lauffray, 1958: pp. 14–15; Martin, 1974: pp. 165–66.

12 Lauffray, 1958: pp. 15–16; Martin, 1974: pp. 171–73.
13 Acts, 9: 11.
14 Martin, 1974: p. 173.
15 Ward-Perkins, 1974: pp. 20–21.
16 Strabo, xiv 1. 37 (646).
17 Bean, 1966: pp. 252–59; Peschlow-Bindokat, 1977: pp. 90–104; *AR*, 1979: pp. 79–81; Hornblower, 1982: pp. 319–23.
18 Bean, 1971: pp. 190–98; Martin, 1974: pp. 149–50.
19 Martin, 1974: pp. 155, 274; Ward-Perkins, 1974: p. 114.
20 Hansen, 1971: pp. 245–51.
21 ibid., p. 251.
22 ibid., pp. 253–61.
23 ibid., pp. 261–84; Martin, 1974: pp. 127–46.
24 See Martin, 1974: pp. 149–50; Ward-Perkins, 1974: p. 19; von Zabern, 1987: pp. 11–44.
25 Bean and Cook, 1955: p. 143; Hornblower, 1982: p. 301.
26 Martin, 1974: p. 147; Ward-Perkins, 1974: p. 19.
27 *TLS*, 1974: p. 768; Hornblower, 1982: p. 301.
28 Bean, 1971: pp. 56–68.
29 Compare Martin, 1974: p. 210 and von Gerkan, 1924: p. 88.
30 See above, note 16; for Amastris see Pliny, *Epist.* x 98.
31 Lyttleton, 1974: pp. 207–8.
32 Stillwell, 1976: pp. 756–57.

6 ETRUSCAN AND ROMAN PLANNING IN ITALY

1 Livy, v 55, 2–5.
2 Livy, v 42, 1–3. Recent excavations at Rome have revealed no evidence of destruction, see *AR*, 1980: p. 64.
3 Livy, vi 4, 6.
4 Livy, v 52, 1–17.
5 Diodorus Siculus, xiv 116, 8–9. For discussion of Rome's origins see Ridgway, 1979: pp. 208–11.
6 Cicero, *De lege agr.* ii 96.
7 The different theories are briefly discussed by Castagnoli, 1971: pp. 5–7.
8 Ward-Perkins, 1974: p. 25.
9 Scullard, 1967: pp. 77–78.
10 Drews, 1981: pp. 132–56.
11 Scullard, 1967: pp. 104–10.
12 Ward-Perkins, 1961: pp. 20–25.
13 ibid., pp. 3–20.
14 ibid., pp. 25–28; Drews, 1981: pp. 140–41.
15 Ward-Perkins, 1961: pp. 28–31.
16 ibid., pp. 47–51; Scullard, 1967: p. 108.
17 Boethius, 1978: pp. 19–20; Drews, 1981: pp. 145–47.
18 Scullard, 1967: pp. 94–96; Drews, 1981: p. 150.
19 De Ruyt, 1973: pp. 584–86; *AR*, 1979/80: pp. 64–65; Drews, 1981:

pp. 150–52.
20 Scullard, 1967: pp. 136–41; Boethius, 1978: p. 65.
21 Ward-Perkins, 1974: p. 25.
22 Chevallier, 1957: p. 446.
23 Grant, 1971: p. 45.
24 Castagnoli, 1971: pp. 26–35 discusses the layout of Pompeii and the problems of its interpretation. For a general description of Pompeii, see Grant, 1971: esp. chs 3 and 4.
25 Castagnoli, 1971: pp. 46–50.
26 Boethius, 1978: p. 21.
27 Scullard, 1967: pp. 209–12; Banti, 1973: pp. 10–11; AR, 1979/80: pp. 68–69.
28 Boethius, 1978: p. 227, note 45.
29 Scullard, 1967: pp. 205–9; Mansuelli, 1972: pp. 111–43; Mansuelli, 1979: pp. 354–59.
30 Mansuelli, 1979: p. 359.
31 Ward-Perkins, 1955: p. 144.
32 Mansuelli, 1972: pp. 124–27.
33 Mansuelli, 1979: p. 362.
34 At Akragas for instance, according to Diodorus Siculus, xi 25, the comprehensive drainage system was not installed until after the defeat at the battle of Himera of the Carthaginians, to whom the Etruscans were allied. The prisoners of war from the battle were employed in constructing the drains.
35 Mansuelli, 1979: p. 355.
36 See above, p. 40.
37 See above, p. 57.
38 Salmon, 1969: pp. 29–39.
39 Servius, Ad Aen. i 422.
40 Vitruvius, i 7. 1.
41 Haverfield, 1913: pp. 68–69; Castagnoli, 1971: p. 96.
42 Castagnoli, 1971: pp. 96–97; Stillwell, 1976: p. 31.
43 Salmon, 1969: p. 33.
44 Ward-Perkins, 1955: p. 145.
45 Meiggs, 1973: pp. 20–26, 111–17.
46 EAA, vi 1965: p. 144; Stillwell, 1976: pp. 716–17.
47 Stillwell, 1976: p. 158.
48 EAA, ii 1959: pp. 926–27; Stillwell, 1976: p. 248.
49 EAA, i 1958: pp. 511–20; Stillwell, 1976: pp. 79–80.
50 For Lucca see EAA, iv 1961: p. 701; Stillwell, 1976: p. 527. For Luni see EAA, iv 1961: p. 731; Stillwell, 1976: p. 532.
51 EAA, vi 1965: pp. 688–90; Stillwell, 1976: pp. 93–94.
52 Financial gain for recruitment is a continuing theme in the late Republic, see Sallust, BJ 84. 4; Appian, BC i 57; Caesar, BC i. 3.
53 Richmond and Holford, 1935: pp. 69–76.
54 Haverfield, 1913: pp. 89–91; Castagnoli, 1971: p. 112.
55 Haverfield, 1913: pp. 86–89; Castagnoli, 1971: pp. 110–12.
56 Ward-Perkins, 1955: pp. 145–51.
57 Frontinus, Strategemata iv 1. 14.

58 Polybius, iv 31.10.
59 Cicero, *Pro Font.* 13.
60 Appian, *BC.* i 7.
61 Salmon, 1969: p. 24.
62 ibid., 1969: p. 166, note 9.
63 See above, note 60.
64 See the confiscations of the Sullan period, Cic. *Ad Fam.* xiii 4. 1–2, *Ad Att.* i 19. 4, *De Domo* 79; see Tacitus, *Ann.* xiv 31 for the effects of the colonists of Camulodunum on the native Trinovantes.
65 Grew and Hobley, 1985: Introduction, p. x, quoting Dilke in Grew and Hobley, 1985: p. 11.
66 Dilke, 1971: pp. 68, 88.
67 Stillwell, 1976: p. 326.
68 Arthur, 1986: p. 41.
69 Richmond and Holford, 1935: p. 70.
70 Salmon, 1969: p. 48 quoting the evidence from Sinuessa, Livy, xxii 14, 3.
71 Richmond and Holford, 1935: pp. 70–71.
72 See above, Aquileia; see also Julius Caesar's legislation concerning Rome, Abbott and Johnson, 1926: no. 24 pp. 289–91.
73 Strabo, v 3. 8 (235).
74 e.g. Turin, Triers and Verona; see also above, note 69.
75 Rome's first aqueduct, the Aqua Appia, was constructed in 312 BC.
76 See Cicero, *Respublica* ii 19. 34; for the hostility of Cato the Elder, see Plutarch, *Cato Maior* 21. 2–23. 3.
77 See Stillwell, 1976: pp. 594–95.
78 Boethius, 1978: pp. 169–74.
79 See above, p. 91.
80 Boethius, 1978: p. 146.

7   PLANNING IN THE ROMAN EMPIRE

1 Aelius Aristides, xiv 93.
2 Salway, 1981: p. 261.
3 e.g. Sabora, see *CIL.*, II 1423; Lewis and Reinhold, II 1966: pp. 341–42. Similarly Augustodunum replaced Bibactre, the native capital of the Aedui, which occupied a nearby hill, Drinkwater, 1983: pp. 131, 143; see also Verulamium, below, pp. 124–26.
4 Apuleius, *Metamorphoses* ii 19.
5 For evidence of competition and benefactions see Dio Chrysostom, xxxiv 48; Cassius Dio, lii 37. 9–10; *CIL*, II 3270 (Castulo, Spain); *CIL*, V 5262 (Pliny's benefactions to Comum).
6 Rivalry for honorific titles between cities was particularly fierce in Asia Minor, see, e.g., Abbott and Johnson, 1926: no. 100 p. 422 (Ephesos) and, generally, Magie, 1950: pp. 588–89, 590.
7 Abbott and Johnson, 1926: no. 101 p. 423. The emperor Antoninus Pius rebuked the citizens of Ephesos for their lukewarm attitude

towards one of their benefactors because he had given a permanent
benefaction in the form of a building rather than the transitory gifts of
games or corn doles.

8 Pliny, *Epist.* x 98–99.

9 Pliny, *Epist.* x 37–38, 39–40, 49–50, 70–71.

10 See Trajan's reply to Pliny concerning the completion of an aqueduct
to supply Nicomedia, Pliny, *Epist.* x 38.

11 See the African cities which are discussed below, pp. 134–40; the plan
of pre-Roman Numantia was Greek-inspired, see Castagnoli, 1971:
p. 87.

12 e.g. in Britain see Tacitus, *Agr.* 21; for the growth of urbanisation in
Galatia see Jones, 1940: p. 69.

13 Tacitus, *Ann.* xi 19 states that Corbulo imposed the Roman form of
urban administration on the Frisii.

14 Strabo, iv 5. 1 (200).

15 For the general layout of Roman forts see Webster, 1973: p. 38;
Webster, 1979: pp. 172–88; Johnson, 1983: pp. 27–35. For the
relationship between fort and civilian settlement, see Jones in Grew
and Hobley, 1985: pp. 86–93; Webster, 1988: pp. 42 (Camulodunum),
56–58 (Glevum), 110 (Isca), 136 (Viroconium), 149–51 (Lindum).

16 Tacitus, *Ann.* xii 32.

17 Frere, 1964: pp. 103–12; Wacher, 1975: pp. 202–25.

18 Grenier, III 1958: p. 287; Drinkwater, 1983: p. 144. It is possible that
there was a temple associated with the forum at Verulamium, see
Wacher, 1974: p. 207.

19 Wacher, 1974: pp. 375–89.

20 ibid., p. 388.

21 Boon, 1974: pp. 36–42; Wacher, 1974: pp. 255–77.

22 Boon, 1974: pp. 53–56, 98.

23 Drinkwater, 1983: pp. 11–12, 133–34, 143.

24 Wheeler, 1964: pp. 71–76; Stillwell, 1976: pp. 119–21.

25 Strabo, iv 1. 12 (186); Pliny, *NH* iii. 37.

26 Grenier, III 1958: pp. 143–56.

27 ibid., pp. 157–71.

28 Wheeler, 1964: pp. 47–52; Ward-Perkins, 1981: pp. 391–96.

29 Ward-Perkins, 1981: pp. 399–407.

30 Wheeler, 1964: p. 46; Stillwell, 1976: pp. 917–19.

31 Ward-Perkins, 1981: pp. 378–83.

32 Wheeler, 1964: pp. 52–57; Ward-Perkins, 1981: pp. 371–78, 382–91.

33 Ward-Perkins, 1981: pp. 372–73.

34 Ward-Perkins, 1974: p. 31; Ward-Perkins, 1981: pp. 307, 373.

35 e.g. see the temple to Asclepius at Cos, Lyttleton, 1974: pp. 205–8;
for the use of axial roads in street planning, see the cities of the
Seleucids, above, p. 80.

36 Ward-Perkins, 1974: p. 31.

37 Ward-Perkins, 1981: pp. 255–63.

38 Plutarch, *Pompey* xlii 5–6.

39 Philostratus, *Vit. Soph.* ii 1 (550).

40 Pausanias, i 20. 7; Hill, 1953: pp. 205–15; Ward-Perkins, 1981: pp. 263–71; Shear, 1981: pp. 357–77; for the agora, see Thompson and Wycherley, 1972: pp. 23–24.
41 See above, p. 54; Bean, 1966: pp. 219–30; for the nymphaeum, see Ward-Perkins, 1981: pp. 268–69.
42 Bean, 1968: pp. 45–59.
43 Lauffray, 1958: pp. 19–20; Martin, 1974: pp. 178–80; Ward-Perkins, 1981: pp. 335–39.
44 Martin, 1974: pp. 180–83; Ward-Perkins, 1981: pp. 354–61.
45 See Hypata, above, note 4.
46 Pliny, *Epist.* x 40.
47 Pausanias, x 4. 1.
48 Pausanias, viii 31. 1. By Strabo's time 'the Great City was a great desert', see Strabo viii 8. 1 (388). Strabo also comments on the disappearance of cities in Aeolis, xiii 3. 6 (622).
49 See above, note 9.
50 Ward-Perkins, 1981: pp. 306, 390–91, 441.
51 ibid., p. 378.
52 Tertullian, *Apologeticus* 38. 4–5.
53 *Theodosian Code* xvi 2. 3.
54 Tertullian, *Apologeticus* 38. 1–3 rejects elections, public meetings, meetings of the local council and other communal gatherings, which were an integral part of ancient urban life.
55 At the Roman colony at Kremna, Pisidia, the public buildings were utilised as veritable quarries for the construction of the churches.
56 Frere, 1988: p. 242.
57 Lactantius, *De mortibus persecutorum* 7; Aurelius Victor, *Vitae* xxxix.
58 Ammianus Marcellinus, xxvii 8. 6, xxviii 3. 1 records the speed with which the cities of Britain recovered after Count Theodosius had dealt with the Saxon and Frankish threat in the second half of the fourth century AD.
59 See Wacher, 1975: p. 222; Salway, 1981: pp. 458–60.

8 THE ANCIENT CITY AND THE URBAN INFRASTRUCTURE

1 Vitruvius, i 8. 1; for a comparison of the advantages and disadvantages of Greek and Roman cities, see Strabo, v 3. 8 (235).
2 Wycherley, 1962: p. 5; Scullard, 1967: p. 77; Boethius, 1978: p. 67.
3 Thucydides, i. 7.
4 See above, p. 15.
5 See above, pp. 15–16.
6 Wycherley, 1962: p. 39; Horst de la Croix, 1972: p. 21.
7 Scullard, 1967: pp. 67–68; for the opposite view that Etruscan towns had walls from their initial foundation, see Horst de la Croix, 1972: p. 26.

8 Horst de la Croix, 1972: p. 21; Hornblower, 1982: p. 298.
9 Horst de la Croix, 1972: p. 22; Winter, 1971: pp. 110–12; Ward-Perkins, 1974: p. 14.
10 Kleiner, 1968: pp. 13, 27–33.
11 Wiegand and Schrader, 1904: Site plan; fig. 18.
12 See Winter, 1971: p. 114; for examples of *diateichismata* see Athens, Boersma, 1970: p. 84; Theangela and Herakleia in Caria, Hornblower, 1982: p. 307.
13 Horst de la Croix, 1972: pp. 27–29.
14 *CIL*, II 3270.
15 Horst de la Croix, 1972: pp. 30–31; Frere, 1988: p. 284.
16 Wacher, 1975: pp. 213, 302.
17 e.g. Old Smyrna, see above, p. 15; Cosa, see above, p. 108.
18 Nash, 1961: p. 418.
19 ibid., p. 411.
20 Livy, xxi 62. 1–4.
21 Roman cities were also defined by the *pomerium*. Caesar's legislation concerning Rome also indicated that the laws were operative within one mile of continuous habitation of the city; see Tabula Heracleensis, Abbott and Johnson, 1926: no 24, esp. pp. 289–90, *ll.* 20–23, 56–58. The duties of the magisterial board in charge of the city's streets was limited to one mile outside the city. A board of two magistrates was responsible for the roads in the countryside, see Abbott and Johnson, 1926: p. 290 *ll.* 50–52.
22 See Saalman, 1968: pp. 22–26. The Kerameikos district of Athens, which included the agora, was renowned for its sleaziness; see Alkiphron, *Epist.* ii 22. 1, iii 12. 2, 28. 2. Similarly the district of Subura at Rome was unsavoury, see Homo, 1971: p. 482.
23 The question of intramural burial is complicated. According to Cicero, *Ad Familiares* iv 12. 3, it was not permitted in Athens on the grounds of religion, although infant burial was apparently exempted; see Boardman and Kurtz, 1971: pp. 70, 92. The burial and cremation of dead bodies in Rome was forbidden by the law of the Twelve Tables, see Lewis and Reinhold, I 1966: p. 108 (Table 10). Similarly the Charter of Urso forbade not only the introduction, burial and cremation of the dead within the city limits but also the construction of cremetoria within half a mile of the city limits; see Abbott and Johnson, 1926: no. 26, p. 303 (Clauses 73 and 74). The people of Tarentum, on the other hand, allowed intramural burial after receiving an oracle; see Polybius, viii 28. 6–8, and it was also practised at Corinth, see Williams, 1984: pp. 11–12. The tombs of rich citizens were often impressive public monuments in their own right. At Termessos, tombs are located on the heights overlooking the city but within the city walls; and at Ariassos an impressive series of tombs was immediately adjacent to the main civic centre.
24 See Athenaeus, 518 C; Abbott and Johnson, 1926: no. 26, p. 304 (Clause 76) limited the size of pottery and tile factories within Urso.
25 Aristotle, *Ath. Pol.* 50 2; Wycherley, 1962: p. 156.
26 Plato, *Phaedrus* 229 b, 230 b.

27 Champlin, 1982: pp. 97–117 for a study of the suburbs of Rome. See also Cleary, in Grew and Hobley, 1985: pp. 78–85.
28 e.g. at Timgad five of the eleven bath buildings were outside the city walls.
29 e.g. see Demosthenes, xliv 53.
30 For the advantages see Pliny, *Epist.* ii 17, although the villa mentioned is approximately 17 miles away.
31 Martin, 1972: pp. 904–7.
32 Pausanias, vi 24. 2.
33 Wycherley, 1962: pp. 69–78.
34 See above, p. 86.
35 Martin, 1972: pp. 907–9; Boethius, 1978; pp. 145–49.
36 Vitruvius, v 1. 1.
37 As recommended by Aristotle, *Pol.* vii 1331a; see Paestum, above, p. 41.
38 e.g. see Megara Hyblaea, Verulamium, Augusta Taurinorum, etc.
39 See the slightly condescending reply of Trajan to Pliny's request that the citizens of Nicaea be allowed to construct a gymnasium, Pliny, *Epist.* x 40. 2.
40 Fronto, *Elements of History* 17.
41 As appears at Rhodes and other cities. The *insulae* of Calleva Atrebatum had internal lanes for access, some of which had metalled surfaces. However, in all little work has been done on the nature of the *insulae* of Roman towns.
42 See below, Appendix.
43 Martin, 1974: p. 209. See also Young, 1951: pp. 147, 149–51, 161–2 (Athens); Waşowicz, 1975: p. 70 (Olbia); *BCH Chronique* 1976: p. 610 (Halieis).
44 Abbott and Johnson, 1926: p. 290, *l.* 54; Carcopino, 1956: pp. 57–59.
45 In AD 71 Vespasian had to undertake the repair of Rome's streets, see *CIL*, VI 931.
46 See Juvenal, III 247 which alludes to the conditions of the streets of Rome in Domitian's day.
47 See above, pp. 11–12.
48 Demosthenes, 1v 22; see Lalonde, 1968: pp. 132–33.
49 See above, p. 33.
50 See above, p. 64, note 41.
51 Fougères, 1898: pp. 162–63.
52 Holland, 1944: pp. 118–22.
53 Dimitrov, 1961: p. 95.
54 Plassart, 1916: p. 155; Chamonard, 1924: p. 86.
55 See above, p. 99.
56 See Abbott and Johnson, 1926: no. 26, p. 304 (Clause 77); *CIL*, II 3270 details the paving of rural roads.
57 Ammianus Marcellinus, xiv 1. 9; Jones, 1940: p. 214; there was no provision for street lighting at Delos, see Charmonard, 1924: pp. 86–87.
58 Libanius, *Orat.* xvi 41, xxii 6.

59 In another of Libanius' speeches the defendant, Tisamenos, tried to force individuals to improve the street lighting by providing lamps outside their own property. Such provision was viewed as being expensive for the individual, not part of the individual's civic duty, and unnecessary at night when the city was asleep; see Libanius, *Orat.* xxxiii 36–37. It was also argued that increased street lighting did not necessarily lessen the risk of crime; ibid, 38. Pedestrians out at night either carried, or were accompanied by a slave carrying, a lamp, see Aristophanes, *Vespae* 250–57; Apuleius, *Metamorphoses* ii 32.

60 See above. p. 1. Pausanias comments on the difficulties which the inhabitants of Stiris had in obtaining adequate supplies of good-quality drinking water; Pausanias, x 35. 8.

61 See Diodorus Siculus, xii 10. 7 (Thourioi); Herodotus, iv 158. 3 (Cyrene). Until the construction of the Aqua Appia in 312 BC Rome relied for water on wells and from the River Tiber; Frontinus, *De Aqueductibus* i 4. Other cities also relied upon river water (e.g. Alexandria, see below, note 88), but in general river water was considered inferior and suitable only for washing and irrigation; see Palladius, *De re rustica* i 17.

62 Piraeus at the start of the Peloponnesian War seems to have relied on public cisterns; see Thucydides, ii 48. 2.

63 See above, p. 32.

64 See above, note 1.

65 Herodotus, iii 60. 1–3.

66 Thompson and Wycherley, 1972: pp. 197–203; Wycherley, 1978: pp. 248–50; see Lang, 1968: *passim.*

67 Burns, 1974: pp. 397–404.

68 ibid., p. 392.

69 Robinson and Graham, 1938: pp. 307–11.

70 Wiegand and Schrader, 1904: pp. 68–70.

71 Hansen, 1971: pp. 246–50; von Zabern, 1987: pp. 13–47.

72 Coulton, in Macready and Thompson, 1987: pp. 72–73.

73 As happened at Syracuse, see Thucydides, vi 101.

74 See below, Appendix.

75 Frontinus compared Rome's aqueducts with the pyramids of the Pharaohs or the famous but useless works of the Greeks; Frontinus, *De Aqueductibus* i 4.

76 e.g. Athens and Argos under Hadrian, see Walker, in Macready and Thompson, 1987: pp. 62–68; Pergamon, see Hansen, 1971: p. 247.

77 Herodes Atticus revitalised the cities of Alexandria Troas in Asia and Canusium in Italy by donating aqueducts; Philostratos, *Vitae* ii 1 (548 and 551). Similarly Procopius describes how the once-populous city of Ptolemais had been reduced because of a shortage of water and was only revitalised when the emperor, Justinian, built an aqueduct; *De Aedific.* vi 2.

78 Grenier, IV 1960: pp. 41–51, 88–97.

79 Cunliffe, 1978: pp. 130–31.

80 For the system of water distribution at Pompeii see von Zabern, 1987: pp. 202–7; according to Frontinus, Rome had 247 distribution towers; see *De Aqueductibus* ii 78.

81 Vitruvius, viii 1. 1; see Coulton, in Macready and Thompson, 1987: p. 82.

82 See above, note 62.

83 Stephens, 1985: pp. 200–1; Coulton, in Macready and Thompson, 1987: pp. 81–82; the aqueduct at Kremna, Pisidia, similarly seems to have supplied the bath house. At Alexandria Troas Herodes Atticus showed specific concern for the scarcity of bath houses as well as the poor quality of the water when suggesting to Hadrian that an aqueduct should be built; see above, note 77.

84 See Walker, in Macready and Thompson, 1987: pp. 60–71, For examples of public latrines, see Athens, Travlos, 1971: pp. 342–44; Lepcis Magna, Ward-Perkins, 1981; p. 382; Ostia, Ward-Perkins, 1981: p. 142, fig. 73.

85 Juvenal, III 11–12.

86 Frontinus, *De Aqueductibus* ii 87, 126; Smith, 1978: p. 154.

87 Pliny, *Epist.* x 37.

88 See above, note 77. Caesar states that Alexandria did not have public fountain houses but the city was riddled with underground channels which brought muddy, turgid water from the Nile to private houses; see *Bellum Alexandrinum* 5. 1–3.

89 See the water accounts of Arsinoë in Egypt where the magistrates provided up to 50 per cent of the costs of supplying water, Lewis and Reinhold, II 1966: pp. 333–34. Philostratos, ii 1 (548) makes it clear that Hadrian had supplied money to construct aqueducts in the villages around Alexandria Troas.

90 Pliny, *Epist.* x 90–91.

91 See above, note 77.

92 See Crouch, 1984: pp. 355–61 for comments on the water supply of Morgantina.

93 Strabo, xiv 1. 37 (646).

94 Robinson and Graham, 1938: p. 38; similarly at Thorikos, Mussche, II 1964: pp. 65–66.

95 Aristotle, *Ath. Pol.* 50. 1; Demosthenes, lv 16–20, 26, records the custom of the Athenians of draining water from private property on to the street.

96 Thompson and Wycherley, 1972: pp. 194–97; Wycherley, 1978: pp. 250–52; *BCH*, 1976: *Chronique*, pp. 771–74.

97 *BCH*, 1976: *Chronique*, pp. 768–71.

98 See above, p. 33.

99 Robinson, 1928: pp. 11, 38; Robinson, 1946: p. 273.

100 See above, p. 47.

101 See above, p. 59.

102 Wiegand and Schrader, 1904: pp. 74–75.

103 Dimitrov, 1961: p. 100.

104 See above, note 86.

105 Pliny, *NH* xxxvi 104–6; Nash, i 1961: p. 258.

106 Livy, v 55. 4–5.
107 Stephens, 1985: pp. 206–7; Wacher, 1975: pp. 51, 126.
108 Grenier, IV 1960: pp. 511–55, 67–68, 85–88, 140–43.
109 See above, p. 177, note 27.
110 Strabo, xiv 1. 21 (640).
111 Strabo ix 1. 19 (397) records the comment of Callimachus that by the third century BC the Eridanos Stream at Athens was so polluted that it was unfit even for cattle to drink.

9 EPILOGUE

1 Ward-Perkins, 1974: p. 8; reviewed in *TLS*, 19 July 1974: p. 768.
2 One is reminded of Juvenal's complaint regarding the influence of the Greeks from the Hellenised east; see Juvenal, iii 58–61.

APPENDIX

1 See above. p. 173, note 40.
2 Thompson and Wycherley, 1972: p. 20.
3 Abbott and Johnson, 1926: no. 24 pp. 291 *ll.* 68–72.
4 e.g. Pergamon; see *OGIS*, 483, *ll.* 35–37.
5 Aristotle, *Oeconomica* ii 2. 4.
6 Polyaenus, *Strategemata* iii 9. 30.
7 *Cod. Just.* VIII 10 12. 5b.
8 Martial, vii 61.
9 Lalonde, 1968: pp. 132–33.
10 Demosthenes, lv 22.
11 *OGIS*, 483 *ll.* 38–40, 60–65.
12 *SIG*³, 313, *ll.* 25–28.
13 Abbott and Johnson, 1926: no. 24, p. 289, *l.* 23. See also Urso, ibid, no. 26, p. 309, sect. civ.
14 Aristotle, *Ath. Pol.* 50 1–2.
15 See above, p. 39.
16 Martin, 1974: pp. 52–53, quoting Dareste-Haussoullier, *Insc. Jur. Gr.* II, no. 36, p. 354.
17 Abbott and Johnson, 1926: no. 26, pp. 307–8 sects. xcix and c.
18 See above, p. 62.
19 See above, p. 65.
20 *Insc. Cret*, IV, 73A, *ll.* 7–10.
21 *OGIS*, 483, *ll.* 100–37. According to Tacitus party walls were banned by Nero in Rome after the fire of AD 64; *Ann.* xv 43.
22 e.g. Finley, 1973: no. 86, p. 142; see also ibid., p. 260, note 116.
23 See Owens, 1983: pp. 46–47.
24 Juvenal, iii 275–78.
25 *OGIS*, 483, *ll.* 79–84.
26 *IG*, I⁴ 4. For similar problems at Epidauros and on Paros see *IG*, IV² i 45 and *IG*, XII v 107.

27 Aristotle, *Ath. Pol.* 50 2.
28 *OGIS*, 483, *ll.* 49–50, 95–101.
29 Plutarch, *Moralia* 811 B.
30 Abbott and Johnson, 1926: no. 24, p. 289, *ll.* 20–23; p. 290, *ll.* 50–55.
31 See above, note 22.
32 Owens, 1983: pp. 49–50.
33 Abbott and Johnson, 1926: no. 24, p. 289, *ll.* 29–31.

BIBLIOGRAPHY

ABBREVIATIONS

AA	*Archäologischer Anzeiger*
AD	*Archaiologikon Deltion*
AJA	*American Journal of Archaeology*
AJAH	*American Journal of Ancient History*
AJPh	*American Journal of Philology*
AntCl	*L'Antiquité Classique*
AntJ	*Antiquaries Journal*
Annuario	*Annuario della scuola archeologica di atene e delle missioni italiane in oriente*
AR	*Archaeological Reports*
Arch	*Archaeology*
BCH	*Bulletin de Correspondance Hellénique*
B.d'A	*Bolletino d'Arte*
BSA	*Annual of the British School at Athens*
CAH²	*Cambridge Ancient History* (2nd edn)
CIL	*Corpus Inscriptionum Latinarum*
CQ	*Classical Quarterly*
EAA	(1958–66) *Enciclopedia dell'Arte Antica e Orientale*, 7 vols, Rome
IG	*Inscriptiones Graecae*
Insc.Jur.Gr.	Dareste, R., Haussoullier, B. and Reinach, T. (1891–1904) *Recueil des Inscriptions Juridiques Grecques*, 2 vols, Rome
Insc.Cret.	*Inscriptiones Creticae*
JRIBA	*Journal of the Royal Institute of British Architects*
JRS	*Journal of Roman Studies*
MDAI(A)	*Mitteilungen des Deutsches Archäologischen Instituts: Athenische Abteilung*
MDAI(I)	*Mitteilungen des Deutsches Archäologischen Instituts: Istanbuler Abteilung*
MEFRA	*Mélanges d'Archéologie et d'Histoire de l'Ecole Française de Rome: Antiquité*
OGIS	Dittenberger, K.F.W. (1903–5) *Orientis Graeci Inscriptiones Selectae*, Leipzig
PBSR	*Papers of the British School at Rome*

REA   Revue des Etudes Anciennes
REG   Revue des Etudes Grecques
Sci.Am.   Scientific American
SIG³   Dittenberger, K.F.W. (1915–24) Sylloge Inscriptionum
                Graecarum, 3rd edn, revised by F. Hiller von Gaertringen,
                Hildesheim
TLS   Times Literary Supplement
TPR   Town Planning Review

Abbott, F.F. and Johnson A.C. (1926) Municipal Administration in the
    Roman Empire, Princeton.
Acta Congressus Madvigiani IV (1958) Urbanism and Town Planning,
    Copenhagen.
Adamestaneau, D. (1973) 'Le suddivisione di terra nel Metapontino', in
    M.I. Finley (ed.), Problèmes de la terre en Grèce ancienne, Paris, 49–62.
Allen, H.L. (1970) 'Excavations at Morgantina, 1967–69', AJA 74,
    354–83.
Arthur, P. (1986) 'The urbanisation of Pompeii: excavations 1980–1981',
    AntJ 66, 29–44.
Banti, L. (1973) Etruscan Cities and their Culture, London.
Bean, G.E. (1966) Aegean Turkey, London.
Bean, G.E. (1968) Turkey's Southern Shore, London.
Bean, G.E. (1971) Turkey Beyond the Maeander, London.
Bean, G.E. and Cook, J.M. (1955) 'The Halicarnassus peninsula', BSA
    50, 84–174.
Berchem, van D. (1970) 'Alexandre et la restauration de Priene', Museum
    Helveticum 27, 198–205.
Berlin de Ballu, E. (1972) Olbia: cité antique du littoral nord de la mer noire,
    Leiden.
Blake, N. (1959) The Widow's Cruise, London.
Boardman, J. (1967) Excavations in Chios 1952–1955: Greek Emborio,
    Oxford.
Boardman, J. (1980) The Greeks Overseas, 3rd edition, London.
Boardman, J. and Hammond, N.G.L. (eds) (1982) Cambridge Ancient
    History, III.3, 2nd edition, Cambridge.
Boardman, J. and Kurtz, D.C. (1971) Greek Burial Customs, London.
Boersma, J.S. (1970) Athenian Building Policy from 561/0 to 405/4 BC,
    Gröningen.
Boethius, A. (1948) 'Roman and Greek town architecture', Göteborgs
    Högskolas Årrkrift 64, Göteborg.
Boethius, A. (1978) Etruscan and Early Roman Architecture, 2nd edition,
    Harmondsworth.
Boon, G.C. (1974) Silchester: The Roman Town of Calleva, revised edition
    of Roman Silchester, London.
Boyd, T.D. and Jameson, M.H. (1981) 'Urban planning and rural land
    division in ancient Greece', Hesperia 50, 327–42.
Boyd, T.D. and Rudolph, W.W. (1978) 'Excavations at Porto Chelli and
    vicinity, preliminary report IV: the lower town of Halieis, 1970–77',
    Hesperia 47, 333–55.

Bradford, J. (1956) 'Aerial discoveries in Attica and Rhodes', *AntJ* 36, 57–69.

Bradford, J. (1957) *Ancient Landscapes: Studies in Field Archaeology*, London.

Bruneau, P. (1968) 'Contribution à l'histoire urbaine de Délos', *BCH* 92, 633–709.

Bruneau, P. and Ducat, J. (1966) *Guide de Délos*, 2nd edition, Paris.

Bruneau, P. *et al.* (1970) *Exploration archéologique de Délos*, XXVII, 'Ilôt de la maison des comédiens', Paris.

Burns, A. (1974) 'Ancient water supply and city planning: a study of Syracuse and Acragas', *Technology and Culture* 15, 389–412.

Burns, A. (1976) 'Hippodamus and the planned city', *Historia* 25, 414–28.

Cambitoglou, A. (1971) *Zagora*, I, Sydney.

Carcopino, J. (1956) *Daily Life in Ancient Rome*, translated by E.O. Lorimer, Harmondsworth.

Castagnoli, F. (1971) *Orthogonal Town Planning in Antiquity*, Cambridge, Massachusetts.

Chamonard, J. (1924) *Exploration archéologique de Délos*, VIII, 'Le quartier du théâtre', Paris.

Champlin, E. (1982) 'The *suburbium* of Rome', *AJAH* 7, 97–117.

Chevallier, R. (1957) Review of F. Castagnoli, *Ippodamo di Mileto e l'urbanistica a pianta ortogonale*, Rome, 1956, *REA* 59, 445–49.

Cleary, A.S. Esmonde (1985) 'The quick and the dead: suburbs, cemetries and the town', in F. Grew and B. Hobley (eds), *Roman Urban Topography*, London, 74–77.

Colburn, O.C. (1967) 'A habitation area of Thurii', *Expedition* 9.3, 30–38.

Coldstream, J.N. (1977) *Geometric Greece*, London.

Coleman, J.E. (1970) 'Excavation of a site (Elean Pylos) near Agraphidochori', *AD 24 B¹ 1969*, 155–61.

Collingwood, R.G. and Richmond, I. (1969) *The Archaeology of Roman Britain*, revised edition, London.

Cook, J.M. (1947) 'Archaeology in Greece', *JHS* 67, 41–43.

Cook, J.M. (1950) 'Archaeology in Greece, 1948–9', *JHS* 70, 10–13.

Cook, J.M. (1958/9) 'Old Smyrna, 1948–1951', *BSA* 53/4, 1–34.

Cook, J.M. (1962) *The Greeks in Ionia and the East*, London.

Coulton, J.J. (1987) 'Roman aqueducts in Asia Minor', in S. Macready and F.H. Thompson (eds), *Roman Architecture in the Greek World*, London, 72–84.

Courbin, P. (1956) 'Une rue d'Argos', *BCH* 80, 183–218.

Croix, de la H. (1972) *Military Considerations in City Planning: Fortifications*, New York.

Crouch, D.P. (1984) 'The Hellenistic water system of Morgantina', *AJA* 88, 353–65..

Crummy, P. (1982) 'The origins of some major Romano-British towns', *Britannia* 13, 125–34.

Cumont, F. (1926) *Fouilles de Dura-Europus 1922–3*, Paris.

Cunliffe, B. (1978) *Rome and Her Empire*, London.

Cunliffe, B. (1985) 'Aspects of urbanization in northern Europe', in F. Grew and B. Hobley (eds), *Roman Urban Topography*, London, 1–5.

Dareste, R., Haussoullier, B. and Reinach, T. (1891–1904) *Recueil des inscriptions juridiques grecques*, 2 vols, Paris.

Demargne, J. (1901) 'Les Ruines de Goulas ou l'ancienne ville de Lato en Crète', *BCH* 25, 282–307.

Demargne, J. (1903) 'Fouilles à Lato en Crète 1899–1901', *BCH* 27, 203–32.

Demargne, P. and Effenterre, van H. (1937) 'Recherches à Dréros', *BCH* 61, 5–32, 333–48.

Desborough, V.R.d'A. (1972) *The Greek Dark Ages*, London.

Dilke, O.A.W. (1971) *The Roman Land Surveyors: An Introduction to the Agrimensores*, Newton Abbot.

Dilke, O.A.W. (1985) 'Ground survey and measurement in Roman towns', in F. Grew and B. Hobley (eds), *Roman Urban Topography*, London, 6–13.

Dimitrov, D.P. (1961) 'Seuthopolis', *Antiquity* 35, 91–102.

Dinsmoor, W.B. (1950) *The Architecture of Ancient Greece*, 3rd edition, London.

Dittenberger, K.F.W. (1903–5) *Orientis Graeci Inscriptiones Selectae*, Leipzig.

Downey, G. (1961) *A History of Antioch in Syria*, Princeton.

Drerup, H. (1964) 'Griechische Architectur zur Zeit Homers', *AA* 180–219.

Drerup, H. (1969) 'Griechische Baukunst in geometrischer Zeit', *Archaeologica Homerica* II, 0, Göttingen.

Drews, R. (1981) 'The coming of the city to central Italy', *AJAH* 6, 133–65.

Drinkwater, J.F. (1983) *Roman Gaul*, London.

Ducat, J. (1973) 'Exploration archéologique d'Himère', *REG* 86, 414–17.

Dunbabin, T.J. (1948) *The Western Greeks*, Oxford.

Effenterre, van H. (1963) 'Voies et plans au nord-ouest du palais de Mallia', *BCH* 87, 229–51.

Ehrenberg, V. (1948) 'The foundation of Thurii', *AJP* 69, 149–70.

Enciclopedia dell'arte antica e orientale (1958–66) 7 vols, Rome.

Evans, A. (1895–6) 'Goulas: the city of Zeus', *BSA* 2, 169–94.

Finley, M.I. (1973) *Problèmes de la terre en Grèce ancienne*, Paris.

Finley, M.I. (1977) *Atlas of Classical Archaeology*, London.

Forrest, W.G. (1980) *A History of Sparta, 950–192 BC*, 2nd edition, London.

Fougères, G. (1898) *Mantinée et l'Arcadie orientale*, Paris.

Frere, S. (1964) 'Verulamium: three Roman towns', *Antiquity* 38, 103–12.

Frere, S. (1987) *Britannia*, 3rd edition, Oxford.

Garland, R. (1987) *The Piraeus: From the Fifth to the First Century BC*, London.

Genière, de la J. (1981) 'Nuove richerche sulla topografia di Selinunte', *Accademia Naz. dei Lincei: Rendiconti della Classe di Scienze Morali e Storiche* 36, 211–17.

Genière, de la J. and Theodorescu, D. (1979) 'Richerche topografiche nell' area di Selinunte', *Accademia Naz. dei Lincei: Rendiconti della Classe di Scienze Morali e Storiche* 34, 385–95.

Gerkan, von A. (1924) *Griechische Städteanlagen*, Leipzig.

Giuliano, A. (1966) *Urbanistica delle città greche*, Milan.

Glaser, F. (1985) *Antike Brunnenbauten (Krēnai) in Griechenland*, Vienna.

Golding, N.H. (1975) 'Plato as a city planner', *Arethusa* 8, 359–71.

Goodchild, R.G. (1952) 'Eusperides, a devastated city site', *Antiquity* 26, 208–12.

Graeve, von V. (1973/4) 'Milet 1963', *MDAI(I)* 23/4, 62–115.

Graham, J.W. (1972) 'Notes on houses and housing – districts at Abdera and Himera', *AJA* 76, 295–301.

Grant, M. (1971) *Cities of Vesuvius*, Harmondsworth.

Grenier, A. (1931–60) *Manuel d'archéologie Gallo-Romaine*, 4 vols, Paris.

Grew, F. and Hobley, B. (eds) (1985) *Roman Urban Topography*, CBA Research Report no. 59, London.

Gruben, G. (1970) 'Der Dipylon – Brunnen B', *MDAI(A)* 85, 114–28.

Hadjimichali, V. (1971) 'Recherches à Lato', *BCH* 95, 167–222.

Hammond, M. (1972) *The City in the Ancient World*, Cambridge, Massachusetts.

Hammond, N.G.L. (1953) 'Hellenic houses at Ammotopos in Epirus', *BSA* 48, 135–40.

Hammond, N.G.L. (1967) *Epirus*, Oxford.

Hansen, E.V. (1971) *The Attalids of Pergamon*, Ithaca and London.

Harden, D. (1971) *The Phoenicians*, London.

Haverfield, F. (1913) *Ancient Town Planning*, Oxford.

Heinrich, E. (1958) 'Die "Inselarchitectur" in des Mittelmeergebietes', *AA*, 89–130.

Hill, D.K. (1932) 'Boundary stones from the Peiraeus', *AJA* 36, 254–59.

Hill, I.T. (1953) *The Ancient City of Athens*, Chicago.

Hiller, von Gaertringen F. (ed.) (1899–1909) *Thera: Untersuchungen, Vermessungen und Ausgrabungen in den Jahren 1895–98*, 4 vols, Berlin.

Hoddinott, R.F. (1975) *Bulgaria in Antiquity*, London.

Holland, L.B. (1944) 'Colophon', *Hesperia* 13, 91–171.

Holloway, R.R. (1978) Review of G. Vallet, F. Villard and P. Auberson *Megara Hyblaea I: Le quartier de l'agora archaïque*, Paris, 1976, *AJA* 82, 560–62.

Hommel, P. (1960) 'Der Abschnitt östlich des Athenatempels', *MDAI(I)* 9/10, 31–62.

Homo, L. (1971) *Rome impériale et l'urbanisme dans l'antiquité*, Paris.

Hopper, R.J. (1968) 'Laureion: a reconsideration', *BSA* 63, 293–326.

Hornblower, S. (1982) *Mausolus*, Oxford.

Jameson, M.H. (1969) 'Excavations at Porto Chelli and vicinity: I', *Hesperia* 38, 311–42.

Jameson, M.H. (1974) 'Excavations at Porto Chelli', *AD* 26B[1], 114–19.

Jantzen, V., Felsch, R.C.S., Hoepfner, W and Willers, D. (1973) 'Die Wasserleitung des Eupalinos', *AA* 88, 72–89.

Jeffrey, L.H. (1976) *Archaic Greece: The City States ca.700–500 BC*, London.

Johnson, A. (1983) *Roman Forts of the First and Second Centuries AD in Britain and the German Provinces*, London.

Jones, A.H.M. (1940) *The Greek City*, Oxford.

Jones, J.E. (1975) 'Town and country houses of Attica in Classical times',

Miscellanea Graeca I, 63–140.

Jones, M.H. (1985) 'New streets for old: the topography of Roman Lincoln', in F. Grew and B. Hobley (eds), *Roman Urban Topography*, London, 86–93.

Judeich, W. (1931) *Topographie von Athen*, 3rd edition, Munich.

Judson, S. and Kahane, A. (1966) 'Underground drainageways in southern Etruria and northern Latium', *PBSR* 21, n.s. 18, 74–99.

Kastenbein, W. (1960) 'Untersuchen am stellen des Eupalinos', *AA* 75, 178–98.

Kinch, K.F. (1914) *Fouilles de Vroulia*, Berlin.

Kirsten, E. (1956) *Die griechische Polis als historisch-geographisches Problem des Mittelmeerraumes*, Bonn.

Klaffenbach, G. (1954) 'Die Astynomeninschrift von Pergamon', *Abhandlungen der deutschen Academie der Wissenschaft*, Berlin.

Kleiner, G. (1966) *Alt-Milet*, Wiesbaden.

Kleiner, G. (1968) *Die Ruinen von Milet*, Berlin.

Kleiner, G. and Müller-Wiener, W. (1971) 'Die Grabung in Milet 1959', *MDAI(I)* 21, 45–92.

Kolb, F. (1984) *Die Stadt im Altertum*, Munich.

Kondis, I.D. (1954) *Symbole eis ten metelen tes rhythmotomias tes Rhodou*, Athens.

Kondis, I.D. (1958) 'Zum antiken Stadtbauplan von Rhodos', *MDAI(A)* 73, 146–58.

Konstantinopoulos, G. (1968) 'Rhodes: new finds and old problems', *Arch* 21, 115–22.

Kriesis, A. (1958) 'Ancient Greek town building', *Acta Congressus Madvigiani* IV, Copenhagen, 39–103.

Kriesis, A. (1965) *Greek Town Building*, Athens.

Lalonde, G.V. (1968) 'A fifth century hieron southwest of the Athenian agora', *Hesperia* 37, 124–33.

Lampl, P. (1968) *Cities and Planning in the Ancient Near East*, New York.

Lang, M. (1968) *Water Works in the Athenian Agora*, Princeton.

Lauffray, J. (1958) 'L'Urbanisme antique en Proche Orient', *Acta Congressus Madvigiani* IV, Copenhagen, 7–26.

Lauter-Bufe, H. and Lauter, H. (1971) 'Wohnhäuser und Stadtviertel des Klassischen Athen', *MDAI(A)* 86, 109–24.

Lavedan, P. (1926) *Histoire de l'urbanisme* I, Paris.

Lewis, N. and Reinhold, M. (1966) *Roman Civilisation: Sourcebook*, 2 vols, New York.

Love, I.C. (1970) 'Excavations at Knidos, 1969', *AJA* 74, 149–55.

Love, I.C. (1972) 'A preliminary report of the excavations at Knidos, 1970', *AJA* 76, 61–76.

Love, I.C. (1972) 'A preliminary report of the excavations at Knidos, 1971', *AJA* 76, 393–405.

Love, I.C. (1973) 'A preliminary report of the excavations at Knidos, 1972', *AJA* 77, 413–24.

Lyttelton, M. (1974) *Baroque Architecture in Classical Antiquity*, London.

McCredie, J.R. (1971) 'Hippodamos of Miletos', in D.G. Mitten, J.G. Pedley and J.A. Scott (eds), *Studies Presented to G.M.A. Hanfmann*, Mainz, 95–100.

MacDonald, C. (1961) 'The ancient mine workings of Laureion', *Greece and Rome*, n.s. 8, 19–23.

MacDonald, W.L. (1965) *The Architecture of the Roman Empire* I, New Haven and London.

Macready, S. and Thompson, F.H. (eds) (1987) *Roman Architecture in the Greek World*, London.

Magie, D. (1950) *Roman Rule in Asia Minor to the End of the Third Century After Christ*, 2 vols, Princeton.

Makaronas, Ch.J. (1966) 'Pella: capital of ancient Macedonia', *Sci. Am.* 215.6, 98–105.

Mansuelli, G.A. (1972) 'Marzabotto: dix années de fouilles et de recherches', *MEFRA* 84, 111–44.

Mansuelli, G.A. (1979) 'The Etruscan city' in D. and F.R. Ridgway (eds), *Italy Before the Romans*, London, 353–71.

Marshall, M.H.B. (1975) 'Urban settlement in the second chapter of Thucydides', *CQ* 25, 26–40.

Martienssen, R.D. (1941) 'Greek cities', *South African Architectural Record* 26, 1–58.

Martienssen, R.D. (1956) *The Idea of Space in Greek Architecture*, Johannesburg.

Martin, R. (1951) *Recherches sur l'agora grecque*, Paris.

Martin, R. (1957) 'Sur deux expressions techniques de l'architecture grecque', *Revue de Philologie* 31, 66–81.

Martin, R. (1972) 'Agora et forum', *MEFRA* 89, 903–33.

Martin, R. (1973) 'Rapport entre les structures urbaines et les modes de division et d'exploitation du territoire', in M.I. Finley (ed.), *Problèmes de la terre en Grèce ancienne*, Paris, 97–112.

Martin, R. (1974) *L'Urbanisme dans la Grèce antique*, 2nd edition, Paris.

Meiggs, R. (1973) *Roman Ostia*, 2nd edition, Oxford.

Mellink, M.J. (1968) 'Archaeology in Asia Minor', *AJA* 72, 125–47.

Mellink, M.J. (1969) 'Archaeology in Asia Minor', *AJA* 73, 203–27.

Metraux, G.P.R. (1972) 'Western Greek land use and town planning in the Archaic period', unpublished thesis, Harvard University.

Miro, de E. (1957) 'Il quartiere Ellenistico-Romano di Agrigento', *Accademia Naz. dei Lincei: Rendiconti della Classe di Scienze Morali e Storiche* 12, 135–40.

Mitchell, H. (1964) *Sparta*, Cambridge.

Müller, C. and Th. (eds) (1841–83) *Fragmenta Historicum Graecorum*, 5 vols, Paris.

Mumford, L. (1961) *The City in History*, London.

Mussche, H.F. (1970) 'Recent excavations at Thorikos', *Acta Classica* 12, 125–35.

Mussche, H.F. (1974) *Thorikos: A Guide to the Excavations*, Brussels.

Mussche, H.F., Bingen, J., Servais, J. and Hackens, T. (1965) 'Thorikos 1963', *Ant Cl* 34, 5–46.

Mussche, H.F. Spitaels, P. and Goemaere-De Poerck, F. (1975) *Miscellanea Graeca* I, Ghent.

Mussche, H.F. *et al.* (1967–73) *Thorikos*, 6 vols, Brussels.

Napoli, M. (1970) *Paestum*, Novaro.

Nash, E. (1961) *Pictorial Dictionary of Ancient Rome*, 2 vols, London.

Nicholls, R.V. (1958/9) 'Old Smyrna: the iron age fortifications and associated remains on the city perimeter', *BSA* 53/54, 35–137.

Owens, E.J. (1983) 'The koprologoi at Athens', *CQ* n.s. 33, 44–50.

Pairault, F.H. (1972) 'L'Habitat archaïque de Casalecchio di Reno près de Bologne: structure planimetrique et technique de construction', *MEFRA* 84, 145–97.

Pallotino, M. (1955) *The Etruscans*, Harmondsworth.

Papageorgiou-Venetas, A. (1981) *Délos: recherches urbaine sur une ville antique*, Munich.

Pelagatti, P. (1964) 'Naxos – relazione preliminare delle campagne di scavo, 1961–4', *B.d'A* 149–65.

Pelagatti, P. (1972) 'Naxos II – richerche topografiche e scavi, 1965–70', *B.d'A*, 211–19.

Pelagatti, P. (1978) 'Sur parco archeologico di Camarina', *B.d'A*, 122–30.

Pendlebury, H.W. and Pendlebury, J.D.S. (1937/8) 'Excavations on the plain of Lasithi III-Karphi', *BSA* 28, 57–141.

Peschlow-Bindokat, A. (1977) 'Herakleia am Latmos', *AA*, 90–104.

Petsas, Ph. (1958) 'New discoveries at Pella – birthplace and capital of Alexander', *Arch* 11, 246–54.

Petsas, Ph. (1964) 'Ten years at Pella', *Arch* 17, 74–84.

Petsas, Ph. (1978) *Pella: Alexander the Great's Capital*, Thessaloniki.

Plassart, A. (1916) 'Quartier d'habitations privées à l'est du stade', *BCH* 40, 145–256.

Plommer, H, (1977) 'Shadowy Megara', *JHS* 97, 75–83.

Popham, M.R. and Sackett, L.H. (1968) *Excavations at Lefkandi, Euboea 1964–1966*, London.

Popham, M.R. and Sackett, L.H. (1972) 'Lefkandi', *Arch* 25, 8–19.

Popham, M.R., Sackett, L.H. and Themelis, P.G. (1980) *Lefkandi I: The Iron Age*, London.

Pound, N.J.G. (1969) 'Urbanisation of the classical world', *Ann. of Assoc. of Am. Geographers* 59, 135–57.

Quilici, L. (1967) *Siris-Heraclea*, Rome.

Rainey, F. (1969) 'The location of archaic Greek Sybaris', *AJA* 73, 261–73.

Richmond, I.A. and Holford, W.G. (1935) 'Roman Verona: the archaeology of its town plan', *PBSR* 13, 69–76.

Rider, B.C. (1964) *Ancient Greek Houses*, 2nd edition, Chicago.

Ridgway, D. and Ridgway, F.R. (eds) (1979) *Italy Before the Romans*, London.

Robertson, D.S. (1943) *A Handbook of Greek and Roman Architecture*, 2nd edition, Cambridge.

Robinson, D.M. (1928–52) *Excavations at Olynthus*, 14 vols, Baltimore.

Robinson, D.M. (1928) *Excavations at Olynthus* II, Baltimore.

Robinson, D.M. (1946) *Excavations at Olynthus* XII, Baltimore.

Robinson, D.M. and Graham, G.W. (1938) *Excavations at Olynthus* VIII, Baltimore.

Robinson, H.S. (1965) *The Urban Development of Ancient Corinth*, Athens.

Roebuck, C. (1972) 'Some aspects of urbanization in Corinth', *Hesperia* 41, 96–127.

Ruyt, De F. (1973) 'Une cité étrusque d'époque archaïque à Acquarossa (Viterbe)', *Ant Cl* 42, 584–86.

Rykwert, J. (1976) *The Idea of a Town*, Princeton.

Saalman, H. (1968) *Medieval Cities*, London.

Salmon, E.T. (1969) *Roman Colonisation Under the Republic*, London.

Salmon, J.B. (1984) *Wealthy Corinth*, Oxford.

Salway, P. (1981) *Roman Britain*, Oxford.

Salway, P. (1985) 'Geography and the growth of towns, with special reference to Britain', in F. Grew and B. Hobley (eds), *Roman Urban Topography*, London, 67–73.

Saugavet, J. (1941) *Alep*, Paris.

Saugavet, J. (1949/50) 'Le Plan antique de Damas', *Syria* 26/27, 314–58.

Schmiedt, G. (1968/9) 'Le richerche sull'urbanistica delle città italiote e siceliote', *Kokalos* 14/15, 397–427.

Scullard, H.H. (1967) *The Etruscan Cities and Rome*, London.

Shear, T.L., Jnr (1969) 'The Athenian agora: excavations of 1968', *Hesperia*, 38, 383–417.

Shear, T.L., Jnr (1973) 'The Athenian agora: excavations of 1971', *Hesperia* 42, 146–56.

Shear, T.L., Jnr (1981) 'From city-state to provincial town', *Hesperia* 50, 356–77.

Smith, N. (1978) 'Roman hydraulic technology', *Sci. Am.* 238.5, 154–61.

Snodgrass, A.M.S. (1971) *The Dark Age of Greece*, Edinburgh.

Snodgrass, A.M.S. (1980) *Archaic Greece: The Age of Experiment*, London.

Stanislawski, D. (1946) 'The origin and spread of the grid-pattern town', *Geographical Review* 36, 105–20.

Stephens, G.R. (1985) 'Civil aqueducts in Roman Britain', *Britannia* 16, 197–208.

Stewart, C. (1952) *A Prospect of Cities*, London.

Stillwell, R. (ed.) (1976) *The Princeton Encyclopedia of Classical Sites*, Princeton.

Taylour, L.W. (1964) *The Mycenaeans*, London.

Theipland, L.M. (1963) 'Excavations besides the north-west gate at Veii, 1957–58', *PBSR* 31, n.s. 18, 33–73.

Thompson, H.A. (1937) 'Buildings on the west side of the agora', *Hesperia* 6, 1–226.

Thompson, H.A. (1940) 'The tholos of Athens and its predecessors', *Hesperia*, Supplement IV.

Thompson, H.A. (1954) 'Excavations in the Athenian agora: 1953', *Hesperia* 23, 31–56.

Thompson, H.A. (1957) 'Activities in the Athenian agora: 1956', *Hesperia* 26, 99–110.

Thompson, H.A. (1959) 'Activities in the Athenian agora: 1958', *Hesperia* 28, 91–108.

Thompson, H.A. (1968) 'Activities in the Athenian agora: 1966–1967', *Hesperia* 37, 36–72.

Thompson, H.A. and Wycherley, R.E. (1972) *The Athenian Agora XIV;*

The Agora of Athens, Princeton.

Tod, M.N. (1948) *A Selection of Greek Historical Inscriptions*, 2 vols, Oxford.

Tomlinson, R.A. (1972) *Argos and the Argolid*, London.

Travlos, J. (1960) *Poleodomike exelixis ton Athenon apo ton proïstikon chronon mekri ton archon tou 19ou ainou*, Athens.

Travlos, J. (1971) *A Pictorial Dictionary of Ancient Athens*, London.

Vallet, G. (1973) 'Espace privée et espace publique dans une cité coloniale d'Occident (Megara Hyblaea)', in M.I. Finley (ed.), *Problèmes de la terre en Grèce ancienne*, Paris, 83–96.

Vallet, G., Villard, F. and Auberson, P. (1976) *Megara Hyblaea I: le quartier de l'agora*, 2 vols, Paris.

Vallois, R. (1966) *L'Architecture Hellénique et Hellénistique à Délos*, Paris.

Vanderpool, E. (1959) 'Roads at the north-west corner of the Athenian agora', *Hesperia* 28, 289–97.

Vermeule, E. (1964) *Greece in the Bronze Age*, Chicago and London.

Villard, F. (1951) 'Megara Hyblaea', *Mélanges d'archéologie et d'histoire* 63, 7–52.

Voza, G. (1963) 'La topografia di Paestum alla luce di alcune recenti indagini', *Archeologica Classica* 15, 223–32.

Wacher, J. (1975) *The Towns of Roman Britain*, London.

Wacher, J. (1978) *Roman Britain*, London.

Ward-Perkins, J.B. (1949) Review of A. Boethius, 'Roman and Greek town architecture', *JRS* 39, 175–77.

Ward-Perkins, J.B. (1955) 'Early Roman towns in Italy', *TPR* 26, 126–54.

Ward-Perkins, J.B. (1961) 'Veii: the historical topography of the ancient city', *PBSR* 29, n.s. 16.

Ward-Perkins, J.B. (1962) 'Etruscan engineering' in *Hommages à Albert Grenier*, Brussels, 1636–43.

Ward-Perkins, J.B. (1974) *Cities of Ancient Greece and Italy: Planning in Antiquity*, London. (Reviewed in *TLS*, 19 July 1974, 768.)

Ward-Perkins, J.B. (1981) *Roman Imperial Architecture*, Harmondsworth.

Warner, M. (1983) 'Selinunte's 200 years of grandeur', *Connoisseur* 213, 130–34.

Waşowicz, A. (1972) 'Traces de lotissements anciens en crimée', *MEFRA* 84, 199–229.

Waşowicz, A. (1975) *Olbia pontique et son territoire*, Paris.

Webster, G. (1973) *The Roman Army*, Chester.

Webster, G. (1979) *The Roman Imperial Army*, 2nd edition, London.

Webster, G. (ed.) (1988) *Fortress into City*, London.

Wheeler, M. (1964) *Roman Art and Architecture*, London.

Wiegand, T. and Schrader, H. (1904) *Priene*, Berlin.

Willetts, R.F. (1965) *Ancient Crete*, London.

Williams II, C.K. (1984) 'The early urbanization of Corinth', *Annuario*, n.s. 44, 9–20.

Winter, F.E. (1971) *Greek Fortifications*, London.

Woloch, G.M. (1983) *Roman Cities*, Winsconsin.

Wycherley, R.E. (1937/8) 'Aristophanes, *Birds*, 995–1009', *CQ* 31/2, 22–31.

Wycherley, R.E. (1938) 'The agora of Miletus', *JRIBA* 45, 1005–11.
Wycherley, R.E. (1951) 'Notes on Olynthus and Selinus', *AJA* 55, 231–36.
Wycherley, R.E. (1951) 'Hellenic cities', *TPR* 22, 103–21.
Wycherley, R.E. (1951) 'Hellenistic cities', *TPR* 22, 177–205.
Wycherley, R.E. (1962) *How the Greeks Built Cities*, 2nd edition, London.
Wycherley, R.E. (1964) 'Hippodamos and Rhodes', *Historia* 13, 135–39.
Wycherley, R.E. (1978) *The Stones of Athens*, Princeton.
Young, R.S. (1949) 'An early geometric grave near the Athenian agora', *Hesperia* 18, 275–97.
Young, R.S. (1951) 'An industrial district of ancient Athens', *Hesperia* 20, 135–288.
Zabern, von P. (1987) *Die Wasserversorgung antiker Städte*, Mainz.

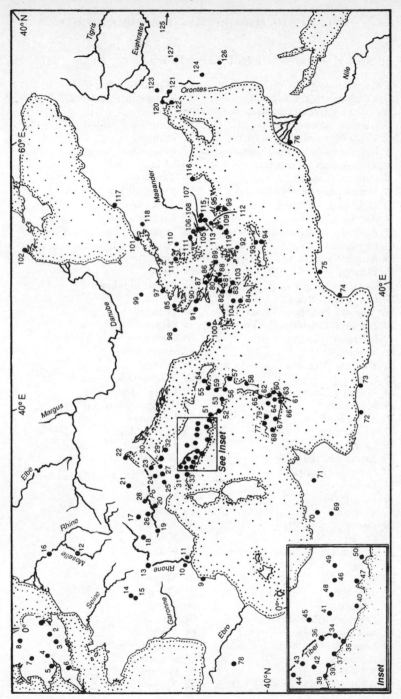

LIST OF SITES

1 Camulodunum (Colchester)
2 Verulamium (St Albans)
3 Calleva Atrebatum (Silchester)
4 Glevum (Gloucester)
5 Venta Silurum (Caerwent)
6 Isca Dumnoniorum (Exeter)
7 Viroconium (Wroxeter)
8 Lindum (Lincoln)
9 Narbo Martius (Narbonne)
10 Nemausus (Nîmes)
11 Arelate (Arles)
12 Augusta Treverorum (Triers)
13 Lugdunum (Lyon)
14 Augustodunum (Autun)
15 Bibactre
16 Colonia Agrippina (Cologne)
17 Comum (Como)
18 Augusta Praetoria (Aosta)
19 Augusta Taurinorum (Turin)
20 Placentia (Piacenta)
21 Verona
22 Aquileia (Veneto)
23 Spina
24 Bononia (Bologna)
25 Marzabotto
26 Ticinum (Pavia)
27 Casalecchio
28 Cremona
29 Ariminum (Rimini)
30 Faventia (Faenza)
31 Lucca
32 Fanum (Fano)
33 Vetulonia
34 Rome
35 Ostia
36 Veii
37 Pyrgi
38 Cosa
39 Tarquinii
40 Terracina
41 Praeneste (Palestrina)
42 San Giovenale
43 Luni sul Mignone
44 Aquarossa
45 Alba Fucens
46 Allifae

47 Minturnae
48 Venafrum (Venafro)
49 Capua
50 Neapolis (Naples)
51 Pompeii
52 Poseidonia/Paestum
53 Elea
54 Tarentum
55 Metapontum
56 Thourioi
57 Croton
58 Locri
59 Herakleia Lucania
60 Syracuse
61 Akrai
62 Megara Hyblaea
63 Heloros
64 Leontini
65 Naxos
66 Camarina
67 Akragas
68 Selinus
69 Thamugadi (Timgad)
70 Cuicul (Djemila)
71 Thugga (Dougga)
72 Sabratha
73 Lepcis Magna
74 Eusperides (Benghazi)
75 Cyrene
76 Alexandria
77 Soluntum
78 Numantia
79 Himera
80 Athens
81 Piraeus
82 Corinth
83 Argos
84 Megalopolis
85 Olynthos
86 Eretria
87 Lefkandi
88 Thorikos
89 Zagora, Andros
90 Demetrias
91 Goritza
92 Thera

93 Lato
94 Dreros
95 Rhodes
96 Lindos
97 Abdera
98 Pella
99 Seuthopolis
100 Kassopeia
101 Constantinople
102 Olbia
103 Halieis (Porto Chelli)
104 Mantinea
105 Miletos
106 Ephesos
107 Herakleia-under-Latmos
108 Priene
109 Knidos
110 Pergamon

111 Old Smyrna
112 Halicarnassus
113 Labraunda
114 Assos
115 Alinda
116 Perge
117 Amastris
118 Nicomedia
119 Cos
120 Antioch-on-the-Orontes
121 Apamea
122 Laodicea-by-the-sea
123 Beroia
124 Damascus
125 Doura-Europos
126 Gerasa (Jerash)
127 Palmyra

INDEX